WITHDRAWN
UTSA Libraries

D0224605

Perspectives in Systematic Musicology

SELECTED REPORTS IN ETHNOMUSICOLOGY, VOLUME XII

RENEWALS 458-4574

Perspectives in Systematic Musicology

Editors
Roger A. Kendall & Roger W. H. Savage

Library
University of Texas
at San Antonio

Department of Ethnomusicology
University of California, Los Angeles

Cover Painting: Vasily Kandinsky, Composition 8, July 1923, Solomon R. Guggenheim Museum, New York, © 2005 Artists Rights Society (ARS), New York/ADAGP, Paris.

Cover Design: Robin Weisz/Graphic Design

Copyright © 2005 The Regents of the University of California
All rights reserved
Printed in the United States of America

ISBN: 0-88287-056-4

**Library
University of Texas
at San Antonio**

Selected Reports in Ethnomusicology is a refereed series published by the Department of Ethnomusicology, University of California, Los Angeles.

Address inquiries to:
Ethnomusicology Publications
Department of Ethnomusicology
University of California
2539 Schoenberg Music Building
Los Angeles, CA 90095-1657

Contents

ACKNOWLEDGMENTS   vii

SYSTEMATIC MUSICOLOGY PAST AND PRESENT
Roger A. Kendall & Roger W. H. Savage   1

Empirical Perspectives

Empirical Perspectives in Systematic Musicology
Roger A. Kendall   13

How Music Influences the Interpretation of Film and Video:
Approaches from Experimental Psychology
Annabel J. Cohen   15

The Perception of Audio-visual Composites:
Accent Structure Alignment of Simple Stimuli
Scott D. Lipscomb   37

Empirical Approaches to Musical Meaning
Roger A. Kendall   69

Subjective Evaluation of Tuning Systems for Piano
Haruka Shimosako & Kengo Ohgushi   103

Auditory Roughness as a Means of Musical Expression
Pantelis N. Vassilakis   119

Reflections on the Nature of Music Learning
Frank Heuser   145

Aesthetic and Philosophical Perspectives

Aesthetic and Philosophical Perspectives in Systematic Musicology
Roger W. H. Savage   157

The Roots of Autonomous Music: Rethinking Autonomy
Before and After Formalism
Angeles Sancho-Velázquez   163

Cuma agus Craiceann/Shape and Skin: Metaphor and
Musical Aesthetics in Tory Island
Lillis Ó Laoire   183

The "Supermen" and the "Normal People": Music, Politics, and
Tradition in 1990s Serbia
Brana Mijatovic   203

Hieroglyph, Gesture, Sign, Meaning: Bussotti's *pièces de chair II*
   Paul Attinello   219

Hermeneutics, Adorno, and the New Musicology
   Roger W. H. Savage   229

Contributors   243

Acknowledgments

We would like to thank Timothy Rice for his invaluable support and efforts. His detailed comments and analyses were instrumental to the conception and completion of this volume. Kelly Salloum, Director of the UCLA Ethnomusicology Publications office, assisted in numerous ways. We would like to thank her, and Publications Coordinators Jeff Janeczko and Youngmin Yu, for shepherding this project through its many stages.

The Editors

I thank my research associates who participated in my experimental studies: Edward C. Carterette and Uday Krishnakumar in the expression experiment, Pantelis Vassilakis in the film experiment, and Koroush Safari and Robin Shields in the timbre experiments. I also thank the numerous graduate and undergraduate students who served as subjects. I am particularly appreciative of Warren Campbell and Jack Heller, whose teachings informed my research. These efforts are dedicated to the memory of my mother, Eleanor T. Kendall (1923-2004).

Roger A. Kendall

I extend my thanks to the many students and friends who have been stimulating conversation partners over the years. I would like to especially thank Angeles Sancho-Velázquez, who was my research assistant and is now a valued colleague. I am also indebted to the students and colleagues who make the Hermeneutics Study Group a lively forum of intellectual inquiry: Sonia Seeman, Charles Sharp, Angela Rodel, Sarah Truher, Paulette Gershen, Alice Hunt, Harmony Bench, Amy Frishkey, Lillis Ó Laoire and Angeles. Finally, I would like to express my enduring gratitude to my wife Pat and daughters Kristen and Laura for their confidence and support. The collection of essays on aesthetics and philosophical issues is dedicated to them.

Roger W. H. Savage

Systematic Musicology Past and Present

ROGER A. KENDALL & ROGER W. H. SAVAGE
University of California, Los Angeles

Guido Adler's 1885 essay "*Umfang, Method und Ziel der Musikwissenschaft*" (The Scope, Method and Aim of Musicology) marks the inception of a disciplinary divide that haunts contemporary musicological research. Adler, who published his seminal essay in the journal *Vierteljahrschrift für Musikwissenschaft* that he founded with Friedrich Chrysander and Philip Spitta in 1884, separates aesthetics, music theory, pedagogy, and comparative ethnography from chronological histories of music. Chrysander's 1863 preface to the first issue of *Jahrbüch für musikalische Wissenschaft* prefigures Adler's schema by acknowledging the multiplicity of the new *Musikwissenschaft*'s disciplinary branches. Adler's formulation delineates the disciplinary fields into which the scholarly study of music falls by distinguishing between historical and systematic research. From the outset, systematic musicology and historical musicology comprise complementary arms of a comprehensive science of music that investigates music's multiple aesthetic and historical facets.

Systematic and historical musicology's inaugural separation belies their common root. By adopting the model of the natural sciences, Adler's schema anchors systematic and historical knowledge of music in the intellectual current that dominates the second half of the nineteenth century. The call for a return to Kant and the rejection of Hegelianism in the nineteenth century mark the rise of positivism as a cultural fact. Adler aligns the science of music with the dominant cultural ethos of his time by erecting a unified framework for a comprehensive science of music. His *Musikwissenschaft* presupposes the ideal of "positive" knowledge that governs the intellectual horizons of the second half of the nineteenth century. Consequently, the division between systematic and historical musicology that Adler institutes is substantive only in the sense that it delineates the different subject matters of musicological inquiry. *Musikwissenschaft*'s historiographical thrust is therefore no less systematic than its suprahistorical complement. Rather, historical and systematic musicology house disciplinary specializations that investigate the complex of aesthetic, psychological, cultural, and historical facts.

The framework that Adler establishes for the study of music reflects nineteenth-century demands by setting out a comprehensive system that aims at a complete scientific knowledge of music. Within this framework, historical research investigates musical notation, musical forms' historical categories, and the compositional laws evinced within different historical periods. Systematic research investigates music theory, aesthetics, pedagogy, and comparative ethnographies. Auxiliary sciences such as history, biography, acoustics, physiology, psychology, poetics, and pedagogy support historical and systematic musicology's subdisciplinary fields. The plurality of subdisciplinary methodologies notwithstanding, Adler's conception of a comprehensive science aims at a unified field of musicological research whose ultimate horizon is the comprehension, evaluation, and discovery of music's supreme laws.

Although the science of music's division into distinct fields intends to systematize the study of music through subdisciplinary specializations, systematic musicology's separation from historical musicology effectively undermines the intended integrity of a comprehensive musicological knowledge. By pitting ostensibly nonhistorical against historical disciplines, this division defines the systematic arm through its difference from historical inquiries. Systematic musicology bears the stigma of this opposition between historical and nonhistorical research aims, methods, and subject matter. Whereas the idea of historiographical inquiry unifies historical musicology's disciplinary intent, systematic musicology's conceptual or methodological unity appears wanting. Debates over systematic musicology's definition that revolve around its intellectual coherence invariably bear the trace of *Musikwissenschaft*'s original division. The burden of defining the unity of a field comprised of "ahistorical" research notwithstanding, this systematic arm preserves the intention of a comprehensive musicology that investigates fundamental questions of music's meaning. Its current configuration reanimates this intention within a new intellectual, cultural, and historical context.

The history that precedes systematic musicology's contemporary refiguration manifests the tension that springs from Adler's distinction. Despite the field's changing arrangements, from the mid-nineteenth into the late-twentieth centuries systematic musicology's difference from historical musicology functions as its defining feature. Waldo Selden Pratt's 1890 reworking of Adler's schema identifies acoustics, aesthetics, pedagogics, and practices as the four areas of systematic inquiry. His later revision (Pratt 1915) extends the field of systematic inquiry to physics and acoustics, music's psychical effects, musical poetics and criticism, aesthetics, notation and documentation, performance techniques, and practical uses of music in theatre, dance, therapy, and education. Hugo Riemann in 1908 evades Adler's systematic-historical division by identifying five principle areas of research. Riemann's division of musicological study into acoustics, tone physiology-psychology, aesthetics, compositional and performance theory, and music history attenuates the tension between systematic and historical branches by recombining them within the subdisciplines he outlines.

The advent of ethnomusicology as a distinct discipline marks this discipline's emancipation from its systematic root. In 1941 Glen Haydon, who was greatly influenced by Adler, set out a six-part classification consisting of acoustics, psychophysiology, aesthetics, pedagogy, anthropology, and music theory. This classification's interpolation with the tripartite division of history, systematic inquiry, and ethnomusicology formalizes these disciplines' separation. By the 1950s, the institutional recognition of ethnomusicology codifies this tripartite division. Despite disciplinary divides and the internecine strife that Bruno Nettl (1995) remarks sometimes accompanies them, historical musicology, systematic musicology, and ethnomusicology remain tied to the aim of a comprehensive interdisciplinary field.

Charles Seeger, whose pandisciplinary approach to musicological inquiry initiates a quasi-reciprocal relation between systematic and historical aims, has a formative place in systematic musicology at the University of California, Los Angeles. For Seeger, historical research investigates the history of musical systems. Systematic studies investigate the systems of musical knowledge within a history of its practices and innovations. Although for Seeger systematic and historical orientations could not be completely joined, neither could they be absolutely sundered. Individual musicological studies would be either historical or systematic. Nevertheless, by acknowledging that musicology's systematic and historical arms are ineluctably intertwined, Seeger's reflections on systematic musicology's scope and methods anticipate a rapprochement that eludes systematic musicology's reflections on itself throughout most of the twentieth century (Seeger 1951).

William Hutchinson, who also taught in the systematic musicology program at UCLA, reiterates the tension that inheres within the history of this discipline. In a 1976 article entitled "Systematic Musicology Reconsidered," Hutchinson identifies the controversy over systematic musicology's definition with the ambiguities and contradictions that inhere in a systematic as opposed to a historical research field. Hutchinson reviews three possible ways of defining systematic musicology. As a comprehensive theoretical science of music, systematic musicology discovers suprahistorical [*über-historische*] phenomena within different historical and cultural traditions. As the selected interdisciplinary study of music, systematic musicology integrates perspectives drawn from cognate or auxiliary disciplines such as acoustics, psychology, physiology, aesthetics, and sociology to develop a more comprehensive knowledge of music. As a discipline whose correlative epistemological orientation corresponds to that of historical musicology, systematic musicology offers a complementary perspective whose ultimate integration within historical research would fulfill Adler's original intention of a comprehensive science of music.

The difficulties that Hutchinson articulates evidence the enduring effects of systematic and historical musicology's separation. By setting musicology's systematic arm against its historical one, this division defines systematic musicology's conceptual unity through its difference from historical research. This difference valorizes systematic musicology's intellectual scope. Privileging historical research for its methodological unity and intellectual coherence prejudices systematic musicology as a polyglot of disciplinary interests that fall outside historical musicology's purview. Conversely, the Greek and Islamic antecedents of acoustics, aesthetics, and music theory evince a concept of systematic musicology that is older than that of historical musicology.

Andrew McCredie (1971: 14), who suggests that as the youngest of systematic musicology's disciplines the psychology of music might serve a central role in unifying the field, attributes this field's lack of inclusion within the academy to a liberal humanism that rejects systematic musicology's scientific tenor. For McCredie, systematic musicology's incompatibility with liberal humanist tenets presents the greatest impediment to an all-encompassing disciplinary approach. This incompatibility, which exacerbates systematic musicology's negative relation to historical musicology's intellectual interests, drives the wedge between them deeper into the humanistic-scientific ground of knowledge in which both are planted. Systematic-scientific and historical-humanistic prejudices are therefore the legacy of a discipline divided within itself while remaining rooted in the nineteenth century's positivist ground.

Institutionalization

Systematic musicology's current status varies among institutions and scholars. A brief overview reveals a number of approaches to the field. Some programs, conferences, and institutions refer explicitly to the term and concept systematic musicology; others simply imply a relationship. The following survey represents a sample of systematic musicology's different institutional configurations world-wide.

Austria

University of Vienna. Austria, specifically the University of Vienna, is where Guido Adler spent the majority of his career in musicology until his retirement in 1927 (he also taught in Prague). A Ph.D. graduate at the University of Vienna in 1880, his considerable influence was felt beyond the some fifty years he spent in international music circles, including the founding of the *Vierteljahrschrift für Musikwissenschaft*, the publishing of Monuments of Music in Austria, and the establishment of scholarly festivals on Haydn and Beethoven. (The University of Georgia Library (http://www. libs.uga.edu) contains the Guido Adler Collection, consisting of 74 boxes of documents.) Today, the University of Vienna houses an Institute for Music Science. The institute provides a diploma and doctorate consisting of two course streams: historical music science, devoted to European art music, and comparative music science. The latter has three independent subdisciplines: systematic music science "of predominantly scientific research methods"; ethnomusicology; and the Viennese school of comparative-systematic music science. The list of principal research professors' specializations includes music history of Austria, song in the nineteenth and twentieth centuries, historical music theory, archaeology, music aesthetics, music understanding, music sound research and psychoacoustics, acoustics (including four staff members), computer analysis methods, theory and method in ethnomusicology, and the musical cultures of Madagascar and American country music. As an institute, this program encompasses the global, umbrella-like structure of Adler's original vision of music science. It is worth noting that the area of "systematic music science" is focused on scientific research methods, as distinct from general music science and comparative music science (http://www.univie.ac.at/Musikwissenschaft/english.html, April 20, 2004).

University of Salzburg. The Institute for Music Science of the University of Salzburg specifically refers to Guido Adler and Friedrich Chrysander as antecedents. The institute describes the field of music science as suffering from a lack of independent research methods leading to a limitation "all too easily on music history" with the other disciplines as mere appendages. The institute proclaims a broader view of music science with three subsections: historical music science, systematic music science, and ethnomusicology. In this case, systematic music science refers to history of music theory, organology, physiology, psychology, aesthetics, sociology, and acoustics (http://www.sbg.ac.at/mus/home.htm, April 1, 2004). The website contains an interesting taxonomy of the musical sciences and notes the paucity of positions in the field.

University of Graz. This university houses an Institute for Music Science with emphasis on systematic music science and historical music science. There is a professor of systematic musicology who oversees studies in a variety of disciplines including cognitive music theory, analysis, and computer applications. The university recently (April, 2004) hosted a Conference on Interdisciplinary Musicology. The director, Richard Parncutt, professor of systematic musicology, Graz, eschews the term systematic musicology (http://gewi.uni-graz.at/~cim04/index2.htm, February 11, 2004).

Germany

The University of Hamburg provides a program and lecture series in music science (http://www.uni-hamburg.de/Wiss/FB/09/Musik/, April 1, 2004). This includes the disciplines of music sociology, historical music science, popular music, and systematic music science (hard sciences). The general structure and content appear consonant with the Austrian model (Richard Parncutt, professor of systematic musicology, University of Graz, personal communication, March 28, 2004). The University of Hamburg is also the address of the International Cooperative in Systematic and Comparative Musicology, Inc. Founded in 1993 as a scientific nonprofit organization, its charter is to further research in "systematic and comparative musicology on an international level." Meetings have been held yearly at locations in Slovakia, Germany, Austria, Belgium, Berlin, Norway, and Finland (http://www.uni-hamburg.de/wiss/fb/09/musik/systematicmusicology.html, February 11, 2004).

The University of Cologne has a Music Science Institute. Under this rubric the entire gamut of musicological studies is covered. The list of lectures includes ethnomusicology, sociology, psychology and cognition, acoustics, music technology, music-theory and analysis, music history, and music performance (*Collegium Musicum*). The interdisciplinary nature of the coursework is exemplified in a course on Beethoven that includes the music's use in the film *A Clockwork Orange* (http://www.uni-koeln.de/phil-fak/muwi/, March, 2004).

The University of Applied Sciences of Magdeburg ad Stendal recently hired a professor of systematic musicology and music theory. Courses taught include psychology of music, acoustics, and sociology of music in addition to the traditional music theory sequence (http://www.sgw.hs-magdeburg.de/musik/, March, 2004).

Belgium

Music at the University of Ghent includes the Institute for Music Science, the primary areas of which are music history and empirical music studies under the label of "systematic music science." Within the university is also the Institute for Psychoacoustics and Electronic Music (IPEM). This institute has been instrumental in expanding research in areas of computer-based modeling of music cognition and perception, and has an active guest lecture series in systematic musicology and cognitive musicology (http://www.ipem.rug.ac.be/, February 14, 2004).

Czech Republic

An indication of activity in *Musikwissenschaft* comes from the contributors to the *Acta Universitatis Palackianae Olomucensis, Gymnica*. Contributors include professors in musical aesthetics, semiotics, and music history that specifically list their background in *Musikwissenshaft* (http://www.upol.cz/UP/Pracovis/aupo/, April 4, 2004). Another journal, *Systematic Musicology*, published since 1993 and since 1998 four times a year, is in association with the Institute of Musicology of the Slovak Academy of Sciences and the University of Hamburg, Germany. Topics of prior issues include music education, sound analysis, status of the field of systematic musicology, psychoacoustics, experimental and empirical music research, computer applications, and acoustics (http://www.uhv.sav.sk/GB/journals.html, February 11, 2004).

Poland

The Institute of Musicology at Warsaw University has a Department of Systematic Musicology with two professors and four other teaching staff. The focus is on interdisciplinary music studies. Although the traditional areas of psychoacoustics, psychology of music, sociology of music, and music theory are included, the institute emphasizes biological and cultural issues through archaeology, cultural anthropology, and ethnomusicology. Apparently these disciplines are studied in a manner less traditional than the institute's Department of Ethnomusicology (http://www.imuz.uw.edu.pl/depts.htm, February 17, 2004).

Greece

Although no programs label themselves as systematic musicology, the empirical areas are represented at Aristotle University. Areas covered by five faculty include music psychology and technology, with specializations in rhythm perception, melodic pattern recognition algorithms, generative theories of musical analysis, and music education. Athens University includes faculty in electroacoustic music and musical semiotics. Ionian University covers music psychology, education, and therapy. In Athens there is an Institute for Research in Music and Acoustics sponsored by the Ministries of Culture and Education (Costas Tsougras, lecturer, musical studies department, Aristotle University of Thessaloniki, personal communication, April 2, 2004).

Korea

Seoul National University provides both undergraduate and graduate programs in musicology, chaired by a graduate of the systematic musicology program at UCLA, Professor Suk Won Yi. The course offerings include graduate and undergraduate acoustics, psychology of music, and aesthetics, as well as graduate courses in semiotics, phenomenology of music, and theories of music analysis. Although the coursework is not explicitly labeled systematic musicology, the interdisciplinary scope of the program is clearly aligned with the essence of the concept (Suk Won Yi, Chair, Department of Musicology, Seoul National University, personal communication, April 23, 2004).

Canada

The King's University College in Edmonton, Alberta, offers a graduate course in systematic musicology. The course includes introductory material in philosophy and aesthetics of music, psychology of music, musical symbolism, musical logic, sociology of music, historiography in music, physiology of sound, and acoustics (http://www. kingsu.ab.ca/calendar/coursede.scr/musi495o.htm, February 12, 2004).

United States

University of Massachusetts. The graduate program in musicology offers a master of music with concentrations in music history/musicology. The upper-division courses in musicology specifically refer to bibliography, specialized topics, and research methods in historical and systematic musicology (http://www.umass.edu/gradschool/catalog/prgms/M/Music.html, April 25, 2004).

University of Arkansas. Under musicology, the university provides a seminar in topics in systematic musicology, apparently oriented to musical grammars and computing. In addition, courses in music cognition, including issues of psychology, philosophy, computer science, musicology, and neuroscience as well as a series in ethnomusicology are offered (http://advancement.uark.edu/catalogofstudies/03-04/html/musy.html).

The Ohio State University. The music program at Ohio State University has a noted program in music cognition. Eight faculty in both music and the department of psychology teach a variety of courses, including cognitive ethnomusicology. The website features lectures that include systematic musicology from both an empirical and philosophical, including postmodern, perspective (http://dactyl.som.ohio-state.edu/courses.html, April 24, 2004).

The University of Washington. The only U.S. university to have an officially titled program in systematic musicology other than UCLA was the University of Washington. The program at the University of Washington was ended in 1995, with the consequence that undergraduate instruction in music technology was also eliminated. The program, when it existed, was known for studies in music cognition and acoustics, with expert faculty in both areas (Ocampo 1995).

Interdisciplinarity

This survey demonstrates systematic musicology's institutional reach. The field's disciplinary components are also now dispersed among scholarly fields with which they intersect. Systematic musicology's inherently interdisciplinary nature facilitates reappropriations of initial borrowings from auxiliary disciplines such as philosophy, acoustics, psychology, and sociology. The filiations of psychoacoustics and the psychology of music with its disciplinary partner facilitate its inclusion in psychology programs. The degree of specialization required to conduct advanced research in psychoacoustics and music cognition challenges attempts to unify the field through a common body of research knowledge. Research publications in scientific journals address an intellectual community versed in the language of this scientific discourse. Aesthetics and the philosophy of music present a similar challenge for a field whose scholarly depth corresponds to interdisciplinary breadth. The multiple affiliations of music aesthetics make it equally amenable to programs in analytic and continental philosophy, music criticism, and cultural studies.

The dispersal of systematic musicology's several fields is most forcefully evident in the development of a discipline whose origins in Adler's schema are all but forgotten. Ethnomusicology, whose academic integrity UCLA acknowledged by instituting the first department of ethnomusicology in the world, traces its roots back to comparative musicology, which Alder places under musicology's systematic umbrella. Ethnomusicology's emancipation from systematic musicology marks the coming-of-age of a discipline whose emphasis on field research and experiences distinguishes it from text-based or laboratory research. By taking on an intellectual life of its own, the comparative ethnography that Adler envisages as a component of systematic musicology becomes an independent constituent of musicology's tripartite physiognomy. Ethnomusicology's intellectual traditions and the changing paradigms that mark its history attest to the autonomy of a discipline whose self-reflexive discourse places it among the contemporary social sciences.

The dispersal of psychoacoustics and music cognition away from scientific departments into specialized domains such as music departments and departments of linguistics evidences another contemporary trend. Few perceptual psychologists are being rehired on retirement. Instead, the traditional science domains are being now housed increasingly in departments of music or with faculty who hold appointments across departments. Musical acoustics is rarely taught anymore in physics departments. The inclusion of these disciplines within music programs reinforces the continuing influences of systematic musicology's interdisciplinary research currents.

The dispersal of sociology of music evinces more complex affiliations that attest to its multiple historical and disciplinary links with cognate fields. This interdisciplinary area of research, which is a later addition to be included within systematic musicology's disciplinary fold, intersects ethnomusicology's and cultural anthropology's interests in social conditions surrounding music's production and reception. Impacted by Frankfurt school critical theory and British cultural studies, this interest provides a foundation for research agendas that distinguish the new cultural musicology's music criticism from its predecessor. The sociology of music's multiple filiations exemplify the complex lines of intellectual influence that run throughout systematic musicology's interdisciplinary constitution. Consequently, its dispersal among related disciplines attests to the integrity of its multidisciplinary stance.

Systematic Musicology at UCLA

Systematic musicology's current configuration at UCLA embraces the interdisciplinary orientation that is the legacy of Adler's intention to establish a comprehensive science of music. This configuration, which consists of a philosophical and empirical arm, reflects the pluralistic perspectives engendered by the different disciplinary histories that ground scholarly inquiry in different intellectual traditions. The systematic musicology program's philosophical arm at UCLA draws on hermeneutics, phenomenology, and critical theory to interrogate how music communicates a meaningful experience that is culturally and historically significant. The program's empirical arm investigates music's communication of meaning by linking the intent of composer and performer to the listener through the disciplines of cognitive psychology, psychoacoustics, acoustics, and experimental semiotics. The perspectives gained through these two research avenues contribute to our growing knowledge and understanding of music's importance as a creative human endeavor. By focusing on questions of music's meaningfulness and communicability, each of these research streams pursues fundamental research at different interdisciplinary intersections within a broader scholarly field.

By pursuing the kind of fundamental research that Adler and Seeger envisaged as the purview of a systematic musicology, the program at UCLA renews these innovators' legacies by cultivating the field's interdisciplinary framework. Systematic musicology's dispersal and ultimate marginalization within the North American academy eclipses its central role in interrogating presuppositions that inform musicological and ethnomusicological studies. Empirical studies in music have undergone nomenclatural changes in the last three decades. Initially, there was psychomusicology, an area that combined theoretical and experimental empirical research in music. This area focused on studies of music perception, music learning, computer modeling, and elements of music theory. This has morphed into the concept of cognitive musicology, a discipline which deemphasizes conducting experiments per se and focuses on notational theory devised and interpreted on the basis of research in music cognition. The major journal of the field, *Music Perception*, emphasizes an all-inclusive interdisciplinary perspective, permitting both cognitive music theory and experimental psychology to symbiotically relate and accepting computer modeling and neural nets, multimedia, traditional psychoacoustics, and cognitive ethnomusicology among its subdisciplines.

Empirical research at UCLA renews interest in the traditional areas of music science that includes acoustics, psychophysiology, and psychoacoustics by incorporating computer research, modern concepts of music cognition, and the sophistication of advanced statistical analysis that is both parametric and nonparametric. The main focus is linking physical frames of reference, such as the vibrational and notational, to the listener's cognitive schema. This research deemphasizes notational music theory and stresses the communication process among composer, performer, and listener in areas such as musical expression, timbre, and multimedia. Nonwestern musical structures such as tunings, modes, and the relationship between theory and perception are uniquely incorporated into the breadth of study. It is a goal of the program to renew the dialog between cultural study and experimental research that was partly abandoned after the formative decades of ethnomusicology, demonstrating the relevance and accessibility of new interpretive tools brought about by the information processing revolution.

Systematic musicology's philosophical dialogue with ethnomusicology and critical musicology constitutes a vital moment both for hermeneutical aesthetics and for the self-reflexive understanding of disciplines that investigate music's cultural, historical, and social relevance. By critiquing the history of music's isolation from reality, hermeneutical inquiry reevaluates intellectual practices and research methods that reverse the principle of music's aesthetic autonomy. Aesthetics and politics, globalization, and the crisis of representation constitute the further horizons of a philosophical discourse whose engagement with critical social theory and the phenomenology of music extends systematic musicology's boundaries. This hermeneutical discourse reanimates the spirit of Adler's aim without succumbing to the seduction of a systematic science that would surpass its historical condition. By participating in the history and intellectual traditions to which it contributes, systematic research enlarges the scope of musicological knowledge by expanding its interdisciplinary course.

The two arms of systematic musicology at UCLA each contribute to the field's pandisciplinary outlook. By preserving the intellectual and scholarly integrity of each, the program carries Adler's and Seeger's legacies into the twenty-first century. In an era in which metatheory and ambitions of totalizing knowledge no longer hold sway, exchanges between the program's scientific and philosophical branches enrich the program's multifaceted research perspectives. These perspectives represent the new direction of systematic musicology at UCLA.

REFERENCES

Adler, Guido
    1885 [1981]   "The Scope, Method and Aim of Musicology." Translated by Erica Muggle-
                  stone. *Yearbook for Traditional Music* 13: 1–21.

Haydon, Glen
    1941   *Introduction to Musicology*. New York: Prentice-Hall.

Hutchinson, William
    1976   "Systematic Musicology Reconsidered." *Current Musicology* 27: 61–69.

McCredie, Andrew
    1971   "Systematic Musicology—Some Twentieth-Century Patterns and Perspec-
                  tives." *Studies in Music* 5: 1–35.

Nettl, Bruno
    1995   "The Seminal Eighties: A North American Perspective of the Beginnings
                  of Musicology and Ethnomusicology." http://www.sibetrans.com/trans/
                  trans1/nettl.htm.

Ocampo, Philip
    1995   *The Online Daily of the University of Washington*. Wednesday, September 27.

Pratt, Waldo Selden
    1890   "The Scientific Study of Music." *Official Report to the Music Teachers'
                  National Association Convention, Detroit*.
    1915   "On Behalf of Musicology." *Musical Quarterly* 1: 1–16.

Reimann, Hugo
    1908 [1928]   *Grundriss einer Musikwissenschaft*. 4th edition. Leipzig.

Seeger, Charles
    1951   "Systematic Musicology: Viewpoints, Orientations and Methods." *Journal of
                  the American Musicological Society* 4(3): 240–248.

Empirical Perspectives

Empirical Perspectives in Systematic Musicology

ROGER A. KENDALL
University of California, Los Angeles

The empirical papers in this volume each have abstracts, so this introduction to them discusses generally the nature of empiricism and how musical meaning relates to scientific study, largely from the perspective of cognitive psychology.

Like many scholarly fields, a pendulum swings between paradigms in empirical research. Currently, empirical areas such as acoustics, electroacoustics, and psycho-acoustics have received less attention, particularly within music departments, than they once did. The area of musical emotion, largely neglected as not evincing sufficient scholarly machinery, has been recently revisited, as is evidenced by the number of papers on the subject submitted for the 8th International Conference on Music Perception and Cognition in 2004. Study of music related to other modalities of perception, particularly visual, has recently enjoyed the interest of scientists. The papers by Cohen, Lipscomb, and Kendall in this volume explore some multimedia questions.

However, it must be noted that, despite these interdisciplinary and multimodal studies, in general music empiricism has been guided by the privileged status of pitch, and, to a lesser extent, rhythm. Multi-variable interactions of pitch, rhythm, timbre, tonality and so forth are really rather rare in experimental cognitive psychology. There appears to be a tendency to focus on music notational theoretic structures. Cognitive music theory or cognitive musicology appropriates concepts, data, and ideas from experimental work, but rarely actually attempts to generate new experiments. This sort of "new music theory" has received reinforcement from the political structure of universities, particularly in the United States; the music-theory concept reigns supreme, even though it is rarely theory of music, but theory of notational grammars. Another emerging area of privileged status is that involving neurophysiology, given impetus and stature by generous governmental grants in medicine and related disciplines, and benefiting from technological revolutions in such areas as magnetic resonance imaging.

It is apparent that all levels of empirical work in music and sound are of value. One great triumph of more than a century of psychoacoustics is the technology of compressed sound. Perceptual coding of musical signals relies on physics, computer science, physiology, and perceptual psychology for its success. The knowledge accumulated from Helmholtz through von Békésy to the present was the foundation for this technology. In another century, neurophysiological understanding may lead to a similar breakthrough and benefit. In the meantime, issues of education, enculturation, preference, and meaning will be pursued. In this volume, Vassilakis discusses roughness in terms of culture and psychoacoustics, Hakuru and Ohgushi extend studies of perceptual preference for different tunings, and Heuser concludes our section with an analysis of educational issues.

I believe that in order to ask cogent and valid questions, one cannot be mired in a single frame of reference. Although scholars will specialize, we must also expand our intellectual horizons. Scholarly phobias and distrust must be dissolved, as is implied in the concept of *Fiat Lux* (Let there be light); the ascendancy of the scientific method did not come from myopic empiricists. At the same time, the intellectual abandonment of scientific discourse in some of the arts is only evidence of the reactionary in search of the paradigm *du jour*; unable to truly participate in epistemological expansion. Instead some adopt theory as technology and impede methodological creativity.

Empiricism is but one path in the search for predictive relationships in our observations. We are all observers; the only difference among disciplines is what we do with our observations. The empirical papers in this section provide examples of current scientific approaches to the music communication process.

How Music Influences
the Interpretation of Film and Video:
Approaches from Experimental Psychology

ANNABEL J. COHEN
University of Prince Edward Island

The quantitative nature of experimental psychology enables researchers to test models of the mental interaction of musical and visual information presented in a film or video. One possibility is that associations (that is, meanings) between musical and visual elements simply add together to produce a composite meaning. However, as demonstrated in psychological experiments, this principle of additivity of associations is sometimes insufficient to account for the influences of music on the interpretation of film and video. In particular, Iwamiya (1994), Lipscomb and Kendall (1994a), and Marshall and Cohen (1988) have pointed to the factor of crossmodal (that is, audiovisual) temporal structure as a determinant of the transmission of associations arising from music in a multimedia context. Limitations on working memory, as reflected in models of educational multimedia (Mayer, Bove, Bryman, Mars, and Tapangeo 1996; Fisch 2000), also constrain the interaction of music and film meanings. Taken together, these factors can be represented by a multi-level Congruence-Associationist framework that provides a foundation for experimental-psychological research directed at understanding the influence of music on the interpretation of film and video.

Music often accompanies film, video, and other electronic multimedia. Music is considered an important factor contributing to the meaning of the production. The present article examines the influence of music in such productions and develops a framework for exploring how this influence is accomplished. (The support of the Social Sciences and Humanities Research Council of Canada (SSHRC) and the research assistance of Robert N. Drew and Susan M. Doucette are gratefully acknowledged.) The particular perspective taken is that of experimental psychology, just one of many approaches that together enable a more complete understanding of phenomena such as music and film and their interaction.

The Experimental Psychological Perspective

Psychology is the study of the mind, behavior, and the relationship between them (Sternberg 1996). It is also the science of behavior and the cognitive (or mental) processes (Baron, Earhard and Ozier 2000). As part of its scientific task, psychology aims to determine how perception of events or objects in the world directly depends on the properties of these events or objects which stimulate the senses. Such information is obtained through repeatable experiments in which human responses are measured under different controlled conditions of external stimulation. Experiments have led to precise accounts of the sensitivity of the eye to color and light, and of the ear to sound frequency and intensity. In addition, research has elucidated complex aspects of perception such as reading, speech, and more recently music. Whereas in the last century much progress has been made in explaining how the eye and ear represent simple and complex information that is either visual or auditory in nature, less is known about how the brain represents multisensory information (that is, auditory plus visual). Yet, the multisensory context is typical of everyday experience. Auditory and visual information co-occur naturally: a passing car produces both visual and auditory impressions; a breeze creates effects that are heard and seen, and a speaker's articulation provides correlated information to both the ear and eye. Film, video, and other electronic multimedia provide another common source of multisensory information although this audiovisual co-occurrence is not necessarily natural.

At the same time as experimental psychology begins to address multisensory integration of information as it naturally occurs (for example, speech sounds and corresponding visible changes of the articulatory facial musculature), there is also interest in understanding the perception of arbitrarily combined multisensory sources of information (such as music and film). Although these two domains—the natural and artificial combination of multisensory information—overlap considerably, there is an important difference. In the natural environment, the co-occurrence of auditory and visual information is subject to the rules of physics. For example, dropping a stone of particular shape and weight onto a hollow wood box of specific dimensions will create a sound having a particular intensity and quality. (Indeed this audiovisual regularity forms a basis for grading shellfish, such as mussels in Prince Edward Island.) In the artificial world of film and video, however, any recorded sound or music can arbitrarily accompany the impact of a stone with the surface below. Nevertheless, film-music scholarship (Gorbman 1987; Kalinak 1992) and the art of film-score composition (cf. Cohen 1994/1996, 2001; Davis 1999; Karlin 1994; Thomas 1997) reveal that the application of music in film is not arbitrary; certain combinations of film and music are more effective than others. From the experimental psychological perspective, the appropriate application of music in film reflects psychological rules. Critics of film music, composers of film scores, and audience members tacitly understand these rules. It is the job of the experimental psychologist to make such implicit rules explicit. Recent research in the psychology of film music has progressed in that direction. The present article reviews this research and provides a framework to assist future advances.

Music and Experimental Psychology: Structure and Meaning

The experimental psychological perspective has a long history of application to music. It recognizes that music depends on the interacting minds of composer, performer, and listener. In the last two decades, however, there has been an enormous increase of research in music cognition as represented in seminal books by Deutsch (1999), Dowling and Harwood (1986), Krumhansl (1990), and Sloboda (1985). This psychological literature focuses on many aspects of music and the human responses to them. For the purpose of examining the influence of music on film perception from a psychological perspective, it is useful to distinguish between two aspects: structure and meaning.

For the purpose of this article, structure refers to systematic relations among sounds that characterize the style or grammar of music originating within any time period or culture. Music theory often provides useful terminology for describing this kind of musical structure. For example, for music within the Western-European tradition, terms such as interval, triad, scale, tonality, and rhythm are useful. Descriptions based on the physical properties of sound (for example, frequency, intensity, and duration) can also be employed. Experimental psychological questions about music structure address such issues as perceptual grouping (for example, where do listeners naturally segment parts of an unfolding musical piece, Clarke and Krumhansl 1990; Frankland and Cohen 2004), tonality (for example, what tone, triad, or scale is most prominent in a section of a musical piece, Cohen 2000a; Krumhansl and Toivianinen 2001), or memory (for example, what structural characteristics of music facilitate melodic memory, Cohen, Trehub, and Thorpe 1989; Dowling, Kwak, and Andrews 1995). Perceiving the structure of music is necessary for music appreciation, but listeners are seldom directly cognizant of it; in the same way, speakers of a language are seldom cognizant of the rules of grammar that govern their use of language.

Most people are oblivious to the structure underlying the music they appreciate. It is the meaning of music that forms their predominant conscious experience. Meaning includes the emotional aspect as well as the associations that the music brings to mind (Sloboda 1985; Juslin and Sloboda 2001). Psychological questions about musical meaning focus on revealing common interpretations of particular musical passages (for example, Hevner 1936; Juslin 1997; Kamenetsky, Hill, and Trehub 1997; Krumhansl 1997), anecdotal details about the significance of particular musical experiences during one's life (Sloboda 1998; Sloboda and O'Neill 2001), and assessment of examples of music that gives rise to deep emotional experience (for example, Gabrielsson and Lindstrom 1993). Questions about musical meaning typically fall outside the realm of much musicological discourse. This situation arises because musicology has fostered a view of the autonomy of pure music, that music does not have meaning beyond the relations of the sounds themselves (Kivy 1990). But as film theorist Kassabian (2001, ch. 1) points out, such a view is inconsistent with the application of music in film, and with the experiments which show agreement among listeners on what a musical excerpt does and does not imply. Musicologist Nicholas Cook (1998) in *Analyzing Musical Multimedia* takes the stance, in contrast to the "music-alone" view, that "music is never alone." For Cook, music is a source of meaning in search of an object. Nowhere is its function clearer than its application in multimedia presentations of visual images to which musical meaning becomes aligned. In his book, however, Cook (1998) does not take the perspective of an experimental psychologist, but, as I have argued elsewhere, an experimental psychologist could test many of his implicit and explicit theoretical ideas about the integration of music and visual images (see Cohen 2000b for a review).

Structure and Meaning in Other Domains

For the purposes of this article, the breakdown of music into structure and meaning is useful because the same dichotomy can also apply to the visual aspect of a presentation. Again, structure refers to the formal characteristics of visual images, and meaning refers to the associations, feelings, or interpretations that the visual images bring to mind. For example, consider the video image of a person running over a hilly terrain. The structural description would include such aspects as the temporal patterning or rhythm of the motion pattern, the size and direction of the up and down excursions, the pattern of dark and light, and so on. These characteristics are independent of the individual moving agent and could indeed arise from many different agents, be they inanimate or animate, animal or human, male or female, and so forth. The meaning of the image (its interpretation), however, is closely tied to the particular identity of the moving agent, whether it is a car about to collapse due to rough terrain or a lost child wandering over unknown territory. The general distinction drawn here has been described in other theoretical frameworks using different though related terminology. For example, the experimental psychologist Garner (1962) distinguished internal and external structure. Internal structure referred to the relations within a set of events (for example, a matrix of black and white squares), and external structure referred to the relations between the entire event set and external objects (for example, the external object that could be represented by a black and white matrix pattern). Musicologist Leonard Meyer (1956) distinguished between internal (musical pattern) meaning and external musical meaning (associations to real-world events). These examples distinguish the two separate categories of structure and meaning as used in the present article. It is also possible to theorize a single, inclusive but more complex dimension of meaning as Kendall (1999; 2005) has done by introducing specially defined concepts of syntax and areferential vs. association/referential meaning. For present purposes, however, the terms structure and meaning as distinguished above serve our goals well by allowing us to readily refer to distinct properties that interact across media.

Indeed, the dichotomy of structure and meaning, so defined, apply to each of the five domains that comprise film, video, and other electronic multimedia (Stam 2000). Three of these domains are auditory: music, speech, and sound effects, and the other two are visual: the film image and written text. Whereas the present article focuses on the relation between music and the visual image, it is useful to appreciate that these two domains reside within a larger physical and mental context, yet a context that can be analyzed according to this dichotomy: structure and meaning. This is not to suggest that structure and meaning, as defined, provide the only way to analyze multimedia materials, but, as will be argued here, it is one way that can help to elucidate the nature of the interactions between various media.

The discipline of experimental psychology entails many subdivisions that can apply to music or other aesthetic domains. Perception focuses on the basic processes underlying hearing and seeing, whereas cognition takes into account the mental processes representing long term experience and their impact on memory (Craik and Lockhard 1972), comprehension (Kintsch 1998) and consciousness (Baars 1997). Social psychology considers how attitudes develop and change (e.g., Bandura 2001; Heider and Simmel 1944). Another field of experimental psychology is that of emotion (for example, Juslin and Sloboda 2001). Whereas these separate fields overlap, an enormous literature and associated experimental methodology have been developed for each of them. A complete psychological theory of film-music would necessarily represent the subdisciplines of perception, cognition, social psychology, and emotion. In addition, such topics as lifespan development (how psychological principles and functions change with age), cross-cultural psychology, gender and individual differences would necessarily be included. One can predict a new subdiscipline of multimedia psychology in which the psychology of film-music would contribute an essential part.

Experiments on the Interaction of Music and Film

Three goals of the experimental-psychological perspective emphasized here are (1) to quantify film-music and film materials that send energy to the eye and ear (known as stimuli); (2) to quantify the mental effects of these stimuli independently and in conjunction; and (3) to describe the effects of the joint (film and music) stimuli in predictive models. These goals can be attained by conducting experiments that examine responses of audience members to specific musical and visual patterns (stimuli) in isolation and in conjunction.

To illustrate further, consider as experimental stimulus materials any two musical and visual excerpts. In one condition of the experiment, these examples would be presented independently (that is, music alone, and visual alone) to volunteer participants who would be asked to judge them for meaning. There is an infinite range of possibilities of music and visual examples. The experimenter would first decide what examples would be most appropriate for addressing the question of interest, and what human responses to these stimuli should be gathered from the participants. Basic principles can be revealed even with very simple materials. For example, Cohen (1993) reported experiments in which stimulus melodies of several seconds in duration were repeating tones and the visual patterns were computer animations of a single object moving up and down on a screen (bouncing ball). As shown in Figures 1 and 2 respectively, melodic notes varied in tempo and pitch height and the bounce of the ball varied in tempo and height. As a measure of meaning, participants used a five-point scale to rate the apparent happiness/sadness of the music and video examples separately presented.

The ratings showed that the judged happiness of the melody background increased for faster tempos and higher pitches, and that judged happiness of the bouncing ball increased for faster tempos of bounce and higher bounces. Thus, the meaning of the music and visual materials was systematically related to physical

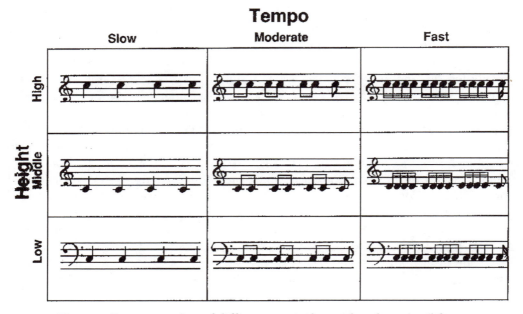

Figure 1. Representation of different musical soundtracks created from
three tempos and three pitch heights of a repeating tone.

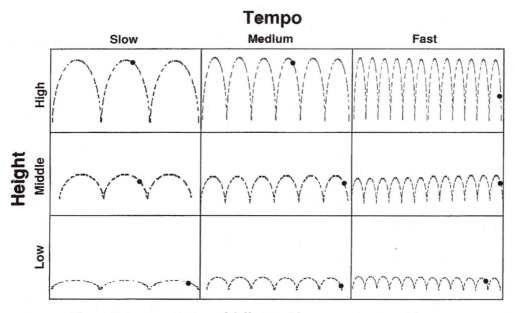

Figure 2. Representation of different video patterns created from
three tempos and three heights of a bouncing ball.

characteristics of the sound and light patterns. Such information about the effect of tempo and pitch height on meaning of musical patterns had been previously revealed in early work of Hevner (1936) but had not been illustrated for visual patterns.

Having determined the meaning of the musical and visual stimuli separately, the next step was to determine the meaning of the musical and visual stimuli in combination. Thus, different participants judged many combinations of the musical and visual patterns (for example, the low, slow melody with the low, slow bounce, and the low, slow melody with the high, fast bounce, and so forth). The question of interest was whether the accompanying music could change the original judgments of the happiness/sadness of the bouncing ball. Indeed it was observed that a ball that bounced high and fast was judged as very happy if the background music was high pitched and fast but was judged less happy if the background music was low pitched and slow (see Figure 3). The statistical analysis of the mean ratings of happiness/sadness arising for the different bounce patterns under the different music backgrounds revealed an effect of both the tempo and the pitch height of the music on the judged happiness of the bouncing ball.

The final stage of the experimental process compared the results from the combined music-video condition to the results of the first stage of the experiment that had obtained meanings of the music and video independently. Recall that the combined results showed that happy music (high, fast tones) decreased the level of sadness (for example, low, slow bounce) of the bouncing ball, and conversely the sad music (low, slow tones) increased the level of happiness (for example, high, fast bounce) of the bouncing ball. Thus, the comparison of the unimodal (auditory *or* visual) and bimodal (auditory *and* visual) conditions suggested that the auditory and visual meanings (that is, associations) systematically combined to produce an overall happiness/sadness judgment.

Even an experiment with simple stimuli, such as those described above, can quickly become complex. For example, presenting a melody based on a major or minor triadic arpeggio rather than just a repeating tone creates yet another dimension of musical meaning for study. Indeed, melodies in the major mode add to the level of happiness of the bouncing ball and melodies in the minor mode decrease it. The temporal relation of the musical and visual patterns is yet another type of variation that might influence the degree to which musical and visual associations combine to create meaning. For example, if the temporal relations are in phase, meanings might combine more effectively than if the temporal relations are out of phase. Thus, studies with stimuli of greater complexity than that of a simple monophonic melody and bouncing ball cannot focus exhaustively on all the physical characteristics of the test stimuli. Careful descriptions of the experimental stimuli are often provided by the authors of these studies (for example, Boltz 2001; Lipscomb and Kendall 1994a) and urge us not to lose sight of the fact that the source of musical influence is ultimately the physical and structural characteristics of the music.

In the study of the bouncing ball just described, participants assessed only one kind of meaning (that on the happiness/sadness dimension). Other dimensions of meaning could of course be investigated. For example, Bolivar, Cohen, and Fentress (1994) asked participants to rate friendliness/aggressiveness of social interactions

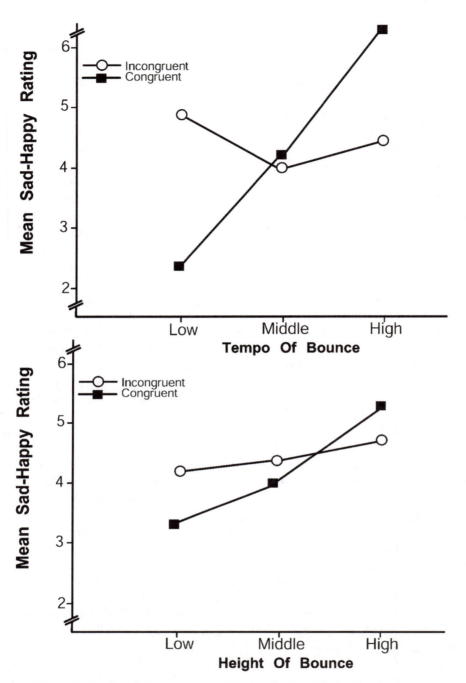

Figure 3. Mean rated happiness of the bouncing ball under congruent
and incongruent audiovisual tempo and height combinations
(data from Cohen 1993).

among wolves, the particular visual material under investigation. Fundamental work of Osgood, Suci, and Tannenbaum (1957) on the Semantic Differential showed that connotative meanings (that is, affective meaning as compared to dictionary definitions or denotative meaning) depend on three different dimensions: evaluation (for example, good-bad), potency (for example, strong-weak), and activity (fast-slow). The degree to which a bipolar adjective pair (for example, strong-weak) loads on each of the three dimensions has been empirically determined through the statistical method of factor analysis (other techniques such as cluster analysis can also provide similar information). A researcher can select from a published source (for example, Osgood et al. 1957) adjective pairs with previously determined loadings on the three dimensions so as to measure the importance of the three dimensions for the meaning of an audio, visual, or audiovisual excerpt. Thus, Marshall and Cohen (1988), Lipscomb and Kendall (1994a), and Sirius and Clark (1994) used three or four different bipolar adjective pairs to represent each of the three connotative dimensions of meaning.

Iwamiya (1994) took a different starting point and used 22 different bipolar adjective pairs that he felt could be applied to audio and visual stimuli drawn from commercially recorded materials. The rating data were then submitted to factor analysis to reveal a number of dimensions on which the connotative judgments were based. Rather than finding only the three traditional dimensions, his data led to five separate dimensions of meaning that he interpreted as tightness, evaluation, brightness, cleanness, and uniqueness. Similarly, Lipscomb and Kendall (1994a) carried out a cluster analysis of the ratings on ten bipolar adjective pairs and revealed two primary factors, one for evaluation and the other that they referred to as a combination of potency and activity.

It is not important that different dimensions or different numbers of dimensions appear in the studies of the diverse investigators. What is important is that within a study, the same dimensions of meaning can be tracked across different experimental conditions. Evidence has been observed both for additivity of audio and visual meaning along particular dimensions and for a more complex interaction between the audio and visual meanings on particular dimensions.

In the experiment of Marshall and Cohen (1988), a two-minute animation was presented that entailed a large and small triangle and a small circle. The animation had been developed within social psychology by Heider and Simmel (1944) to illustrate that people form stereotypes even of inanimate objects. People who see this short animation generally characterize the large triangle as a bully victimizing the two smaller geometric figures. The question that Marshall and Cohen posed was whether two contrasting examples of background music would alter observers' attitudes toward these figures. Thus baseline information about the meaning of the music and visual stimuli was first obtained on twelve bipolar adjective rating scales (for example, powerful/powerless). For the visual stimulus, the participants judged each of the three film characters (large and small triangle and small circle) and the film overall. In the second part of the study, other participants were presented with one combination of the music and film and judged the film and film characters on the same twelve bipolar adjective ratings. With this information, it was possible to determine whether the meaning of the visual material changed when the music was added to it, and, if so, whether the change was systematically related to the meaning of the music. Judgments of individual characters in the film led to a surprising finding. It appeared that the degree of meaning along a particular dimension ascribed to each of the film characters depended on the particular background music. In particular, the activity rating for the three geometric characters differed significantly under the two music backgrounds, although the overall activity rating of the two kinds of music did not differ.

In relating the change in meaning of the film characters to the different background music, Marshall and Cohen (1988) postulated that an interaction of the temporal structure of the film and music influenced visual attention, such that the focus of visual attention differed under the two different musical backgrounds. Thus, the attributes of the music were differentially ascribed to the visual attentional focus that differed for each of the two pieces of music. They argued that if music through structural similarity directs attention to a particular feature of the film and provides particular connotative information, then this particular connotation can become associated with the attended visual feature (see also Cook 1998: 69 for discussion). This joint process of the emergence of congruent music-visual temporal structure followed by ascription of meaning (associations) led to the postulation of the Congruence-Associationist Framework for understanding the effects of film music in film and video presentations.

Association

Although Marshall and Cohen (1988) focused on both temporal-structural congruence and association, in some cases, association alone is sufficient to account for effects of music in the interpretation of a film. In a further study reported by Cohen (1993), two one-minute feature-film excerpts (a fight scene between two men and an encounter between a man and woman) and two orchestrated music excerpts (suitably entitled "Conflict" and "Say hello to love") provided the stimulus materials. Semantic differential (that is, bipolar adjective rating) judgments were obtained to reflect the evaluation, potency, and activity dimensions for each of the music and video excerpts, and these judgments revealed large differences in meaning between the two music excerpts and between the two film excerpts. When the music and video excerpts were combined, there was a change in meaning for only one of the video excerpts. This excerpt showed an interaction between a man and a woman that could be interpreted as either a romantic or an aggressive encounter. The different background musical examples altered the interpretation systematically and raised or lowered the ratings on the semantic differential scales accordingly. The other visual excerpt of two men fighting was unambiguous, and the music had no strong impact on its meaning. Thus, when a visual excerpt is ambiguous, the associations from the background music can assist in establishing the context and disambiguating the interpretation.

Similarly, ratings of friendliness/aggressiveness of background music systematically influenced the judged friendliness/aggressiveness of the social interactions of wolves depicted in short film clips (Bolivar et al. 1994). Using music and film excerpts having various degrees of perceived finality or closure, Thompson, Russo, and Sinclair

(1994) showed a direct (linear) influence of musical closure on the perceived closedness or finality of a film excerpt. More recently, Boltz (2001) showed that positive or negative music significantly biased the interpretation of film clips drawn from Alfred Hitchcock mysteries. These examples are only some that show rather straightforward additivity of associations of music that influences the interpretation of a film.

Music-Visual Structural Congruence

In spite of the many examples whereby associations from music appear to combine directly with associations generated by the visual information, the connection between music and film may not necessarily be this straightforward in all, or even most, cases. The complication has been introduced earlier when we noted that, in the study by Marshall and Cohen (1988), two music excerpts having the same value on the activity dimension led to different ratings of activity of the three geometric "characters" in the presentation. It was suggested that similar temporal structure of the music and film altered the visual attention pattern and directed attention toward one character under one music soundtrack and to a different character under the other music soundtrack.

The importance of temporal structural congruence has also been addressed in several other studies of effects of the film music. Iwamiya (1994), for example, shifted by 500 ms the audio and visual channels of short excerpts drawn from commercially available laser discs (other bases of mismatch were applied to other excerpts in the materials examined). He asked participants to rate their perceived degree of match of the original and altered versions of the excerpts. Not surprisingly the degree of perceived match of the music and visual information was enhanced in the synchronized as compared to the asynchronized condition. The other form of mismatch that Iwamiya explored entailed presentation of a new music background with the original visual material and this also reduced the degree of matching. Participants also rated audiovisual stimuli independently and in conjunction on 22 rating scales previously mentioned. The influence of higher order factors (for example, cleanness and uniqueness) was direct only when the music and visual materials were well matched; however, for the lower order factor, brightness, the influence on meaning was direct regardless of degree of matching. The results of this study are consistent with a three-stage process in which an analysis of the meaning of the separate audio and visual stimuli is first assessed. This process itself has more than one level, in that some features of the stimuli are simple (for example, brightness) whereas others (for example, uniqueness) require comparisons with past experience for their complete analysis. A second process entails comparison of the properties of the audio and visual stimuli, the outcome of which is an assessment of the degree of matching. A third and final process ascribes information from the audio channel to the visual focus of attention. Information from lower-order audio features, such as intensity, is passed to the output of the visual analysis regardless of the degree of match between the music and visual materials. Information from higher-order auditory analyses involving memory and cognition is passed to the visual analysis only if the music and visual material match each other well. Thus, association alone cannot explain how the music influences the visual interpretation. Audiovisual incongruence (both structural and associationist) produces a bottleneck.

Like Iwamiya (1994), Lipscomb and Kendall (1994a) focused on the degree of matching of music-visual pairs. Their stimuli were derived from the motion picture *Star Trek IV: The Voyage Home*, and all soundtracks were taken from the film score composed by Leonard Rosenman. All possible combinations of five video and music excerpts were created making special effort to temporally align the accent patterns of the video and audio, especially in the twenty combinations that were novel. For each visual excerpt, participants in the experiment were presented with each of the five music soundtrack excerpts and they were asked to select the soundtrack that was the best-fit for the excerpt. Almost all participants chose the excerpt that had been created originally by the composer for the excerpt. Participants and composer obviously perceived the visual and music materials according to the same psychological principles and could detect that the originally intended soundtrack made the best match to the visual excerpt.

Because the authors took special effort to temporally align the soundtracks with the visual accent pattern in the visual clip, it is unlikely that temporal synchrony of the original pair provided the basis for matching. Had the film clip and audio track been deliberately desynchronized, as in the case of Iwamiya (1994), this would have provided a basis for the higher rating of the composer's original soundtrack. Thus, we are left with the possibility that the associations brought to mind by the music originally composed for the excerpt blended better with the associations elicited by the visual excerpt than did the associations elicited by the four other music excerpts arbitrarily assigned to each visual clip. The best match of course might not necessarily result from identity of music and visual associations but rather from the complementarity of the two sources of information.

To further explore the basis of the perceived matching, Lipscomb and Kendall (1994a) asked other participants to provide ratings for the five visual and five music excerpts on ten bipolar adjective dimensions. Mean ratings on the scales differed significantly for different music soundtracks when each film excerpt was held constant. The evaluation judgments were typically highest for the original audio and visual combination confirming the previously observed "best-fit" results. An analysis of the structure of the music suggested that meaning on particular dimensions relied on particular features for the music (for example, high potency ratings arose for complex harmonic structure, rubato, and complex rhythm; high activity ratings arose for allegro tempo and steady pulse). Consideration of all of this information led Lipscomb and Kendall (1994a: 91) to postulate a multistage process to account for the contribution of film music to the overall film production, and more specifically the role of music/visual congruence on attentional focus. They posit the importance of an initial comparison process that examines the relation of the accent structure of the visual and audio material. If these two accent structures match, then attention will be directed to the composite. If the focus of attention is on both audio and visual materials due to this joint accent structure, then associations from the audio source will flow through to the visual source. If there is no match between the audio and visual accent structure, then the direction of attention will shift from the audiovisual pair and associative information from the audio source will not be transmitted further.

Marshall and Cohen (1988), Lipscomb and Kendall (1994a), and Iwamiya (1994) all have focused on the importance of music-visual temporal-pattern matching on the ascription of associations of music to the visual source. Additional studies have explored the role of shared musical-video temporal congruencies. Bolivar et al. (1994) used two examples of each music-visual stimulus excerpt of wolf social interactions. Each film clip lasted only several seconds. Temporal match was greater in one music-visual pair than the other. An increased degree of audiovisual synchrony of these very short excerpts, however, did not increase the influence of the background music on the meaning of the film. Lipscomb (1998, 1999; Lipscomb and Kendall 1994b) reported that synchrony played a role for very simple audiovisual patterns but that as the materials became more complex and realistic, the role of synchrony decreased. Sugano and Iwamiya (1998) have also shown the sensitivity of a perceiver to the synchrony of audio-visual periodicity using very simple computer generated displays.

Capacity-Limited Working Memory

The research reviewed in this article suggests that much of the influence of music on the interpretation of film may be explained by association and by structural congruence. The review, however, also makes clear that not all musical information that might influence the interpretation of film exerts such an influence. The brain is limited in the amount of information it can handle at any one time. In making sense of a film or video, mental processes must relate incoming information to past experience stored in long-term memory. This task requires working memory, of which there is a limited supply (Baddeley 1992; Snyder 2000). Although the focus of the present article is primarily on entertainment media, two education-theoretic models provide a precedent for considering the concept of capacity limitation in the development of a framework for understanding multimedia representation. The first model is provided by Mayer and his colleagues in educational psychology at the University of California at Santa Barbara. The second model comes from Fisch at the Children's Television Workshop in New York.

Mayer's cognitive theory of meaningful multimedia learning incorporates elements from several other cognitive-psychological theories: dual-coding theory (Paivio 1990), cognitive-load theory (Mousavi, Low, and Sweller 1995), and generative theory (Wittrock 1989). Meaningful learning requires that the learner engage in active cognitive processes such as selecting words, selecting images, organizing words, organizing images, and integrating words and images (compare Mayer et al. 1996: 64–66). All of these processes entail building representations be they visual or verbal (auditory) or building connections between the different types of representations or creating logical sequences of them.

Most of the work of Mayer and his colleagues has focused on visual and verbal (auditory) material (for example, Mayer 1989; Mayer and Anderson 1991; Mayer and Moreno 1998). However, Moreno and Mayer (2000) explicitly examined the role of music and sound effects (auditory adjuncts) in the design of multimedia instructional messages. They evaluated two competing hypothetical effects of the role of background music, sound effects, or both on learning. The first hypothesis was that entertaining auditory adjuncts, like music, increase both arousal level and the overall level of attention and, consequently, the amount of processing capacity. The second hypothesis was that extraneous (incoherent) sound requires processing capacity and consequently depletes processing resources. Thus, the hypotheses differ in their effect on working memory and processing capacity.

Moreno and Mayer (2000) examined the effect of adding music and environmental sound to multimedia instructional material presented to students who were learning about lightning or the braking system of a car. Presentation of music as part of the multimedia instruction did not enhance learning as measured by memory for verbal material and transfer of information. The results were interpreted as inconsistent with the arousal hypothesis and as consistent with the coherence hypothesis, that is, that extraneous entertaining audio materials depleted processing resources. The music, however, had been arbitrarily selected and played throughout the entire narrative. This is not the way that music is typically used in film. For film, music is specifically chosen or composed to complement the narrative and it is spotted in only at specific points in the drama. Hence, the negative results of Moreno and Mayer (2000) may well apply to irrelevant sounds, and the authors themselves state that it is necessary to conduct additional studies in which the coordination of the sounds is directly manipulated. They conclude that problems arise due to auditory adjuncts because auditory adjuncts "do their damage by limiting the amount of relevant verbal material the learner selects for processing in working memory and by reducing the learner's resources for building connections between verbal and visual representations of the to-be-learned material" (Moreno and Mayer 2000: 124). Clearly, in their view, music and sound effects that are poorly integrated with the narrative can deplete working memory capacity. At the same time, it can be argued, following Boltz (2001), that music can also assist the efficient use of working memory capacity by providing useful context, or "advance organizers" in the words of Fisch (2000), to be discussed below.

Fisch (2000) proposes a model that focuses on allocation of working memory resources while watching television. The model consists of a theoretical construct with three basic components: processing of a narrative, processing of educational content, and distance, that is the degree to which the educational content is integral or tangential to the narrative. Fisch (2000) developed a model to represent how information about the narrative and the educational content can be simultaneously extracted.

The primary assumption of the model is that comprehension of television draws on the limited capacity of working memory. Working memory is required to encode and retain information from the production and integrate it with knowledge stored in long-term memory. Demands on working memory are reflected in longer response times and poorer performance in secondary tasks that are concurrent with viewing. According to the model, narrative and educational content use the same processing resources. Competition for resources increases with decreasing connection of the story and the educational content. When the educational content is integral to the story, then the parallel processes become complementary rather than competitive, and the comprehension of the educational content is likely to be strengthened.

Based on his capacity model, Fisch (2000) predicts several ways in which television program characteristics would result in greater comprehension and retention of educational content. It is suggested here that several of these characteristics can be implemented via music. Music can be used to foreshadow (Boltz 2001; Boltz, Schulkind, and Kantra 1991) and provide what Fisch refers to as "advance organizers" of both the narrative and the educational content or deeper message. Such advance organizers decrease demands for processing both narrative and educational content respectively. By associating the same music with different aspects of the content (be it narrative or educational) the distance between diverse content can be reduced and consequently decrease competition between resources. Music can increase the interest of a presentation and thereby increase transmission of content (although, the work of Mayer and his colleagues earlier described cautions against such a role for irrelevant music). Fisch (2000) also distinguishes between two kinds of capacity limitations in watching television: those related to more peripheral perceptual and attentional mechanisms, and those related to controlled processing (that is, the ability to thoughtfully process and store information). It can be argued that music can play a role in both, and this role would need to be clarified through future research. To this end, empirical investigations of music and film from a memory perspective have begun to define independent and integrative aspects of the auditory and visual modalities (see Boltz 2004; Cohen 1995).

Congruence-Associationist Framework of the Mental Representation of Multimedia

The present article has reviewed studies that have examined the role of film music on the interpretation of a film or video presentation. It has emphasized two principles: association and structural congruence. Association accounts for the direct transfer of meanings elicited by music to the film context, setting the mood, or disambiguating plot. On the other hand, structural congruence, through principles of grouping, influences attention to specific visual information. It was hence argued that, under certain circumstances, the impact of associative principles was to some extent governed by the structural congruence of audio and visual materials. In other words, associations would be applied to the focus of attention that was under control of structural congruence. However, it was also noted that the musical and visual channels operate within the broader context of other domains such as printed or written text, sound effects, and speech. Drawing on the literature from educational multimedia, the processing of multimedia relies on limited-capacity working memory and feeds back from and forward to long-term memory. This literature also emphasizes that narrative is primary, and the audience member is actively engaged in constructing a narrative. A final assumption, developed elsewhere (Cohen 2001 with respect to film music) is that vision generally predominates over audition. Thus, the narrative created is primarily a visual one (for example, according to film theorist Mitry 1990: 235, "the logical development and principle significations are based on the development of images, not on verbal associations"). Putting all of this together, a framework for representing the processing of multimedia is proposed below as shown in Figure 4.

The framework consists of five parallel channels representing each of the five domains that contribute to multimedia presentations: printed/written text, speech, music, sound effects, and visual images (Stam 2000). Each channel represents a separate but interacting information processing system. At the first stage, surface (physical) information is received by the sense organs and is analyzed at the next stage into structural characteristics (for example, accent patterns, contours, motions) and meaning characteristics (associations brought to mind). At this stage, interactions among the five domains may take place. For example, if cross-domain temporal accents coincide, then attention will be focused at these loci of information. Given the dominance of vision, coincident accents may focus visual attention on that part of the visual scene

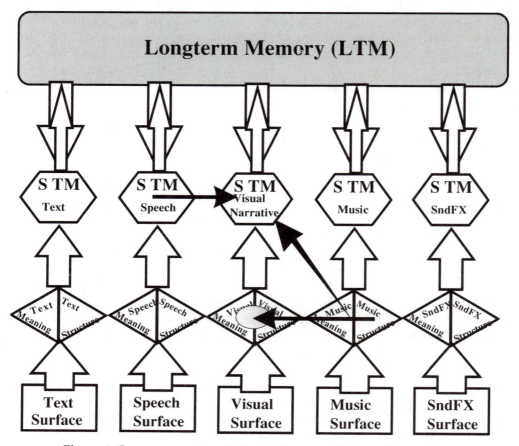

Figure 4. Congruence-Associationist Framework for understanding
how music influences the interpretation of film and video.

that is structurally congruent with the music. An example of this visual focus is shown by the arrow in figure 4 from music structure to the visual channel, highlighting here a portion of the total visual information depicted in the shaded oval. At the next short-term memory (STM) stage, preattended and attended information is processed in working memory and to some extent leaks through to long-term memory (LTM) above. LTM is the repository of knowledge gained through lifelong experience. It is the source of inferences and contexts that an individual actively generates in order to make sense of the external world, known initially through the surface information. The inferences generated via LTM are sent down to working memory. Working memory also receives information sent up from the surface. It is here at the site of working memory that the matching process occurs. The best match between the bottom-up information from the surface and the top-down information from LTM enters consciousness (Cohen 2001; Grossberg 1995) and contribute to the *working narrative*. The narrative plays out primarily in the visual domain and information from the other channels feed into it. The working narrative is the audience member's representation of the story based on the cues from the separate media domains that are deciphered with the help of LTM.

Music plays a role in creating the working narrative (in the diagram, the visual narrative) in several ways. It directs attention to certain features in the visual image domain (see the horizontal arrow from music structure), it feeds information directly to the working narrative (see the diagonal arrow directed from music meaning to the STM Visual Narrative), and it provides associations that establish inferences in LTM. For the sake of clarity, only a few of the many possible interactions between domains are shown. Given the limitations of working memory, only some of the available information ever reaches consciousness and the working narrative.

Elements of the present framework were first presented by Marshall and Cohen (1988) and Cohen (1990), who focused primarily on the influence of music-visual structural congruence on attention and the consequent directing of musical meaning to a visual focus. Cohen (1999, 2000a, 2001) expanded this framework to reflect the contribution of long-term memory on the establishment of inferences and the development of a working narrative based on matching between short-term and long-term memory. The present framework presents a more complete context, extending now to the additional domains of scripted text and sound effects. The review of the educational multimedia literature further justifies the emphasis of this framework on the limited capacity of working memory and the role of active cognitive processes in creation of a working narrative.

In conclusion, experimental psychology research on the effects of film music is in its infancy. The present article has reviewed some of the progress that has been made and provides the Congruence-Associationist framework for considering several challenging issues that lie ahead. The framework illustrates an orderly complexity that underlies the influence of music on the interpretation of film, video, or other electronic multimedia. The framework may help both to stimulate new questions and to interpret results of experiments aimed toward understanding the ways in which music enhances communication between the mind of a director and the mind of an audience member.

REFERENCES

Baars, B. J.
1997   *In the Theater of Consciousness: The Workspace of the Mind.* New York: Oxford University Press.

Baddeley, A. D.
1992   "Working Memory." *Science* 255: 556–559.

Bandura, A.
2001   "Social Cognitive Theory of Mass Communication." *Media Psychology* 3: 265–299.

Baron, R.A, Earhard, B., and Ozier, M.
2000   *Psychology.* 2d ed. Scarborough: Allyn & Bacon.

Bolivar, V., Cohen, A. J., and Fentress, J.
1994/1996   "Semantic and Formal Congruency in Music and Motion Pictures: Effects on the Interpretation of Visual Action." *Psychomusicology* 13: 28–59.

Boltz, M.
2001   "Musical Soundtracks as a Schematic Influence on the Cognitive Processing of Filmed Events." *Music Perception* 18: 427–455.
2004   "The cognitive processing of film and musical soundtracks." *Memory and Cognition* 32: 1194–1205.

Boltz, M., Schulkind, M., and Kantra, S.
1991   "Effects of Background Music on the Remembering of Filmed Events." *Memory and Cognition* 19: 593–606.

Clarke, E. F. and Krumhansl, C. L.
1990   "Perceiving Musical Time." *Music Perception* 7: 213–251.

Cohen, A. J.
1990   "Understanding musical soundtracks." *Empirical Studies of the Arts* 8: 111–124.
1993   "Associationism and Musical Soundtrack Phenomena." *Contemporary Music Review* 9: 163–78.
1995   "One-trial memory integration of music and film: A direct test." Paper presented at the Annual Meeting of the Canadian Acoustical Association, Quebec City.
1994/1996   Ed. "The Psychology of Film Music [Special two-issue volume]." *Psychomusicology* 13.
1999   "The Functions of Music in Multimedia: A Cognitive Approach." In S.W. Yi, ed., *Music, Mind, & Science.* Seoul: Seoul University Press, pp. 53–69.
2000a   "Film Music: A Cognitive Perspective." In D. Neumeyer, J. Buhler, and C. Flinn, eds., *Music and Cinema.* Middletown, CT: Wesleyan University Press, pp. 360–377.
2000b   "Musicology Alone." Review of *Analysing Musical Multimedia*, by Nicholas Cook (Oxford University Press). *Music Perception* 17: 247–260.
2001   "Music as the Source of Emotion in Film." In P. Juslin, and J. Sloboda, eds., *Music and Emotion.* Oxford: Oxford University Press, pp. 249–272.

Cohen, A. J., Trehub, S. E., and Thorpe, L. A.
    1989   "Effects of Uncertainty on Melodic Information Processing. "*Perception and Psychophysics* 46: 18–28.

Cook, N.
    1998   *Analysing Musical Multimedia*. Oxford: Clarendon Press.

Craik, F. I. M., and Lockhardt, R. S.
    1972   "Levels of Processing: A Framework for Memory Research." *Journal of Verbal Learning and Verbal Behavior* 11: 671–684.

Davis, R.
    1999   *Complete Guide to Film Scoring*. Boston: Berklee Press.

Deutsch, D.
    1999   *Psychology of Music*. 2d ed. N.Y.: Academic.

Dowling, J., and Harwood, D.
    1986   *Music Cognition*. N.Y.: Academic.

Dowling, W. J., Kwak, S. Y., and Andrews, M. W.
    1995   "The Time Course of Recognition of Novel Melodies." *Perception & Psychophysics* 57: 136–149.

Fisch, S. M.
    2000   "A Capacity Model of Children's Comprehension of Educational Content on Television." *Media Psychology* 2: 63–91.

Frankland, B. W., and Cohen, A. J.
    2004   "Parsing of Melody: Quantifying and Testing Group Preference Rules of Lerdahl & Jackendoff's (1983) *Generative Theory of Tonal Music*." *Music Perception* 21: 499–543.

Gabrielsson, A., and Lindstrom, S.
    1993   "On Strong Experiences of Music." *Musik Psychologie*, Band 10: 118–139.

Garner, W. L.
    1962   *Uncertainty and Structure as Psychological Concepts*. N.Y.: Wiley.

Gorbman, C.
    1987   *Unheard Melodies: Narrative Film Music*. Bloomington: Indiana University Press.

Grossberg, S.
    1995   "The Attentive Brain." *American Scientist* 83: 438–49.

Heider, F., and Simmel, M.
    1944   "An Experimental Study of Apparent Behavior." *American Journal of Psychology* 57: 243–259.

Hevner, K.
    1936   "Experimental Studies of the Elements of Expression in Music." *American Journal of Psychology* 57: 243–259.

Iwamiya, S.
    1994/1996   "Interaction Between Auditory and Visual Processing when Listening to Music in an Audiovisual Context: 1. Matching 2. Audio Quality." *Psychomusicology* 13: 133–154.

Juslin, P.
    1997   "Emotional Communication in Music Performance: A Functionalist Per-
                    spective and some Data." *Music Perception* 14: 383–418.
Juslin, P., and Sloboda, J. A.
    2001   *Music and Emotion.* Oxford, UK: Oxford University Press.
Kalinak, K.
    1992   *Settling the Score.* Madison: University of Wisconsin Press.
Karlin, F.
    1994   *Listening to the Movies.* N. Y.: Schirmer.
Kassabian, A.
    2001   *Hearing Film: Tracking Identifications in Hollywood Film Music.* N.Y.:
                    Routledge.
Kamenetsky, S. T., Hill, D. S., and Trehub, S. E.
    1997   "Effect of Tempo and Dynamics on the Perception of Emotion in Music."
                    Psychology of Music 25: 149–160.
Kendall, R.
    1999   "A Theory of Meaning and Film Music." Joint meeting of the Acoustical
                    Society of America and the European Acoustics Association, Berlin. Invited
                    paper.
    2005   "Empirical Approaches to Musical Meaning." *Selected Reports in Ethnomusi-
                    cology*, Vol. 12: 69–102.
Kintsch, W.
    1998   *Comprehension: A Paradigm for Cognition.* Cambridge: Cambridge Univer-
                    sity Press.
Kivy, P.
    1990   *Music Alone: Philosophical Reflections on the Purely Musical Experience.*
                    Ithaca, NY: Cornell University Press.
Krumhansl, C. L.
    1990   *Cognitive Foundations of Musical Pitch.* N.Y.: Oxford University Press.
    1997   "An Exploratory Study of Musical Emotions and Psychophysiology." *Cana-
                    dian Journal of Psychology* 51: 336–352.
Krumhansl, C. L., and Toivianinen, P.
    2001   "Tonal Cognition." In R. J. Zatorre, and I. Peretz, eds., *The Biological Founda-
                    tions of Music.* N.Y.: New York Academy of Sciences, pp. 77–91.
Lipscomb, S. D.
    1998   "Synchronization of Musical Sound and Visual Images: Issues of Empirical
                    and Practical Significance in Multimedia Development." Abstract in *Journal
                    of the Acoustical Society of America* 104: 1780.
    1999   "Cross-Modal Integration: Synchronization of Auditory and Visual Compo-
                    nents in Simple and Complex Media." Abstract in *Journal of the Acoustical
                    Society of America* 105: 1274.
Lipscomb, S. D., and Kendall, R.
    1994a/1996   "Perceptual Judgment of the Relationship Between Musical and Visual Com-
                    ponents in Film." *Psychomusicology* 13: 60–98.

1994b   "Sources of Accent in Musical Sound and Visual Motion." In I. Deliege, ed., *Proceedings 3ICMPC*. Liege: Belgium, pp. 451–452.

Marshall, S. E. and Cohen, A. J.
1988   "Effects of musical soundtracks on attitudes toward animated geometric figures." *Music Perception* 6: 95–112.

Mayer, R. E.
1989   "Systematic Thinking Fostered by Ilustrations in Scientific Text." *Journal of Educational Psychology* 81: 240–246.

Mayer, R. E., and Anderson, R. B.
1991   "Animations Need Narration: An Experimental Test of a Dual-Coding Hypothesis." *Journal of Educational Psychology* 83: 484–490.

Mayer, R. E., Bove, W., Bryman, A., Mars, R., and Tapangeo, L.
1996   "When Less is More: Meaningful Learning from Visual and Verbal Summaries of Science Textbook Lessons." *Journal of Educational Psychology* 88: 64–73.

Mayer, R. E., and Moreno, R.
1998   "A Split-Attention Effect in Multimedia Learning: Evidence for Dual Processing Systems in Working Memory." *Journal of Educational Psychology* 90: 312–320.

Meyer, L.
1956   *Emotion and Meaning in Music*. Chicago: University of Chicago Press.

Mitry, J.
1990   *The Aesthetics and Psychology of the Cinema*. (Abridged edition by Mitry). C. King (trans/1997; original unabridged French ed. 1963). Bloomington, IN: Indiana University Press.

Moreno, R., and Mayer, R. E.
2000   "A Coherence Effect in Multimedia Learning: The Case for Minimizing Irrelevant Sounds in the Design of Multimedia Instructional Messages." *Journal of Educational Psychology* 92: 117–125.

Mousavi, S. Y., Low, R., and Sweller, J.
1995   "Reducing Cognitive Load by Mixing Auditory and Visual Presentation Modes." *Journal of Educational Psychology* 87: 319–334.

Osgood, C.E., Suci, G. J., and Tannenbaum, P.H.
1957   *The Measurement of Meaning*. Urbana: University of Illinois Press.

Paivio, A.
1990   *Mental Representations: A Dual-Coding Approach*. 2d ed. N.Y.: Oxford University Press.

Sirius, G., and Clarke, E. F.
1994/1996   "The Perception of Audiovisual Relationships: A Preliminary Study." *Psychomusicology* 13: 119–132.

Sloboda, J.
1985   *The Musical Mind: The Cognitive Psychology of Music*. New York: Oxford University Press.
1998   "Everyday Uses of Music Listening." In S. W. Yi, ed., *5th ICMPC Proceedings*. Seoul: Seoul National University, pp. 55–60.

Sloboda, J., and O'Neill, S.
    2001   "Emotions in Everyday Listening to Music." In P. Juslin, and J. Sloboda, eds.,
                    Music and Emotion. Oxford: Oxford University Press, pp. 415–429.

Snyder, B.
    2000   *Music and Memory.* Cambridge, MA: MIT.

Stam, R.
    2000   *Film theory.* Malden, MA: Blackwell.

Sternberg, R. J.
    1996   *Cognitive Psychology.* Ft. Worth, TX: Harcourt Brace.

Sugano, Y., and Iwamiya, S.
    1998   "On the Matching of Music and Motion Picture Using Computer Graphics
                    and Computer Music." *Proc. 5ICMPC*: 465–468.

Thomas, T.
    1997   *Music for the Movies.* 2d ed. Los Angeles: Silman-James.

Thompson, W. F., Russo, F. A., and Sinclair, D.
    1994/1996   "Effects of Underscoring on the Perception of Closure in Filmed Events."
                    Psychomusicology 13: 9–27.

Wittrock, M. C.
    1989   "Generative Processes of Comprehension." *Educational Psychologist* 24:
                    345–376.

The Perception of Audio-visual Composites: Accent Structure Alignment of Simple Stimuli

SCOTT D. LIPSCOMB
Northwestern University

This investigation examines the relationship between musical sound and visual images when they are paired in simple animated sequences. Based on a model of film music proposed in 1996 by Lipscomb and Kendall, the study focuses specifically on the relationship of points perceived as accented musically and visually. The following research questions were answered: (1) What are the determinants of "accent" (salient moments) in the visual and auditory fields? and (2) Is the precise alignment of auditory and visual strata necessary to ensure that an observer finds the combination effective? In this experimental study, two convergent methods were used: a verbal scaling task and a similarity judgment task. Three alignment conditions were incorporated: consonant (accents in the music occur at the same temporal rate and are perfectly aligned with accents in the visual image), out-of-phase (accents occur at the same rate, but are perceptibly misaligned), or dissonant (accents occur at different rates). Results confirmed that VAME ratings are significantly different for the three alignment conditions. Consonant combinations were rated highest, followed by out-of-phase combinations, and dissonant combinations received the lowest ratings. Subject similarity judgments in response to these simple stimuli divided clearly into three dimensions: visual component, audio component, and alignment condition, further confirming the significance of the alignment of accent strata.

In contemporary society, the human sensory system is bombarded by sounds and images intended to attract attention, manipulate state of mind, or affect behavior.[1] Patients awaiting a medical or dental appointment are often subjected to the "soothing" sounds of Muzak as they sit in the waiting area. Trend-setting fashions are displayed in mall shops blaring the latest Top 40 selections to attract their specific clientele. Corporate training sessions and management presentations frequently employ not only communication through text and speech, but a variety of multimedia types for the purpose of attracting and maintaining attention, for example, music, graphs, and animation. Recent versions of word processors allow the embedding of sound files, animations, charts, equations, pictures, and information from multiple applications within a single document. Even while standing in line at an amusement park or ordering a drink at the local pub, the presence of television screens providing aural and visual "companionship" is now ubiquitous. In each of these instances, music is assumed to be a catalyst for establishing the mood deemed appropriate, generating desired actions, or simply maintaining a high level of interest among participants within a given context.

Musical affect has also been claimed to result in increased labor productivity and reductions in on-the-job accidents when music is piped into the workplace (Hough 1943; Halpin 1943–1944; Kerr 1945), though these studies are often far from rigorous in their method and analysis (McGehee and Gardner 1949; Cardinell and Burris-Meyer 1949; Uhrbock 1961). Music therapists claim that music has a beneficial effect in the treatment of some handicapped individuals and as a part of physical rehabilitation following traumatic bodily injury (Brusilovsky 1972; Nordoff and Robbins 1973; an opposing viewpoint is presented by Madsen and Madsen 1970). Individuals use music to facilitate either relaxation or stimulation in leisure activities. With the increase in leisure time during the 1980s (Morris 1988), many entertainment-related products began to utilize music to great effect in augmenting the aesthetic affect of these experiences. Executives of advertising agencies have realized the impact music has on attracting a desired audience, as evidenced recently by the use of classic rock songs to call baby-boomers to attention or excerpts from the Western art music repertoire to attract a more "sophisticated" audience.

One of the most effective uses of music specifically intended to manipulate perceptual response to a visual stimulus is found in motion pictures and animation. The present study investigated the relationship of events perceived as salient (accented), both aurally and visually. As a result, this study focused on an aspect of the motion picture experience that had never before been addressed explicitly in music perception literature. Many studies had examined associational and referential aspects of both sound and vision. Some investigations had even examined explicitly the relationship of music to visual images in the context of the motion picture experience. However, none have proposed an explicit model based on stratification of accent structures or set out to test the audio-visual relationship on the basis of accent structure alignment.

Before considering the specific interrelationship between the aural and visual components of animated sequences, several issues were carefully examined. First, what are the determinants of "accent" (points of emphasis) in the visual and auditory fields? Second, is it *necessary* for accents in the musical soundtrack to line up precisely with points of emphasis in the visual modality in order for the combination to be considered effective? The ultimate goal of this line of research is to determine the *fundamental principles governing interaction* between the auditory and visual components in the motion picture experience.

Related Literature

To the present, there has been little empirical work specifically directed at studying the symbiotic relationship between the two primary perceptual modalities normally used in viewing films (Lipscomb 1990; Lipscomb and Kendall 1996). In the field of perceptual psychology, interaction between the aural and visual sensory modalities is well documented (see, for example, Radeau and Bertelson 1974; Staal and Donderi 1983; Bermant and Welch 1976; Ruff and Perret 1976; Massaro and Warner 1977; Regan and Spekreijse 1977; and Mershon, Desaulniers, Amerson, and Kiever 1980). For a detailed discussion of film music research (Tannenbaum 1956; Thayer and Levenson 1984; and Marshall and Cohen 1988), see Lipscomb (1995) and Lipscomb and Kendall (1996). The latter paper was included in a special issue of *Psychomusicology* (vol. 13) devoted to the topic of film-music research, including investigations by a wide array of scholars (Thompson, Russo, and Sinclair 1996; Bolivar, Cohen, and Fentress 1996; Lipscomb and Kendall 1996; Bullerjahn and Güldenring 1996; Sirius and Clarke 1996; Iwamiya 1996; and Rosar 1996). Though the list is not long, there have been many approaches to the study of combined sound and image. Marilyn Boltz and her colleagues have investigated the relationship between the presence of musical sound and memory for filmed events and their duration (Boltz 1992; Boltz 2001; and Boltz, Schulkind, and Kantra 1991). Krumhansl and Schenck (1997) investigated the relationship between dance choreography by Balanchine and the music that inspired it, Mozart's *Divertimento No. 15*. In a study by Vitouch (2001), subjects, after seeing a brief film excerpt with one of two contrasting musical soundtracks, provided a written prediction of how the plot would continue, revealing that anticipations of future events are "systematically influenced" by the accompanying musical sound (p. 70). None of these investigations, however, addressed the synchronization between the musical and visual components of the motion picture experience.

Proposed Model and Its Foundation

What is the purpose of a musical soundtrack? An effective film score, in its interactive association with the visual element, need not attract the audience member's attention to the music itself. In fact, the most successful film composers have made a fine art of manipulating audience perception and emphasizing important events in the dramatic action without causing a conscious attentional shift. When watching a film, a typical audience member's perception of the musical component often remains at a subconscious level (Lipscomb 1989).

Marshall and Cohen (1988) provided a paradigm to explain the interaction of musical sound and geometric shapes in motion entitled the "Congruence-Associationist model." They assumed that, in the perception of a composite A-V presentation, separate judgments were made on each of three semantic dimensions (Evaluative, Potency, and Activity; see Osgood, Suci, and Tannenbaum 1957) for the music and the film, suggesting that these evaluations were then compared for congruence at a higher level of processing.

A model proposed by Lipscomb and Kendall (1996) suggests that there are two implicit judgments made during the perceptual processing of the motion picture experience: an association judgment and a mapping of accent structures (see Figure 1). The association judgment relies on past experience as a basis for determining whether or

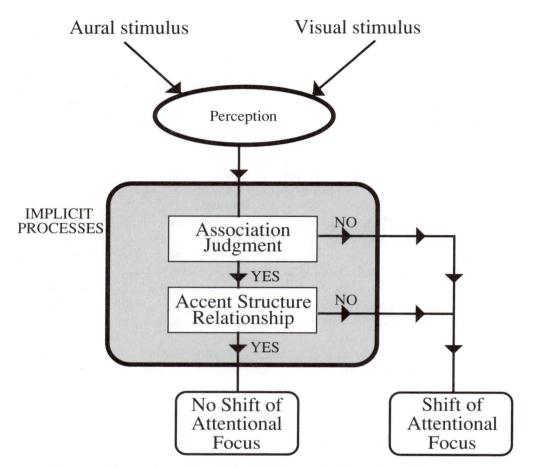

Figure 1. Lipscomb and Kendall's (1996) model of Film Music Perception.
Reprinted with permission of *Psychomusicology*.

not the music is appropriate within a given context. For example, a composer may have used legato string lines for "romantic" scenes, brass fanfares for a "majestic" quality, or low-frequency synthesizer tones for a sense of "foreboding." The ability of music to convey such a referential "meaning" has been explored in great detail by many investigators, for example, Heinlein (1928), Hevner (1935 and 1936), Farnsworth (1954), Meyer (1956), Wedin (1972), Eagle (1973), Crozier (1974), McMullen (1976), Brown (1981), and Asmus (1985).

The second implicit judgment (mapping of accent structures) consists of matching emphasized points in one perceptual modality with those in another. Lipscomb and Kendall (1996) proposed that, if the associations identified with the musical style were judged appropriate and the relationship of the aural and visual accent structures were perceived as consonant, attentional focus would be maintained on the symbiotic composite, rather than on either modality in isolation.

Musical and Visual Periodicity. In the repertoire of mainstream motion pictures, one can find many examples that illustrate the film composer's use of periodicity in the musical structure as a means of heightening the effect of recurrent motion in the visual image. The galley rowing scene from Miklos Rosza's score composed for *Ben Hur* (1959) is an excellent example of the mapping of accent structures, both in pitch and tempo of the musical score. As the slaves pull up on their oars, the pitch of the musical motif ascends. As they lean forward to prepare for the next thrust, the motif descends. Concurrently, as the Centurion orders them to row faster and faster, the tempo of the music picks up accordingly, synchronizing with the accent structure of the visual scene. A second illustration can be found in John Williams' musical soundtrack composed for *ET: The Extraterrestrial* (1982). The bicycle chase-scene score is replete with examples of successful musical emulation of the dramatic on-screen action. Synchronization of the music with the visual scene is achieved by inserting 3/8 patterns at appropriate points so that accents of the metrical structure remain aligned with the pedaling motion.

In the process of perception, the perceptual system seeks out such periodicities in order to facilitate data reduction. Filtering out unnecessary details in order to retain the essential elements is required because of the enormous amount of information arriving at the body's sensory receptors at every instant of time. "Chunking" of specific sensations into prescribed categories allows the individual to successfully store essential information for future retrieval (Bruner, Goodnow, and Austin 1958).

Therefore, in the context of the decision-making process proposed by Lipscomb and Kendall (1996), the music and visual images do not necessarily have to be in perfect synchronization for the composite to be considered appropriately aligned. As the Gestalt psychologists found, humans seek organization, imposing order upon situations that are open to interpretation according to the principles of good continuation, closure, similarity, proximity, and common fate (von Ehrenfels 1890; Wertheimer 1925; Köhler 1929; and Koffka 1935). In the scenes described above, the fact that *every* rowing or pedaling motion was not perfectly aligned with the musical score is probably not perceived by the average member of the audience, even if attention were somehow drawn to the musical score. Herbert Zettl (1990: 380) suggests the following simple experiment. To witness the structural power of music, take any video sequence you have at hand and run some arbitrarily selected music with it. You will be amazed how frequently the video and audio seem to match structurally. You simply expect the visual and aural beats to coincide. If they do not, you apply psychological closure and make them fit. Only if the video and audio beats are, or drift, too far apart, do we concede to a structural mismatch—but then only temporarily.[2]

The degree to which the two strata must be aligned before perceived synchronicity breaks down has not yet been determined. The present experimental investigation manipulated the relationship of music and image by using discrete levels of synchronization. If successful in confirming a perceived difference between these levels, future research will be necessary to determine the tolerance for misalignment.

Accent Structure Alignment

Two issues had to be addressed before it was possible to consider accent-structure synchronization. First, what constitutes an "accent" in both the visual and auditory domains? Second, which specific parameters of any given visual or musical object have the capability of resulting in perceived accent?

The term "accent" will be used to describe points of emphasis (salient moments) in both the musical sound and visual images. David Huron (1994) defined "accent" as "an increased prominence, noticeability, or salience ascribed to a given sound event." When generalized to visual images as well, it is possible to describe an AV composite in terms of accent strata and their relationships one to another.

Determinants of Accent. In the search for determinants of accent, potential variables were established by considering the various aspects of visual objects and musical phrases that constituted perceived boundaries. Fraisse (1982: 157) suggested that grouping of constituent elements results "as soon as a difference is introduced into an isochronous sequence." Similarly, in a discussion of Gestalt principles and their relation to Lerdahl and Jackendoff's (1983) generative theory of tonal music, Deliege (1987: 326) stated that "in perceiving a difference in the field of sounds, one experiences a sensation of accent." Boltz and Jones (1986: 428) propose that "accents can arise from any deviation in pattern context."

Following an extensive review of the literature relating to the perception of accent in both the aural and visual modalities, a limited number of potential variables were utilized in creating a musical stimulus set and a visual stimulus set that—considering each modality in isolation—resulted in a reliably consistent perception of the intended accent points. Accents were hypothesized to occur at moments in which a change occurs in any of these auditory or visual aspects of the stimulus. This change may happen in one of two ways. First, a value that remains consistent for a period of time can be given a new value (a series of soft tones may be followed suddenly by a loud tone or a blue object may suddenly turn red). Second, change in the direction of a motion vector will cause a perceived accent (melodic contour may change from ascending to descending or the direction of an object's motion may change from horizontal left to vertical up). The variables selected for use in the following experiments are listed in Table 1, along with proposed values for the direction and magnitude characteristics.

Method

This study was a quasi-experimental investigation, consisting of a post-test-only, repeated measures factorial design. The experiment was preceded by a series of exploratory studies that assisted in selecting stimulus materials. The main experiment incorporated two independent methods of data collection: verbal ratings and similarity judgments.

Subject Selection

Every participant was required to have seen at least four mainstream, American movies during each of the past ten years, ensuring at least a moderate level of

Table 1
Proposed variables to be utilized in the initial exploratory study
labeled with direction

| Variables | Vectors | |
	Direction	Magnitude of Change
Musical		
Pitch	up/unchanging/down	none/small/large
Loudness	louder/unchanging/softer	none/small/large
Timbre	simple/unchanging/complex	none/small/large
Visual		
Location	left/unchanging/right	
	up/unchanging/down	none/small/large
Shape	simpler/same/more complex	none/small/large
Color		
hue	red-orange-yellow-green- blue-indigo-violet	none/small/large
saturation	purer/unchanging/more impure	none/small/large
brightness	brighter/unchanging/darker	none/small/large

"enculturation" with this genre of synchronized audio-visual media. Musical training was the single between-subjects grouping variable considered, using the following three levels: untrained (less than two years of formal music training), moderate (two to seven years of formal music training), and highly trained (more than seven years of formal study).

Stimulus Materials

Prior to the main experiment, a series of exploratory studies was run to determine auditory and visual stimuli that are consistently interpreted by subjects as generating an intended accent point. The sources of musical and visual accent delineated in Table 1 were used as a theoretical basis for creating MIDI files and generating computer animations for use as stimuli in this experiment. Both the sound files and the animations were limited to approximately five seconds in length, so that a paired comparisons task could be completed by subjects within a reasonable period of time, as discussed below.

The points of accent were periodically spaced within each musical and visual example. Fraisse (1982: 156) identified temporal limits for the perceptual grouping of sound events. The lower limit (approximately 120 ms apart) corresponded closely to the separation at which psychophysiological conditions no longer allowed the two events to be perceived as distinct. The upper limit (between 1500 and 2000 ms) represented the temporal separation at which two groups of stimuli are no longer perceptually linked (Bolton 1894; MacDougall 1903). Fraisse suggested a value of 600ms as the optimum for both perceptual organization and precision. Therefore, the first independent variable utilized in the present experimental procedure, that is, variance of the temporal interval between accent points, consisted of values representing a median range between the limits explicated by Fraisse. This variable had three discrete levels: 500ms, 800ms, and 1000ms. The first and last temporal values allowed the possibility of considering the nesting of accents (within every 1000ms interval two accents 500ms apart may occur). The 800ms value was chosen because it allowed precise synchronization with the visual stimulus at the rate of 20 frames per second (fps), yet it aligned with the other accent periodicities only once every 4 seconds, which is beyond Fraisse's (1982) upper limit for the perceptual linking of stimuli. (The specific relationships are: 1000ms = 20 frames; 800ms = 16 frames, and 500ms = 10 frames.) Seven musical patterns and seven animation sequences utilizing each temporal interval were generated, from which the actual stimuli were selected in a second exploratory study.

The manner in which audio and visual stimuli were combined served as the independent variable manipulated by the investigator. Three possible levels of juxtaposition were utilized: consonant, out-of-phase, and dissonant (Yeston 1976; Monahan, Kendall, and Carterette 1987; Lipscomb and Kendall 1996). Figure 2 presents an idealized visual representation of these three relationships. In each pair of accent strata (one depicting the visual component, the other the audio component), points of emphasis are represented by pulses [⌐⌐] in the figure. *Consonant* relationships (Figure 2a) may be exemplified by accent structures that are perfectly synchronized. Accent structures that are *out-of-phase* (Figure 2b) share a common temporal interval between consecutive points of emphasis, but the strata are offset such that they are perceived as out of synchronization. Juxtaposition of the 500ms periodic accent structure and the 800ms periodic accent structure mentioned in the previous paragraph would result in a *dissonant* relationship (Figure 2c).[3] Because of the possibility of nesting the 500ms stimulus within the 1000ms stimulus, it was necessary to distinguish between identical consonance (synchronization of a 500ms temporal interval in both the audio and visual modalities) and nested consonance (synchronization of a 500ms temporal interval

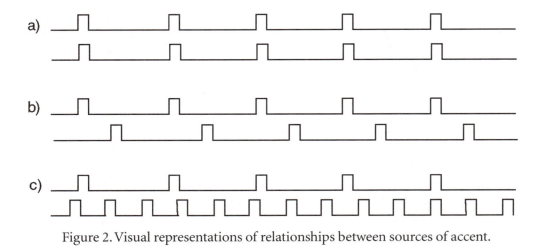

Figure 2. Visual representations of relationships between sources of accent.

in one modality and a 1000ms temporal interval in the other). The same distinction was considered in the out-of-phase relationship between the 500ms and the 1000ms periodicities.

Exploratory Studies

A series of exploratory studies was run in order to select auditory and visual stimuli that illustrate, as clearly as possible, the presence of accent structures in both perceptual modalities, so that subjects were capable of performing tasks based on the alignment of these two strata. For all experimental procedures, Roger Kendall's *Music Experiment Development System* (MEDS, version 3.1e) was utilized to play the auditory and visual examples and collect subject responses. The author programmed for incorporation into MEDS a module that allowed quantification and storage of temporal intervals between consecutive keypresses on the computer keyboard at a resolution well below .01ms. This facility allowed the subjects to register their perceived pulse simply by tapping along on the spacebar.[4]

Subjects were asked to tap along with the perceived pulse created by the stimulus while either viewing the animation sequences or listening to the tonal sequences. In the exploratory study, stimuli were continuously looped for a period of about thirty seconds so that subjects had an adequate period of time to determine accent periodicities. It was hypothesized that the position of these perceived pulses coincided with points in time when significant changes in the motion vector (magnitude or direction) of the stimulus occurred. The purpose of the exploratory studies was to confirm this hypothesis and to determine the audio and visual stimuli that produced the most reliably consistent sense of accent structure.

Main Experiment

There are two methodological innovations incorporated into this study that warrant brief discussion. First, a system of "convergent methods" was utilized to answer the research questions. Kendall and Carterette (1992a) proposed this alternative to the single-method approach used in most music perception and cognition research. The basic technique is to "converge on the answer to experimental questions by applying multiple methods, in essence, simultaneously investigating the central research question as well as ancillary questions of method" (p. 116). In addition, if the answer to a research question is the same, regardless of the method utilized, much greater confidence may be attributed to the outcome. The present investigation incorporated a verbal-scaling procedure and a similarity-judgment task.

Second, rather than using semantic differential bipolar opposites in the verbal scaling task (Osgood et al. 1957), verbal attribute magnitude estimation (VAME) was utilized (Kendall and Carterette 1992b and 1993). In contrast to semantic differential scales, VAME provides a means of assigning a specific amount of a given attribute within a verbal scaling framework (good–not good, instead of good–bad).

Since two convergent methods were utilized, two independent groups of subjects were required for this experiment. Group One was asked to watch every audio-visual composite in a randomly-generated presentation order and provide a VAME response, according to a consistent set of instructions (see Lipscomb 1995). When the OK button was pressed after a response, location of each button on its respective scroll bar was quantified using a scale from 0 to 100 and stored for later analysis. A repeated measures analysis of variance (ANOVA) was used as the method for determining whether or not there was a significant within-subjects difference between the responses as a function of accent structure alignment and/or the between-subjects variable: level of musical training.

Group Two was asked, in a paired-comparison task, to provide ratings of "similarity" on a continuum from "not same" to "same," according to a consistent set of instructions (see Lipscomb 1995). The quantified subject responses were submitted for multidimensional scaling (MDS) in which distances were calculated between objects—in this case, A-V composites—for placement within a multi-dimensional space (Kruskal 1964a, 1964b, and 1978). The resulting points were plotted and analyzed in an attempt to determine sources of commonality and differentiation. The results were confirmed by submitting the same data set for cluster analysis in order to identify natural groupings in the data.

Alternative Hypotheses

It was hypothesized that Group One would give the highest verbal ratings of synchronization and effectiveness to the consonant alignment condition (composites in which the periodic pulses identified in the exploratory studies were perfectly aligned). It was also hypothesized that the lowest scores would be given in response to the out-of-phase condition (combinations made up of identical temporal intervals that are offset), while intermediate ratings would be related to composites exemplifying a *dissonant* relationship. In the latter case, the musical and visual vectors may be perceived as more synchronized because of the process of closure described by Zettl (1990: 380). It was hypothesized that similarity ratings provided by Group Two would result in a multi-dimensional space consisting of at least three dimensions, including musical stimulus, visual stimulus, and accent alignment.

Experimental Procedure

Auditory examples for this experiment consisted of isochronous pitch sequences and visual images were computer-generated animations of a single object (a circle) moving on-screen. Since the stimuli for this experiment were created by the author, a great degree of care was taken in the exploratory study portion to ensure reliability in responses to the selected stimuli (for a detailed discussion of the exploratory studies, see Lipscomb 1995: 53–65). As a result of these carefully controlled preliminary procedures, from the seven audio examples and seven visual examples created, two audio and two visual stimuli were selected for use in the main experiment (Figures 3 and 4).

Subjects

Subjects for this experiment were forty UCLA students (ages 19 to 31) enrolled in general education classes in the Music Department, either Psychology of Music taught by Lipscomb in Fall, 1994 or American Popular Music taught by Keeling in

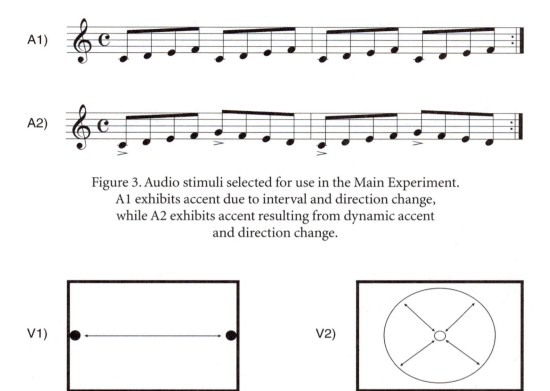

Figure 3. Audio stimuli selected for use in the Main Experiment.
A1 exhibits accent due to interval and direction change,
while A2 exhibits accent resulting from dynamic accent
and direction change.

Figure 4. Visual stimuli selected for use in the Main Experiment.
V1 exemplifies side-to-side continuous motion,
while V2 illustrates apparent near-to-far-to-near continuous motion.

Summer Session II, 1994). The forty subjects (24 males and 16 females) were randomly assigned to two groups before performing the experimental tasks. Group One (n = 20) responded using the VAME verbal rating scale and Group Two (n = 20) provided similarity judgments between pairs of stimuli. For each group of subjects, the number of subjects falling into each level of musical training is provided in Table 2.

Stimulus Materials

The A-V composites utilized in the main experiment were created by combining the two audio and the two visual stimuli selected in the exploratory study into all possible pairs (n_{AV} = 4). For ease of discussion, these stimuli will heretofore be referenced using the following abbreviations: A1 (Audio 1) consists of a repeated ascending melodic contour), A2 (Audio 2) consists of an undulating melodic contour, V1 (Visual 1) represents left to right apparent motion (that is, *translation in the plane* along the x-axis), and V2 (Visual 2) represents front to back apparent motion (*translation in depth* along an apparent z-axis).

Table 2
Number of subjects falling into each cell of the
between-subjects design (Experiment One)

	Musical Training		
Exp. Task	Untrained	Moderate	Trained
VAME	10	7	3
Similarity	10	8	2

In addition to these various A-V composites, the method of audio-visual align-ment was systematically altered. As explained previously, three alignment conditions were utilized: consonant, out-of-phase, and dissonant. It was important to create composites in which the A-V alignment was out-of-phase by an amount that was easily perceivable by the subjects. Friberg and Sundberg (1992) determined the amount by which the duration of a tone presented in a metrical sequence must be varied before it is perceived as different from surrounding tones. This amount is 10ms for tones shorter than 240ms or approximately 5% of the duration for longer tones (p. 107). The out-of-sync versions in this study were offset by 225ms—a value well beyond the just-noticeable difference (JND) for temporal differentiation and also a value that does not nest within or subdivide any of the three IOIs used in this study (500ms, 800ms, and 1000ms).

Stratification of accent structures. In the exploratory study, both the audio and visual stimuli were shown to create a perceived periodic accent where certain moments in the stimulus stream were considered more salient than others. It is possible—using all combinations of synchronization (consonant, out-of-phase, and dissonant) and IOI interval (500ms, 800ms, and 1000ms)—to generate 14 different alignment conditions for each A-V composite (Table 5). Notice that there are two distinct types of consonant and out-of-phase composites. The first is an *identical consonance*, for example, a 1000ms IOI in the audio component perfectly aligned with a 1000ms IOI in the visual component. The second type is referred to as a *nested consonance*, for example, a 500ms IOI in the audio component that is perfectly aligned with—but subdivides—a 1000ms IOI in the visual component (or vice versa). The corresponding pair of out-of-phase composites is referred to as *out-of-phase (identical)* and *out-of-phase (nested)*. Therefore, the total stimulus set consisted of 56 A-V composites (4 A-V combinations x 14 alignment conditions). Each composite was repeated for a period of approxi-mately 15 seconds, before requiring a subject response. The order of stimulus presenta-tion was randomized for every subject.

Experimental Tasks

Group One. Each subject in this group was asked to respond to every A-V composite on two VAME scales: "not synchronized–synchronized" and "ineffective–effective." After viewing each of the composites, subjects were given a choice of either

Table 3
The 14 alignment conditions for A-V composites
in Experiment One

Music IOI	Visual IOI	Audio-visual Alignment
500ms	500ms	consonant
500ms	500ms	out-of-phase
500ms	1000ms	consonant
500ms	1000ms	out-of-phase
500ms	800ms	dissonant
1000ms	1000ms	consonant
1000ms	1000ms	out-of-phase
1000ms	500ms	consonant
1000ms	500ms	out-of-phase
1000ms	800ms	dissonant
800ms	800ms	consonant
800ms	800ms	out-of-phase
800ms	500ms	dissonant
800ms	1000ms	dissonant

providing a response or repeating the stimulus. The response mechanism is shown in Figure 5. The order in which the two VAME scales were presented was also randomized.

Group Two. The similarity scaling task required comparison of all possible pairs of stimuli. Therefore, it was necessary to utilize only a subset of the composites used in the VAME task in order to ensure that the entire procedure could be run within a reasonable time period (30 to 45 minutes). Only the 800ms MIDI and animation files were utilized, eliminating nesting and varying temporal interval from consideration. The alignment conditions were simply consonant (800ms IOI MIDI file and 800ms IOI FLI animation, perfectly aligned), out-of-phase (800ms IOI MIDI file and 800ms IOI FLI animation, offset by 225ms), and dissonant (1000ms IOI MIDI file and

Figure 5. Scroll bar used to collect Group One subject responses.

800ms IOI FLI animation). The triangular matrix of paired comparisons included the diagonal (identities) as a means of gauging subject performance, that is, if identical composites are consistently judged to be "different," it is likely that the subject did not understand or was unable to perform the task. Therefore, the total stimulus set consisted of 12 different A-V composites (4 A-V combinations x 3 alignment conditions), resulting in 78 pairs of stimuli. All paired-comparisons were randomly generated, so that the subject saw one A-V composite and then a second combination prior to providing a similarity judgment.

Results

Group One Data Analysis and Interpretation

A repeated measures ANOVA was performed on the subject responses to each of the VAME rating scales provided by Group One, considering two within-groups variables (4 A-V combinations and 14 alignment conditions) and one between-groups variable (3 levels of musical training).[5] At $\alpha = .025$, neither the synchronization ratings ($F_{(2,17)} = 1.62, p < .227$) nor the effectiveness ratings ($F_{(2,17)} = .66, p < .528$) exhibited any significant difference across levels of musical training. However, there was a highly significant within-subjects effect of alignment condition for both the synchronization ratings ($F_{\lambda(13,221)} = 88.18, p < .0005$) and the effectiveness ratings ($F_{\lambda(13,221)} = 48.43, p < .0005$). The only significant interaction that occurred was an interaction between A-V combination and alignment condition for both synchronization ($F_{(39,663)} = 3.05, p < .0005$) and effectiveness ($F_{(39,663)} = 2.94, p < .0005$). In general, there was a high correlation between subject responses on the synchronization and effectiveness scales ($r = .96$), confirming the strong positive relationship between ratings of synchronization and effectiveness.

Mean subject responses to the VAME scales are represented graphically in Figures 6a to 6d. Each graph represents a different A-V combination. There is a striking consistency in response pattern across A-V composites, as represented in these graphs. This consistency is confirmed by Figure 7, providing a comparison of these same responses across all four A-V combinations by superimposing Figures 6a to 6d on top of one another. In the legend to this figure, the labels simply refer to a specific alignment condition of a given A-V combination (V1A2_C refers to the consonant alignment condition of Visual #1 and Audio #2).[6] There is a relatively consistent pattern of responses, based on alignment condition. In general, the consonant combinations receive the highest mean ratings on both verbal scales. The identical consonant composites (for example, alignment conditions V5A5_C, V10A10_C, and V8A8_C in Figure 7) are consistently given higher ratings than the nested consonant composites (alignment conditions V5A10_C and V10A5_C in Figure 7), with the exception of V10A5_C4, which received a mean rating almost equal to that of V10A10_C4.[7] (Remember that there is no nested consonant composite for the 800ms stimuli.)

The second highest mean ratings were given in response to the out-of-phase (identical) composites (V5A5_O, V10A10_O, and V8A8_O). The lowest mean ratings were always given in response to the out-of-phase (nested) composites (V5A10_O and V10A5_O) and the dissonant composites (V5A8_D, V10A8_D, V8A5_D, and

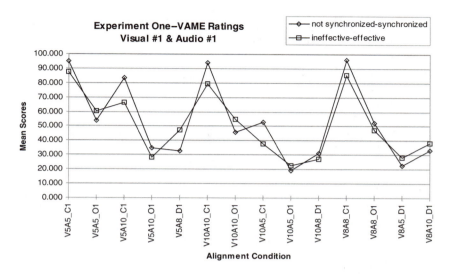

Figure 6a. Mean subject ratings to the two VAME scales when viewing the combination of Visual #1 and Audio #1 across alignment conditions. For an explanation of x-axis labels, see endnote #6.

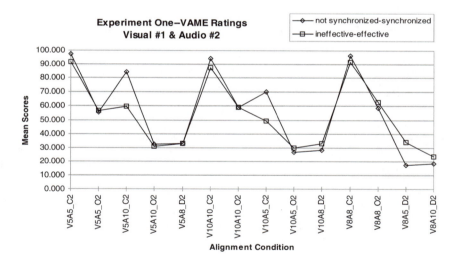

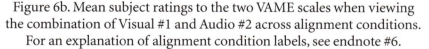

Figure 6b. Mean subject ratings to the two VAME scales when viewing the combination of Visual #1 and Audio #2 across alignment conditions. For an explanation of alignment condition labels, see endnote #6.

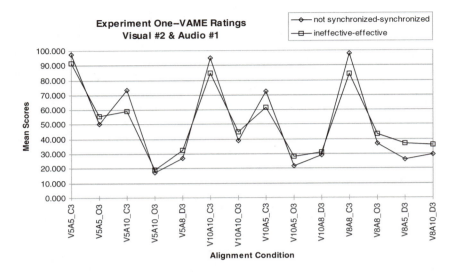

Figure 6c. Mean subject ratings to the two VAME scales when viewing
the combination of Visual #2 and Audio #1 across alignment conditions.
For an explanation of alignment condition labels, see endnote #6.

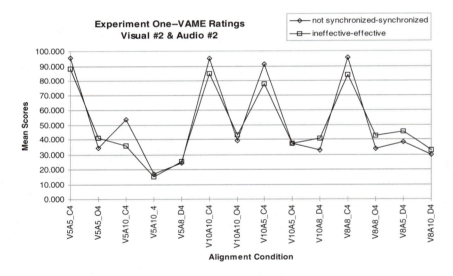

Figure 6d. Mean subject ratings to the two VAME scales when viewing
the combination of Visual #2 and Audio #2 across alignment conditions.
For an explanation of alignment condition labels, see endnote #6.

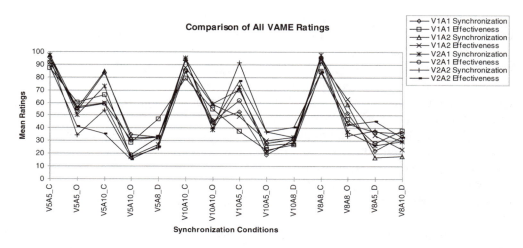

Figure 7. Comparison of all VAME responses across A-V composite and alignment conditions. For an explanation of alignment condition labels, see footnote #6.

V8A10_D) with the former usually being rated slightly higher than the latter. Notice also that the widest spread of mean responses to any of the A-V composites is associated with the nested consonant composites: V5A10_C and V10A5_C. Therefore, the relationship between subject responses on the two VAME scales and accent structure alignment may be represented as shown in Table 4. This ordering of response means is different from that proposed initially as an alternative hypothesis.

Recall that, based upon Zettl's (1990) theory related to closure in the perception of musical and visual vectors, the dissonant conditions were predicted to be perceived as more synchronized and effective than those of the out-of-phase conditions. The responses of Group 1 reveal, however, that higher ratings were given to the out-of-phase conditions than to the dissonant conditions. It is still possible to explain these results in terms of closure, as described by Zettl. However, the process of closure appears to have been applied in a manner different from that predicted at the outset.

Subject responses revealed that the out-of-phase conditions were perceived as more synchronized and more effective than the dissonant conditions, in contrast to the results predicted. In hindsight, perhaps this result makes more sense than the

Table 4
A-V composites arranged from highest response to lowest
on the VAME scales

Identical Consonant Composites	Highest
Nested Consonant Composites	↑
Out-of-Phase (Identical) Composites	
Out-of-Phase (Nested) and Dissonant Composites	Lowest

proposed alternative hypothesis. It appears that, in the process of viewing the present collection of audio-visual composites, subjects sought out recurrent periodicities and considered those that shared the same IOI between accent points to be more synchronized and more effective than those with different IOIs, even if these periodicities were misaligned to a highly perceptible degree. Future research will be required to distinguish between the importance of absolute accent structure alignment and the influence of such matched periodicities.

Collapsing Alignment Conditions Across A-V Composites. The subject VAME responses were collapsed across alignment conditions. When compared to a single measurement, such multiple measures of a single condition provide increased reliability (Lord and Novick 1968). Therefore, the mean of all synchronization ratings given in response to the consonant alignment condition (V1A1_C, V1A2_C, V2A1_C, and V2A2_C) was calculated and compared to the mean ratings for the out-of-phase and dissonant alignment conditions. The ratings of effectiveness were collapsed as well. An ANOVA on the collapsed data set revealed that the significant interaction between A-V composite and alignment condition observed over the complete data set fell to a level not considered statistically significant (synchronization—$F_{\lambda(6,102)} = 1.98959, p < .056$; effectiveness—$F_{\lambda(6,102)} = 2.18760, p < .117$).[8] Further justification for collapsing the data in this manner can be derived from the VAME data set. Figure 8 represents mean ratings for both VAME scales across all A-V combinations at every IOI. Notice the contour similarity across every consonant, out-of-phase, and dissonant combination, that is, the consonant pairs consistently received the highest rating, the dissonant pairs received the lowest rating, and the out-of-phase pairs received a rating in between the other two. In addition, the subject responses to the nested conditions exhibited the most influence of specific A-V combinations. Therefore, eliminating these conditions further justified collapsing alignment conditions (consonant, out-of-phase, and dissonant) across the various A-V combinations. For the remainder of this investigation,

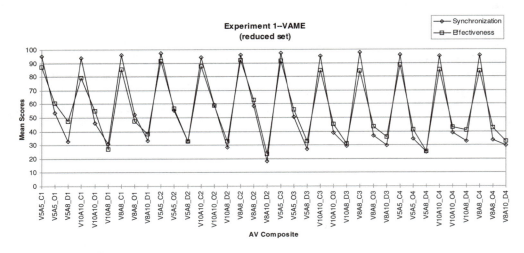

Figure 8. VAME ratings for all consonant, out-of-phase, and dissonant combinations across all A-V composites.

only three alignment conditions will be considered: consonant, out-of-phase, and dissonant, eliminating the nested conditions.

Analysis and Interpretation of Data Collapsed Across Alignment Conditions. An ANOVA across the collapsed data set confirmed that there is no statistically significant difference between the level of musical training for either the synchronization ratings ($F_{(2,17)} = 1.699$, $p < .2125$) or the effectiveness ratings ($F_{(2,17)} = .521$, $p < .603$). Once again, however, analysis reveals a highly significant effect of alignment condition for both verbal ratings: synchronization ($F_{\lambda(2,16)} = 162.274$, $p < .0001$) and effectiveness ($F_{\lambda(2,16)} = 91.591$, $p < .0001$). The interaction between level of musical training and alignment condition was not significant for either synchronization ($F_{\lambda(4,32)} = 1.575$, $p < .2048$) or effectiveness ($F_{\lambda(4,32)} = 2.662$, $p < .0504$).

Regardless of musical training, subjects are clearly distinguishing between the three alignment conditions on both VAME scales (Figure 9). Consonant combinations were given the highest ratings with a steep decline between consonant and out-of-phase combinations, followed by an even lower rating for the dissonant pairs. Interestingly, the effectiveness ratings were consistently less extreme than the ratings of synchronization. For example, when the mean synchronization rating was extremely high (the consonant alignment condition), the effectiveness rating was slightly lower. However, when the synchronization ratings were lower (for the out-of-phase and dissonant alignment conditions), the effectiveness ratings were slightly higher. This suggests that, while synchronization ratings varied more consistently according to alignment condition, ratings of effectiveness may have been tempered slightly by other factors inherent in the A-V composite.

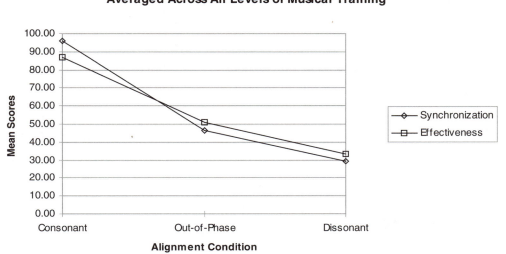

Figure 9. Mean VAME ratings for Experiment One averaged across all levels of musical training.

Group Two Data Analysis and Interpretation

A repeated measures ANOVA was also performed on the similarity ratings provided by Group Two, using one within-groups variable (78 paired comparisons) and one between-groups variable (3 levels of musical training). There was no statistically significant effect of either musical training ($F_{(2,17)}$ = .40, p < .676) or the interaction between musical training and similarity ratings ($F_{(154, 1309)}$ = .56, p < 1.000). As one would expect, however, the similarity ratings did vary at a high level of significance ($F_{(77,1309)}$ = 24.86, p < .0005). Therefore, the null hypothesis is rejected, because subject ratings of similarity between A-V composites did, in fact, vary significantly as a function of A-V alignment.

Multidimensional Scaling. The triangular mean similarity matrix was submitted for multidimensional scaling (MDS) analysis. Figure 10 provides the MDS solution in three dimensions, accounting for 99.884% of the variance at a stress level of only .01189. The twelve stimuli separated clearly on each dimension. All composites using Audio #1 are on the negative side of the "Audio" dimension (x-axis) and all composites incorporating Audio #2 are on the positive side. Likewise, all composites utilizing Visual #1 are on the negative side of the "Visual" dimension (z-axis) and all composites using Visual #2 are on the positive side. Finally, all of the composites that are considered dissonant, fall within the negative area of the "Sync" dimension (y-axis) and all consonant and out-of-phase composites fall on the positive side, practically on top of one another.

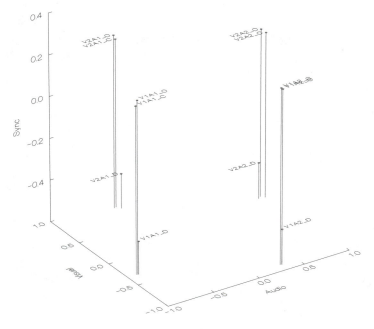

Figure 10. Multidimensional scaling solution for the
similarity judgments in Experiment One.

Notice how tightly the stimuli clustered within this three-dimensional space when viewed from above (across the Visual and Audio dimensions).[9] To further examine the group membership among the various A-V composites, the same triangular matrix was submitted for cluster analysis.

Cluster Analysis. Cluster analysis provides a method for dividing a data set into subgroups without any *a priori* knowledge considering the number of subgroups nor their specific members. The tree diagram presented in Figure 11 graphically illustrates the clustering of A-V composites used in the present study.

As is readily apparent when considering this cluster diagram from right to left, the initial branching of A-V composites into subgroups clearly separates the composites according to the visual component. All composites on the upper branch utilize Visual One (V1) and all composites on the lower branch utilize Visual Two (V2). The next subdivision separates the composites according to audio component, as labeled in the diagram. The third subdivision separates the composites with the same IOIs (consonant and out-of-phase composites) from those composites in which the audio and visual components are of differing IOIs (dissonant composites). Finally, the fourth subdivision divides the consonant composites from the out-of-phase composites

Notice also the mirroring relationship within the lower cluster of six composites (those using V2), based upon alignment condition (see Figure 12a). The closest cross-cluster relationship between those composites incorporating A1 and those using A2 is the dissonant condition, neighbored by the consonant condition, and working

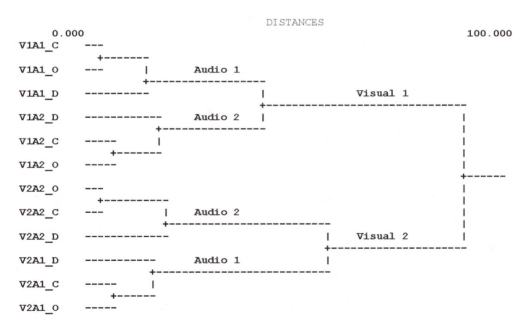

Figure 11. Cluster Analysis tree diagram—complete linkage (farthest neighbor)—
for similarity ratings provided by subjects in Experiment One, Group Two.

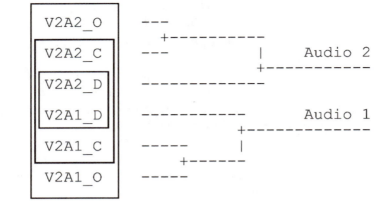

Figure 12a. Illustration of the mirroring relationship between elements
in the upper cluster of composites incorporating Visual One.

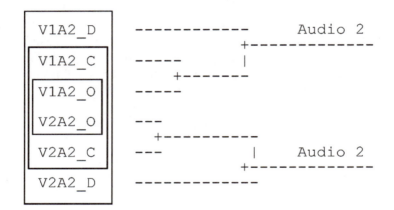

Figure 12b. Illustration of the mirroring relationship between elements
in the middle cluster of composites incorporating Audio Two
with either Visual One or Visual Two.

outward finally to the out-of-phase condition. A similar mirroring is apparent when comparing the composites that incorporate A2, whether combined with V1 or V2 (Figure 12b). In this case, the alignment condition of the closest pair (V1A2_O and V2A2_O) is out-of-phase, working outward to consonant, then dissonant. It is worthy of notice that, when considering the main (visual) branches of the cluster solution in Figure 11, the two neighbor composites (V1A2_O and V2A2_O) share the same audio track *and alignment condition*. These relationships within the cluster branching structure further confirmed the role of alignment condition in the subject ratings of similarity.

Conclusions

Summarizing the results of the main experiment, both of the converging methods (VAME ratings and similarity judgments) substantiated the fact that alignment condition between audio and visual components of an A-V composite were a determining factor in the subject responses. In the VAME scores, verbal ratings of "synchronization" and "effectiveness" did, in fact, vary as a function of A-V alignment. In general, the highest ratings on both scales were given in response to the identical consonant composites followed (in order of magnitude) by nested consonant composites, and then out-of-phase identical composites. The lowest ratings were consistently given to either the out-of-phase (nested) or dissonant composites. Collapsing VAME ratings across alignment condition confirmed the relationship between consonant, out-of-phase, and dissonant pairs, revealing that the ratings of effectiveness were consistently less extreme than the synchronization ratings.

In the similarity judgments, an analysis of variance confirmed that there was a significant difference between ratings given to composites exemplifying the various alignment conditions. MDS revealed three easily interpretable dimensions. Cluster analysis confirmed the three criteria utilized by subjects in the process of determining similarity. In decreasing order of significance, these were the visual component, the audio component, and alignment condition. The fact that the alignment condition plays a significant role in both the multidimensional scaling solution and in the cluster analysis confirms the importance of including "Accent Structure Relationship" as one of the Implicit Judgments in the model of Film Music Perception (Figure 1).

Discussion

Research Questions Answered

The first question posed was: What are the determinants of 'accent'? A review of related literature revealed numerous potential sources of accent in both the aural and visual domains. Several researchers and theorists proposed that introducing a change into a stimulus stream results in added salience (accent). The exploratory study confirmed that hypothesized accent points using parameters (both aural and visual) gleaned from this literature review were, in fact, perceived by subjects and reproduced in a tapping procedure. Particularly reliable in producing an event perceived as musically salient were pitch contour direction change, change in interval size, dynamic accent, and timbre change. Likewise, particularly reliable in producing events perceived as salient in the visual domain were translations in the plane (top-to-bottom, side to side, left-bottom-to-right-top, and so forth) and translation in depth (near-to-far).

The second research question—and the main source of interest in the present study—concerned whether accent structure alignment between auditory and visual components was a necessary condition for the combination to be considered effective when viewing an A-V composite. This question is answered very clearly by the VAME responses of Group One. Calculation of the Pearson correlation coefficient revealed that subject ratings of synchronization and effectiveness shared a strong positive relationship ($r = .96$). Therefore, A-V combinations that were rated high in synchronization also tended to be rated high on effectiveness and vice versa. In addition, results of multidimensional scaling and cluster analysis revealed clear influence of the synchronization condition. We may conclude that, when using simple audio and visual stimuli, accent structure alignment does appear to be a necessary condition in order for an A-V combination to be considered effective.

As a result, in addition to the overwhelming evidence supporting the important referential aspect of the role played by film music, it is imperative that attention be given to the manner in which the audio and visual components are placed in relation to one another. More specifically, the present study has shown that the manner in which salient moments in the auditory and visual domains are aligned results in a significantly different perceptual response to the resulting composite. Therefore, in light of the findings of the present investigation, it is important to reconsider the results of investigations that simply juxtaposed sound upon image with little attention to the manner in which they were combined (Tannenbaum 1956; Thayer and Levinson 1984; and Marshall and Cohen 1988). Marshall and Cohen (1981) appear to have taken this aspecti of animation into consideration when they proposed their "Congruence-Associationist" model, in which semantic association and temporal congruence form the basis for judgments concerning the appropriateness of an audio-visual combination. In a following published discussion of these results, Bolivar, Cohen, and Fentress (1996: 32) state that "the greater [the] temporal congruence the greater the focus of visual attention to which the meaning of the music consequently can be ascribed." Further research will be required to determine the relationship between accent structure alignment (temporal congruence) and referential meaning (association).

Suggestions for Further Research

The most important issue to be addressed in a series of future investigations is whether accent structure alignment remains a necessary condition when viewing more complex stimuli. The present author is currently in the process of preparing a paper that reports findings of an experiment utilizing moderately complex stimuli (experimental animations by Norman McLaren) and highly complex stimuli (actual movie excerpts from Brian DePalma's *Obsession*, 1977).

Future research is also needed to determine the relative importance of referential (associational) and accent structure (syntactic) aspects within the motion picture or animation experience. These results would help further revise the model of Film Music Perception. Accuracy of the model could also be enhanced by experimental designs incorporating more complex A-V interrelationships. For example, instead of simply having consonant, out-of-phase, and dissonant alignment conditions, it would be possible to create a whole series of consonant alignment periodicities using a basic subset of temporal patterns. Monahan and Carterette (1985) performed a study of this kind using pitch patterns with the four rhythmic patterns: iambic, dactylic, trochaic, and anapest. These four rhythmic patterns could provide the basis for creating a series of animations and a series of pitch patterns. The two could then be combined in all possible pairs for use in a similarity scaling procedure to determine what aspects of the A-V composite are particularly salient to an observer. An investigator could incorporate this same stimulus set into a tapping procedure to determine whether subjects tap with the audio, the video, some underlying common pulse, or a complex combinatory rhythmic pattern.

A significant limitation of the present study is that only a small number of audio and visual stimuli were used in order to ensure that subjects could complete the experimental tasks within a reasonable amount of time. In future investigations, the use of blocked designs would allow incorporation of a larger number of stimuli and, hence, improve the investigator's ability to generalize results.

Currently, the temporal duration by which visual images and sounds must be offset in order to be perceived as misaligned (j.n.d. or just noticeable difference, in psychophysical terminology) remains undefined. In the present study a liberal amount was selected (225ms) in order to ensure that the offset amounts were well beyond any psychophysiological or perceptual limitations. Friberg and Sundberg (1992) determined that, when introducing a temporal duration change into a series of isochronous tones, the variation could be perceived at temporal intervals as small as 10ms. The amount of temporal offset in a cross-modal perception task would likely be significantly longer, but that determination must be made through rigorous scientific investigation. Such an experimental design should incorporate stimuli of varying levels of complexity, in order to determine whether the j.n.d. is a constant or relative value.

Much research is needed to assist in the quantification of various parameters of the audio-visual experience. Reliable metrics are needed to express accent prominence, as well as complexity of a musical passage, a visual image, or an A-V combination in quantitative terms. Creating a method to quantify the degree of referentiality in a musical or visual excerpt would be helpful in further developing the model of Film Music Perception.

Finally, the present investigation selected one between-groups variable of interest, that is, musical training. It would also be equally relevant to run a series of similar studies, using visual literacy as a potential grouping variable.[10] In fact, incorporating both musical training and visual literacy would allow consideration of the musical training by visual literacy interaction, which might prove very interesting indeed.

Conclusion

Scientific investigations into the relationship of visual images and musical sound in the context of motion pictures and animation provide a relatively new area of study. The art forms themselves have only existed for a century. However, given the sociological significance of the cinematic experience, it is quite surprising that there is still only a small amount of research literature available addressing issues involved in the cognitive processing of ecologically valid audio-visual stimuli. The present series of experiments, along with those proposed above, will provide a framework upon which to build a better understanding of this important, but underrepresented, area of research.

NOTES

1. The author would like to acknowledge the assistance of both the University of California, Los Angeles and The University of Texas at San Antonio. In addition, the support of Northwestern University has been integral to continuing research efforts. Without the use of the research facilities provided, funding for necessary equipment, and colleagues with whom the results could be discussed, completion of this project would not have been possible. I would especially like to thank Dr. Roger A. Kendall for his invaluable assistance.

2. For another interesting experience of this type, view *The Wizard of Oz* while listening to Pink Floyd's *Dark Side of the Moon* (1973) as the musical soundtrack. If you start the music on cue with the third roar of the MGM lion, you will be surprised how well the audio and visual components appear synchronized at certain transitional points in the film. Though songwriter Roger Waters has remained silent on the matter, both drummer Nick Mason and engineer Alan Parsons deny any intended relationship (MTV, 1997).

3. Even when using extreme differences between temporal intervals and periodicity, it is inevitable that, at some point in time, the two strata will align for a simultaneous point of accent. This possibility occurs, as mentioned, every four seconds when using the 800ms temporal interval with the 500ms or every eight seconds when combined with the 1000ms intervals. The fifth pulse in the upper stratum of Figure 5c illustrates such a coincidental alignment.

4. More information about MEDS is available from Dr. Roger A. Kendall directly at: Dept. of Ethnomusicology, UCLA, Los Angeles, CA 90095-1657 (kendall@ucla.edu). In addition to the KeyPress module, the author also incorporated commands into MEDS, allowing selection of any of the digital or analog audio tracks available on the laserdisc recording. These capabilities were necessary for later experiments.

5. The data set for the main experiment (both synchronization and effectiveness ratings) failed the likelihood-ratio test for compound symmetry, violating one assumption of the ANOVA model. Therefore, when appropriate, transformed F- and *p*-values were provided using Wilks' *lambda* (F_λ), which did not assume compound symmetry.

6. In Figures 6a to 6d, the x-axis labels consist of acronyms formed to identify the specific combination represented. These acronyms consist of the visual stimulus IOI (5, 8 or 10), the aural stimulus IOI (5, 8 or 10), and the alignment condition (C for consonant, O for out-of-phase, or D for dissonant). In each case, the actual IOI value in milliseconds is divided by 100 to make the labels shorter. For example, the label V5A8_D identifies a composite consisting of a visual stimulus with an IOI of 500 ms and an aural stimulus with an IOI of 800 ms resulting in a dissonant alignment condition. Each graph represents a different combination of visual and aural stimuli.

7. Recall that this is the Visual pattern that, because of the results of the exploratory study, was changed from the originally hypothesized accent periodicity to that perceived by all subjects in the tapping task. Perhaps some of the subjects in Experiment One perceived composite V10A5_C4 as nested and others (sensing an accent point at both the nearest and farthest location of visual apparent motion) considered it an identical consonance.

8. Running a second ANOVA on this same data set caused the probability of alpha error (α) to increase. The data from each of three experiments were analyzed independently for significant differences and then one final ANOVA was run across the entire data set, including subject responses from all three experiments. Included in these three experiments are the main experiment reported in this paper and two additional experiments that are presently being prepared for publication. Since the alpha error level was set *a priori* to .025, the resulting level of confidence remained above 95% (.975 x .975). The single exception to this rule was the analysis

of the data from the main experiment reported herein. One ANOVA was already run on the complete data set. Along with the following ANOVA on the collapsed data set and the final ANOVA across all three experiments, the resulting level of confidence was reduced to about 93% (.975 x .975 x .975).

9. They cluster so tightly in fact that, when the similarity matrix was forced into two dimensions, it became immediately apparent that the MDS solution was degenerate. Therefore, results of the MDS solution will be supported by consideration of cluster analyses. For a complete discussion, see Lipscomb (1995).

10. Visual literacy refers to an individual's capability to process visual sensory input. For instance, individuals trained as artists, animators, or film directors tend to be more aware of elements in their visual environment.

REFERENCES

Asmus, E.
1985   "The effect of tune manipulation on affective responses to a musical stimulus." In G.C. Turk, ed., *Proceedings of the Research Symposium on the Psychology and Acoustics of Music*. Lawrence: University of Kansas, pp. 97–110.

Bermant, R.I. and Welch, R.B.
1976   "Effect of degree of separation of visual-auditory stimulus and eye position upon spatial interaction of vision and audition." *Perceptual and Motor Skills* 43: 487–493.

Bolivar, V.J., Cohen, A.J., and Fentress, J.C.
1996   "Semantic and formal congruency in music and motion pictures: Effects on the interpretation of visual action." *Psychomusicology* 13: 28–59.

Bolton, T.L.
1894   "Rhythm." *American Journal of Psychology* 6: 145–238.

Boltz, M.
1992   "Temporal accent structure and the remembering of filmed narratives." *Journal of Experimental Psychology: Human Perception and Performance* 18: 90–105.
2001   "Musical soundtracks as a schematic influence on the cognitive processing of filmed events." *Music Perception* 18(4): 427–454.

Boltz, M. and Jones, M.R.
1986   "Does rule recursion make melodies easier to reproduce? If not, what does?" *Cognitive Psychology* 18: 389–431.

Boltz, M., Schulkind, M., and Kantra, S.
1991   "Effects of background music on the remembering of filmed events." *Memory and Cognition* 19: 593–606.

Brown, R.W.
1981   "Music and language." In *Documentary report of the Ann Arbor Symposium*. Reston, VA: pp. 233–265.

Bruner, J., Goodnow, J.J., and Austin, G.A.
1986   *A study of thinking*. 2nd ed. New Brunswick: Transaction Publishers.

Brusilovsky, L.S.
    1972   "A two year experience with the use of music in the rehabilitative therapy of mental patients." *Soviet Neurology and Psychiatry* 5(3–4): 100.

Bullerjahn, C. and Güldenring, M.
    1996   "An empirical investigation of effects of film music using qualitative content analysis." *Psychomusicology* 13: 99–118.

Cardinell, R.L. and Burris-Meyer, H.
    1949   "Music in industry today." *Journal of the Acoustical Society of America* 19: 547–548.

Crozier
    1974   "Verbal and exploratory responses to sound sequences varying in uncertainty level." In D.E. Berlyne, ed., *Studies in the new experimental psychology: Steps toward an object psychology of aesthetic appreciation.* New York: Halsted Press, pp. 27–90.

Deliege, I.
    1987   "Grouping conditions in listening to music: An approach to Lerdahl and Jackendoff's Grouping Preference Rules." *Music Perception* 4(4): 325–360.

Eagle, C.T.
    1973   "Effects of existing mood and order of presentation of vocal and instrumental music on rated mood response to that music." *Council for Research in Music Education* 32: 55–59.

Farnsworth, P.R.
    1954   "A study of the Hevner adjective list." *Journal of the Aesthetics of Artistic Criticism* 13: 97–103.

Fraisse, P.
    1982   "Rhythm and tempo." In D. Deutsch, ed., *The psychology of music.* New York: Academic Press, pp. 149–180.

Friberg, A. and Sundberg, J.
    1992   "Perception of just-noticeable displacement of a tone presented in a metrical sequence of different tones." *Speech Transmission Laboratory—Quarterly Progress and Status Report* 4: 97–108.

Halpin, D.D.
    1943–1994   "Industrial music and morale." *Journal of the Acoustical Society of America* 15: 116–123.

Heinlein, C.P.
    1928   "The affective characters of major and minor modes in music." *Journal of Comparative Psychology* 8: 101–142.

Hevner, K.
    1935   "Expression in music: A discussion of experimental studies and theories." *Psychological Review* 42(2): 186–204.
    1936   "Experimental studies of the elements of expression in music." *American Journal of Psychology* 48: 246–269.

Hough, E.
    1943   "Music as a safety factor." *Journal of the Acoustical Society of America* 15: 124.

Huron, D.
    1994   "What is melodic accent? A computer-based study of the *Liber Usualis*." Paper presented at the Canadian University Music Society Theory Colloquium Calgary, Alberta, June.

Iwamiya, S.
    1996   "Interactions between auditory and visual processing when listening to music in an audio visual context: 1. Matching 2. Audio Quality." *Psychomusicology* 13: 133–153.

Kendall, R.A. and Carterette, E.C.
    1992a   "Convergent methods in psychomusical research based on integrated, interactive computer control." *Behavior Research Methods* <u>24</u>(2): 116–131.
    1992b   "Semantic space of wind instrument dyads as a basis for orchestration." Paper presented at the Second International Conference on Music Perception and Cognition, Los Angeles, CA, February.
    1993   "Verbal attributes of simultaneous wind instrument timbres: I. von Bismarck adjectives." *Music Perception*, 10(4): 445–467.

Kerr, W.A.
    1945   "Effects of music on factory production." *Applied Psychology Monographs*, no. 5. California: Stanford University.

Koffka, K.
    1935   *Principles of Gestalt psychology*. New York: Harcourt, Brace.

Köhler, W
    1929   *Gestalt Psychology*. New York: Liveright.

Krumhansl, C.L. and Schenck, D.L.
    1997   "Can dance reflect the structural and expressive qualities of music? A perceptual experiment on Balanchine's choreography of Mozart's *Divertimento No. 15*." *Musicae Scientiae* <u>1</u>(1): 63–85.

Kruskal, J.B.
    1964a   "Multidimensional scaling by optimizing goodness of fit to a nonmetric hypothesis." *Psychometrika* 29: 1–27.
    1964b   "Nonmetric multidimensional scaling: A numerical method." *Psychometrika* 29: 115–129.
    1978   *Multidimensional Scaling*. Beverly Hills, CA: Sage Publications.

Lerdahl, F. and Jackendoff, R.
    1983   *A generative theory of Tonal Music*. Cambridge, MA: MIT Press.

Lipscomb, S. D.
    1989   "Film music: A sociological investigation of influences on audience awareness." Paper presented at the Meeting of the Society of Ethnomusicology, Southern Lipscomb, S. D. California Chapter, Los Angeles, March.
    1990   "Perceptual judgment of the symbiosis between musical and visual components in film." Unpublished master's thesis, University of California, Los Angeles.
    1995   "Cognition of musical and visual accent structure alignment in film and animation." Unpublished doctoral dissertation, University of California, Los Angeles.

Lipscomb, S.D. and Kendall, R.A.
    1996   "Perceptual judgment of the relationship between musical and visual components in film." *Psychomusicology* 13(1): 60–98.

Lord, F.M. and Novick, M.R.
    1968   *Statistical theories of mental test scores.* Menlo Park, CA: Addison-Wesley Publishing.

MacDougall, R.
    1903   "The structure of simple rhythm forms." *Psychological Review, Monograph Supplements* 4: 309–416.

Madsen, C.K. and Madsen, C.H.
    1970   *Experimental research in music.* New Jersey: Prentice Hall.

Marshall, S.K. and Cohen, A.J.
    1988   "Effects of musical soundtracks on attitudes toward animated geometric figures." *Music Perception* 6: 95–112.

Massaro, D.W. and Warner, D.S.
    1977   "Dividing attention between auditory and visual perception." *Perception and Psychophysics* 21: 569–574.

McGehee, W. and Gardner, J.E.
    1949   "Music in a complex industrial job." *Personnel Psychology* 2: 405–417.

McMullen, P.T.
    1976   "Influences of distributional redundancy in rhythmic sequences on judged complexity ratings." *Council for Research on Music Education* 46: 23–30.

Mershon, D.H., Desaulniers, D.H., Amerson, T.C. Jr., and Kiever, S.A.
    1980   "Visual capture in auditory distance perception: Proximity image effect reconsidered." Journal of Auditory Research 20: 129–136.

Meyer, L.B.
    1956   *Emotion and meaning in music.* Chicago: University of Chicago Press.

Monahan, C.B. and Carterette, E.C.
    1985   "Pitch and duration as determinant of musical space." *Music Perception* 3(1): 1–32.

Monahan, C.B., Kendall, R.A., and Carterette, E.C.
    1987   "The effect of melodic and temporal contour on recognition memory for pitch change." *Perception and Psychophysics* 41(6): 576–600.

Morris, Phillip, Companies Inc.
    1988   *Americans and the arts: V.* New York: American Council for the Arts.

MTV
    1997   "The Pink Floyd/Wizard of Oz connection." Retrieved May 13, 2002, from: http://www.mtv.com/news/articles/1433194/19970530/story.jhtml.

Nordoff, P. and Robbins, C.
    1973   *Therapy in music for handicapped children.* London: Gallancz.

Osgood, C.E., Suci, G.J., and Tannenbaum, P.H.
    1957   *The measurement of meaning.* Urbana: University of Illinois Press.

Pink Floyd
    1973   *Dark Side of the Moon.* Capitol CDP 7 46001 2.

Radeau, M. and Bertelson, P.
    1974   "The after-effects of ventriloquism." Quarterly Journal of Experimental Psychology 26: 63–71.

Regan, D. and Spekreijse, H.
    1977   "Auditory-visual interactions and the correspondence between perceived auditory space and perceived visual space." Perception 6: 133–138.

Rosar, W.H.
    1996   "Film music and Heinz Werner's theory of physiognomic perception." *Psychomusicology* 13: 154–165.

Ruff, R.M. and Perret, E.
    1976   "Auditory spatial pattern perception aided by visual choices." *Psychological Research* 38: 369–377.

Sirius, G. and Clarke, E.F.
    1996   "The perception of audiovisual relationships: A preliminary study." *Psychomusicology* 13: 119–132.

Staal, H.E. and Donderi, D.C.
    1983   "The effect of sound on visual apparent movement." *American Journal of Psychology* 96: 95–105.

Tannenbaum, P. H.
    1956   "Music background in the judgment of stage and television drama." *Audio-Visual Communications Review* 4: 92–101.

Thayer, J.F. and Levenson, R.W.
    1984   "Effects of music on psychophysiological responses to a stressful film." *Psychomusicology* 3: 44–54.

Thompson, W.F., Russo, F.A., and Sinclair, D.
    1996   "Effects of underscoring on the perception of closure in filmed events." *Psychomusicology* 13: 9–27.

Uhrbock, R.S.
    1961   "Music on the job: Its influence on worker morale and production." *Personnel Psychology* 14: 9–38.

Vitouch, O.
    2001   "When your ear sets the stage: Musical context effects in film perception." *Psychology of Music* 29: 70–83.

von Ehrenfels, C.
    1890   "Über Gestaltqualitäten." *Vierteljahrschrift für wissenschaftliche Philosophie* 14: 249–292.

Wedin, L.
    1972   "A multidimensional study of perceptual-emotional qualities in music." *Scandinavian Journal of Psychology* 13: 1–17.

Wertheimer, M.
    1925   *Über Gestalttheorie.* Erlangen: Weltkreis-Verlag.

Yeston, M.
    1976   *The stratification of musical rhythm.* New Haven, CT: Yale University Press.

Zettl, H.
    1990   *Sight, sound, motion: Applied media aesthetics.* 2nd ed. Belmont, CA: Wadsworth Publishing Co.

Empirical Approaches to Musical Meaning

ROGER A. KENDALL

University of California, Los Angeles

Various approaches to the scientific study of musical meaning are presented. An exposition on the fundamental nature of empirical investigation discusses meaning in terms of operational definitions. Traditional research based on variants of the semantic differential and adjective checklist techniques are critiqued. The overlapping domains of affect, mood, and emotion are briefly analyzed and found wanting of specificity and relevance. In an effort to broadly outline different methodological approaches that minimize the influence of semantic space on purely musical communications, three experiments are presented. First, timbre is investigated by similarity measures leading to multidimensional analysis. Second, the perception of intended performer expression is approached using a non-verbal categorization paradigm. Third, perceived audio-visual relationships are operationalized through a rating scale implying a continuum of referentiality.

Empiricism has approached musical meaning with both vigor and trepidation. On the one hand, notational models provide the privileged status that symbols have among scientists. On the other hand, meanings irreducible to symbols are often ignored for fear of scholarly retribution. This conflict continues and accelerates.

I provide one path through this conflict, focusing on the strengths and weaknesses of various aspects of empirical musical meaning. As exemplars spanning elements of empirical meaning, three previously unpublished experimental studies that illustrate degrees of reliance on words and explicit meanings are offered.

This path may not please those who "fall victim to the seduction of language" (Caputo 1987: 51, quoting Husserl), since the meanings are derived from simple responses to complex events, where the surface features of words are relatively unimportant, but the underlying meaning of a perceptual event identified by words is multidimensionally important. The mode of expression is often numerical, visual and graphical, rather than verbal and semantical.

The reification-of-concepts syndrome present in most musical scholarship often reduces complex events to single concepts such as pitch. I am not convinced that the "new musicology" overcomes this limitation with its exploitation of the fuzziness of the language with which it is seduced. At the same time, the limitations of empirical approaches will be all to clear from the exposition below. Let us consider the funda-mental nature of empiricism.

The Empirical Investigation Process

Antony Flew (1984: 319) in *A Dictionary of Philosophy* writes, "Organized empiri-cal science provides the most impressive result of human rationality and is one of the best candidates for knowledge." While there is no doubt that many would disagree, the ability of the empirical approach to provide prediction among variables is unsur-passed. Figure 1 diagrams the empirical research process. The central circular path emphasizes that the building of a theory or model is a continuing process through time, rather than a one-shot affair. I claim that the essential elements of problem statement—hypothesis building, data gathering, and hypothesis confirmation and disconfirmation, leading to a noncontradictory array of relationships among variables

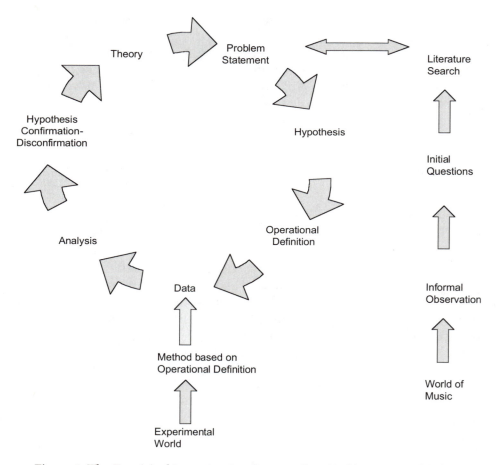

Figure 1. The Empirical Investigation Process (inspired by an unpublished class handout of Warren C. Campbell, University of Connecticut).

known as a theory—pervade all scholarship, whether empirical or non-empirical. What, then, distinguishes empiricism from other approaches is the criterial attribute of the *operational definition*. Unlike dictionary, or constitutional, definitions, the problem statements of empiricism are operationalized in a rule involving an action/operation, which links independent observations with the variables. Therefore, a musical concept like meaning must be actualized by a rule of the form "meaning is when a listener responds to a chosen musical element by X," where X is an action or activity that is observable and recordable. Often this observation involves the concept of measurement, that is, the assignment of a value to a variable. I would note, however, that all research involves measurement, even if it is as peripheral as selecting a domain of study; that selection values one domain over another and is therefore measurement.

Most empiricism employs numerical measurement of variables, using the models of statistics to define the degree of prediction from the currently observed to hypothetical groups of other observers beyond that current observation. This leads to the power of prediction suggested by Flew (1984). It also leads some to reject the approach of empiricism on the grounds that it is somehow mechanistic and even nonhumanistic. It is worth noting, however, that science, as we understand it in the twenty-first century, is not uncovering immutable law, but discovering, via the interpretation of observations using the empirical investigation process, predictable and reliable relationships among variables defined by the insights of humans. In fact, many theories can coexist regarding the same frame of reference as long as they remain internally consistent. Thus there is Newtonian mechanics as a system juxtaposed with various forms of quantum physics. This has lead Kuhn (1962) to articulate a theory of scientific paradigm shifting: when a series of hypotheses based on previous theory are disconfirmed leading to a critical mass of problems (a crisis), a new approach is offered leading to new theory, and thus new variable relationships (see Caputo 1987: 214–222 for an interesting connection of Kuhn's concepts to contemporary philosophy). Thus science is a highly interpretive endeavor driven by the desire to predict; when such prediction fails, theories are modified until they are driven out by new paradigms.[1]

The role of theory in current empiricism is well illustrated by this dialogue between Heisenberg and Einstein (Heisenberg 1971: 63, found at the American Institute of Physics web site: http://www.aip.org/history/heisenberg/p07c.htm):

Heisenberg: "We cannot observe electron orbits inside the atom.... Now, since a good theory must be based on directly observable magnitudes, I thought it more fitting to restrict myself to these, treating them, as it were, as representatives of the electron orbits."

"But you don't seriously believe," Einstein protested, "that none but observable magnitudes must go into a physical theory?"

"Isn't that precisely what you have done with relativity?" I asked in some surprise.

"Possibly I did use this kind of reasoning," Einstein admitted, "but it is nonsense all the same.... In reality the very opposite happens. It is the theory which decides what we can observe."

In the empirical arena of musical meaning, this argument has special relevance. Such research demands the linking of two or more frames of reference, rather than relying solely on a single notational frame as does most music theory or grammars. Music cognition links the perceptual/behavioral frame of reference with notation, physiology, acoustics, and many other domains, and is the most active of the area of empirical music research. An important issue is the extent to which observation can reveal the "real" nature of behavior, the genesis of which cannot be verbalized. It is thus useful to distinguish between explicit, verbal behaviors, and those behaviors that are implicit.

In the behavioral frame of reference, implicit knowledge is that replicable behavior that cannot be adequately explicitly verbalized. An example of this is performer expressiveness (returned to below), or as a nonmusical example, the ability to speak expressively. Explicit knowledge is that replicable behavior that is amenable to explicit verbalization. An example is recalling facts and dates surrounding a composer and her compositions. Both of these forms of knowing interact to produce the myriad behaviors that the experimenter can observe. From the observations based on theory and data collected from the experimental world defined by the researcher, inferences are made on the not-directly-observable operations of the mind.[2]

It is useful to model the relationships among frames of reference in musical communication before continuing on to empirical definitions of musical meaning.

In this model, the behavioral systems of traditional Western art music are represented by the composer, performer, and listener (see Campbell and Heller 1981). The ideation of the composer is recoded to a physical frame of reference, the music notation. This in turn is recoded by the performer to the physical frame of the acoustical

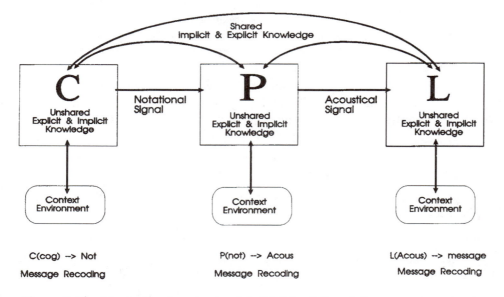

Figure 2. The Music Communication Model (Kendall and Carterette 1990: 132).
Copyright *Music Perception*, the Regents of the University of California.
(Used by permission)

signal, with the addition of expressive messages initiated by the performer (thus there are multiple messages transmitted in parallel). These physical frames of reference have received a privileged status in scholarship: The notational signal is the domain of traditional music theory, and is usually studied in terms of description (common-practice harmony) or prescription (any number of *a priori* structures, including dodecaphonicism). The acoustical signal is the domain of the empirical field of acoustics, which has increasingly linked itself to the behavioral frame of reference; in fact, current means of audio compression, used on the web and for DVD, have as much to do with perceptual models as they do with vibrational models.

The music communication model emphasizes that without implicit and explicit knowledge structures, and the links between them in the chain of communication, music would not exist. (It is striking that although such cognitive components are criterial for the existence of music, much music scholarship, including ethnomusicological approaches, ignores systematic exploration of this domain.) Shared knowledge structures permit intended messages between composer and performer to be transmitted to the listener. The receipt of intended messages provides *derived* meaning, that is, meaning decoded from the intents of composer and performer. It is also possible for the listener to produce *imposed* meanings, meanings that are outside of intent; these meanings explain how listeners can structure musical experiences without sharing much of the knowledge structures of either composer or performer. The fact that music has certain properties based on cognitive universals (such as pitch circularity with the octave and limited short-term memory) explains how a large variety of unfamiliar music can produce meanings. The concept of culture itself must be dependent on shared knowledge structures constrained by cognitive universals.

The idea of a knowledge structure, involving implicit knowledge, was proposed by Bartlett (1932) in the invention of the concept of schemata. The term schemata is intentionally vague, defined in different ways by various psychologists. Basically it is the manifestation of nonrandom behaviors via nonverbalizable rules. The structure of schemata, and the definition thereof, can only be inferred through the process of empirical investigation linking the implicit perceptual frame of reference with other frames, since the schemata themselves are contained within the 'black box' of the mind. The relation of musical meaning to schemata is thus of central importance to research in empirical musicology.

Operationally Defining Musical Meaning

Early approaches to empiricism in music mainly focused on physical frames of reference through the disciplines of acoustics and mathematics. Psychoacoustics, a branch of psychophysics, linked perception to vibrational, physiological, and music notational phenomena through the seminal work of Helmholtz (1954 [1863]) whose influence is still strongly evident today. As research progressed into the twentieth century, psychologists defined, and continue to argue about, the hierarchy of sensation, perception, and cognition. Schemata, as used by Bartlett (1932) and Neisser (1976), clearly deal with higher-order mental processes. Empirical definitions operationalize meaning relative to such cognitive operations.

Kate Hevner (1935a, 1935b, 1936) performed some of the first important work in the cognition of musical meaning. She operationalized musical meaning in terms of an adjective checklist, that is, groups of adjectives within which the subject selected one or more appropriate terms for each musical selection played. The eight groups of six to eleven adjectives each were arranged in a circle, with the following representative terms for each: I: *dignified*; II: *sad*; III: *dreamy*; IV: *serene*; V: *graceful*; VI: *happy*; VII: *exciting*; VIII: *vigorous* (wrapping to dignified, I) (Gabrielsson and Lindstrom 2001: 231). The methods and analysis procedures were remarkably sophisticated for their time. In Hevner (1937: 626) a summary of subject responses relative to six musical factors is provided. Major and minor modes resulted in strongest responses to happy and sad, respectively. This result has been confirmed in a large number of studies (for example, Crowder 1984, 1985, Scherer and Oshinksy, 1977). Although it has been suggested that this association occurs "at least from 7–8 years of age" (Gabrielson and Lindstrom 2001: 239), Pinchot and Crowder (1990: 189) found that children as young as three could reliably respond to happy and sad face icons for the major vs. minor association (I return to nonverbal responses below).

Other musical factors included tempo; slow tempo (sometimes defined relative to personal tempo, where moderate is 600 msec/pulse) was associated with such adjective groups as I. *dignified/solemn*; III. *dreamy/sentimental*; IV. *serene/gentle*. Fast tempo was associated with VI. *happy/bright*; VII. *exciting/elated*. High pitch was associated with V. *graceful/sparkling* and low pitch with II. *sad/heavy*. Other musical factors included rhythm (flowing vs. firm resulting in happy/bright and dignified/solemn, respectively), harmony (simple vs. complex producing serene/gentle/graceful/sparkling and exciting/elated respectively) and melody (ascending vs. descending, this factor producing little differentiation in adjective responses). (See Gabrielsson and Lindstrom (2001: 230–239) for an extensive analysis of Hevner's results and the results of other scholar's experiments using this and similar techniques.)

Hevner was very aware of the limitations of this technique. She admonished researchers to select pieces of music that do not change mood over time, and notes that there are interactions among the various musical variables, such that a minor piece of music with certain rhythmic and harmonic characteristics might not be "sad." She (Hevner 1936) overcame, to a certain extent, the first limitation by inventing a method by which pieces of music were divided into sections and then rated by section. The most famous example is the collected checklist responses to *Reflections on Water* by Debussy. When subjects responded to the piece as a whole, the responses were spread among the eight adjective clusters. However, when the piece was divided into three sections indicated by a signal from the experimenter, subjects responded to the first section using clusters V and VII, the second section using cluster IV, and the third section clusters IV and V. A few more recent studies have essentially used this approach, although with fancier names labeling the methodology (see Namba et al. 1991).

Categorization of meanings using adjective checklists produces highly variable responses. Sufficient time must be given for all of adjectives to be selected, and while the music is continuously playing, this can easily interfere with the subjects' attention to musical changes. The data are not easily amendable to analysis, which is often simply a set of counts as to the number of times a given adjective was selected by a group of subjects. Rating scales provide a solution to some of these issues.

Osgood, Suci, and Tannebaum wrote the seminal work *Measurement of Meaning* in 1957. Rather than using checklists, they simply used a rating scale with bipolar adjectives, for example:

boring _____:_____:_____:_____:_____:_____:_____ interesting

The usefulness of this approach lies in the fact that a number can be assigned (0 for completely boring and 6 completely interesting), producing a ratio-measurement scale, unleashing the power of parametric inferential statistics as well as dimensional analysis (see Experiment 1, below). This method is called the *semantic differential*.

Osgood et al. (1957: 26) write, "What is meant by 'differentiating' the meaning of a concept? When a subject judges a concept against a series of [rating] scales . . . each judgment represents a selection among a set of given alternatives and serves to localize the concept as a point in the semantic space (26). They note the contrast with this differentiating operational definition of meaning and the behaviorist definition of meaning that connects the meaning of a sign in a particular context to the "representational mediation process to which it elicits" (Osgood et al. 1957: 26).

The use of interval scales such as the semantic differential provides a powerful basis for numerical analysis. Each scale can be seen as a point in a multidimensional semantic space, such that there are N-1 dimensions for N scales. In addition, the variability of the subject responses among scales can be analyzed for relationships, creating data reduction allowing one to classify (give structure to) the various scales producing a magnitude of the relation of each scale to these factors. This factor analysis was an important outcome of the rating of a large number of words in a thesaurus by Osgood et al. (1957: 50–68). (Factor Analysis differs from Principal Components Analysis in that the former does not involve all of the variance of the design, whereas the latter does.) Such factors are often given labels based on which adjective scale relates most strongly to a given factor. The main factor was *Evaluation*, the highest loading factor being "good–bad." The next factor was *Potency*, the highest loading scale being "hard–soft" and including "strong–weak." The third factor was *Activity*, the highest loading scale being "active–passive."

The semantic differential has been used in a very large number of music studies, including the communication of affective states by performance expressiveness (Senju and Ohgushi 1987) and the changing associative dimensions of the variations in Ravel's *Bolero* (Asada and Ohgushi 1991). Marshall and Cohen (1988, see also Cohen this volume) studied the influence of two musical soundtracks combined with a two-minute animation containing a large and small triangle and a circle. Twelve rating scales incorporating bipolar adjectives related to the activity, evaluation, and potency factors of the semantic differential were employed by subjects to rate the animation alone or the animation with each of the two soundtracks. Although the two musical examples were judged to have approximately the same activity level, the "characters" of the animation were interpreted differently between soundtracks; the large triangle was more active under one soundtrack and the small triangle more active under the other. Lipscomb and Kendall (1994) employed a rating scale of fitness in addition to semantic differential responses to ascertain how interchanging the soundtracks among five visual and musical scenes in *Star Trek IV* (music by Leonard Rosenman) influenced the listener. In general, results demonstrated that listeners unfamiliar with the movie could determine the correct match between the intended music and the video scene. Both Cohen (this volume) and Lipscomb (this volume) note that in multimedia contexts, associational as well as syntactical elements act in symbiosis (see Experiment 3 below).

Kendall and Carterette (1993a, 1993b), in order to interpret timbral relationships, conducted an extensive investigation into the nature of adjectival rating scales. At first, they attempted to use bi-polar adjectives drawn from the work of von Bismarck (1974a, 1974b), who used 28 rating scales from 69 previously used in psychoacoustical and psycholinguistic research. Subjects listened to 35 synthetic tones varying in harmonic spectral properties, envelopes, and noise. Factor analysis of the correlated ratings yielded four main factors: dull–sharp, compact–scattered, empty–full, colorless–colorful. The dull–sharp scale as the main rating scale seemed somewhat surprising, since the descriptive, rather than empirical, literature is replete with the concept of timbral brightness.

Kendall and Carterette (1993a) attempted to replicate von Bismarck's findings, but used natural instrument timbres in dyads from a previous experiment. They were unable to replicate the findings, and in fact found that the data failed to differentiate among the timbres at all. Kendall and Carterette (1993a) concluded that the terms used in translation from the German were not cross-culturally valid, and that the words used related to synthetic timbres but not to natural timbres. Importantly, they stated, "It occurred to us that a central problem in the use of bipolar opposites is that the "opposite" is, in fact, not an antipode. Is *dull* the opposite of *sharp* when used to describe sound? What is the opposite of a *rich* sound? *Poor*?"

Our solution was to simply negate an attribute, therefore, *sharp* vs. *not sharp*, for example. In fact we studied two different versions of the verbal attribute magnitude estimation (VAME), as we called it. One version used a scale labeled with an adjective and its negation at opposite poles, and the other labeled the scale "sharp," for example, and asked for a rating on a continuous scale from 0 to 100 as to the amount of the attribute, that is, the amount of *sharpness* in the sound. Subsequent use of these modifications of the differential technique produced interpretable results for both the von Bismarck (1974a) adjectives and adjectives derived from Piston's *Orchestration*, demonstrating timbral factors of *power, stridency, plangency,* and *reediness.*

Emotion and Meaning

A recent book, *Music and Emotion* (Juslin and Sloboda 2001), provides clues as to the current empirical understanding of meaning. In this book, it is quite clear that the term "emotion" refers to any adjectival process that uses emotive words. Hevner (1935a, 1935b, 1936) and Meyer (1956) reappear in many chapters.

I would point out that Hevner was very careful about the use of terms. The titles of her research papers use the term "expression," not "emotion." Within the book *Music and Emotion* (Juslin and Sloboda 2001), some authors write in terms that clearly suggest meaning or expression rather than emotion. Scherer (2001: x) in the foreword of the volume states that "It has often been claimed that music is the language of the emotions" and goes on to present two interpretations of the term "emotion." The first interpretation implies that the patterns within music serve to suggest emotions, similar to Langer's (1942) writings, and sometimes termed "physiognomic emotion."[3] The other interpretation is that music must involve emotion considering the contributions of so many people involved in the music communication process. This latter definition is a self-fulfilling, indeed, negative one.

Leonard Meyer (2001: 341) is clearly not convinced of the catch-all phrase "emotion" in this context. He states: "I begin by proposing a number of distinctions [among concepts of music and emotion] because, despite its empirical outlook and methodology, the psychological analysis of human emotional experiences . . . h[as] lacked conceptual specificity and precision." He goes on to wonder if such terms as "aroused," "tired," "bewildered," or "curious" are emotional terms, let alone emotions themselves. In fact, the principal editors of the volume *Music and Emotion* (Sloboda and Juslin 2001: 73) write: "What is an emotion? This question . . . has not yet received a definitive answer. There are many reasons for this state of affairs. One reason is that emotions are difficult to define and measure."

Leonard Meyer's (1956) *Emotion and Meaning in Music* has been important in modernizing and fleshing out of the essential position of Hanslick (1957 [1854]), that musical meanings are more important than semantic meanings in experiencing music. For Meyer (1956), an essential and often neglected concept in musical emotions is that induced by the patterning of tension and release coupled with cognitive expectations of the listener; such musical meaning is embodied within the music itself (see Experiment 3 below). Hanslick (1957 [1854]: 21) remarks "Definite feelings and emotions are unsusceptible of being embodied in music." It could be said that a better title for Meyer's (1956) book is "Emotion *as* Meaning in Music," since clearly the concept of emotion he elucidates is neither the commonsense use of the term nor the psychologically intense state of affairs found in life events nor the epiphanies reported in musical peak experiences (for example, Maslow 1968).

Words about emotions are not necessarily the result of emotions. Kendall and Carterette (1991, 1993a) set forth a caution: Music has *musical* meanings that are far more significant than superimposed semantic meanings from adjectival operational definitions of the type outlined above. The forced overlap of semantic-space schemata onto musical-space schemata, as in the semantic differential and adjectival description approach, produces an uncertain and fragile composite; the approach is in danger of misdirecting scholarly attention to language perception rather than the apprehension of sound patterns organized in time. Research in the Music Cognition and Acoustics Laboratory (MCAL) at UCLA has focused on reducing dependence on such adjectival approaches, using them only in interpretation of the results of other methods. Three different problems with and empirical solutions to musical meaning are outlined in the MCAL experiments below.

Experiment I: Multidimensional Scaling of Timbral Relations among Pitch Chroma

Timbre has been negatively defined as that perceptual attribute that remains when pitch and loudness are held constant. It is clear, however, that a clarinet playing concert Eb3 has a quite different timbre than when playing Bb5 at the same pitch and loudness; that is why the 'registers' of the clarinet are given the names *chalumeau* (written E3–E4), *throat* (written F4–Bb4), and *clarion* (written B4–C6). The same variance of timbre across playing range is true of nearly every instrument, yet the identity of the source remains constant. This fact was an argument used by Mursell (1937) to diffuse the psychoacoustical bases for Seashore's (1938) Cartesian, acoustic-based approach to music psychology and music talent.

One operational definition in timbre communication has revolved around identification of the instrument (Berger 1964; Grey 1977; Saldanha and Corso 1964; Wedin and Goude 1972). Results were extremely variable, ranging from 33% to 85% correct (Handel 1989) and can be attributed to the range of instruments, overlapping similarity of timbres, listener background, tessitura of the isolated single tones used for a given instrument, and the relatively variable reproduction contexts using tape playback (see Hajda, Kendall, Carterette, and Harshberger 1997, for an extensive review). An important consideration is the familiarity of the listeners with the names of the instruments as connected to their sonic attributes. The solution is to find an empirical technique that minimizes such explicit knowledge.

Multidimensional Scaling

This writer considers the use of multidimensional scaling methodologies to be one solution to a myriad series of limitations in verbal-attribute response mechanisms. First, it is important to understand what a dimension is in this context. Figure 3 provides an illustration of the distances in miles between three cities, labeled A, B, and C.

In the top figure, the distance between cities AB (10 miles) plus the distance between cities BC (20 miles) is equal to the distance between cities AC (30 miles). In this case (AB + BC = AC) the cities exist on a single line, and thus are represented by a one-dimensional geometry. If, however, as in the bottom figure, the distance between AB (10 miles), and BC (27 miles) is greater than the distance between AC (30 miles). In this case, a two-dimensional geometry is required, and with three points this forms a triangle. For *N* distances, *N-1* dimensions may be necessary to represent orthogonally the geometrical configuration of the data points. Of course, the multidimensional scaling (MDS) statistical algorithm provides a best fit between an experimenter-specified number of dimensions and a larger number of data points. Thus it, like factor analysis, is a means of specifying relationships in terms of data reduction.

In music perception studies, the subject ratings of the similarity between pairs of stimuli are treated as a distance. That is, pairs of timbres, say oboe and flute, are played, and the subject is asked to rate the similarity of the sounds. That rating becomes the

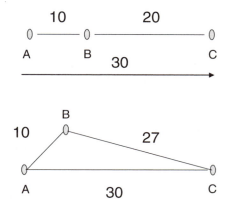

Figure 3. A City-Distance example of dimensionality.

distance between oboe and flute. A matrix of all pairs of similarity ratings in the stimulus set is subjected to multidimensional analysis. This procedure was first applied to timbres by Miller and Carterette (1975) and Grey (1975) and was revitalized and extended in Kendall and Carterette (1990). The stability of recent results suggests that methodological uncertainties in early studies have been overcome.[4]

One finding in Kendall and Carterette (1990) was that, with the combination of orchestral wind instruments including alto saxophone in dyads, a two-dimensional circular configuration was obtained, suggesting that some attributes of timbre, like pitch, wrap back to a given origin point.

Almost all studies of timbre have used a single pitch, often near Eb4. For reasons of tessitura, the Kendall and Carterette studies (1990, 1993a, 1993b, 1999) have used the pitch Bb4. Almost no comparative data across pitch chroma are available, and such is the goal of the present study.

The MDS technique through similarity judgment provides a means of operationalizing timbre relative to the schemata of the listener. It is hypothesized that the single judgment of similarity by the listener has, at its basis, multiple criteria. For example, if one is asked to rate the similarity of two paintings, the myriad attributes of the paintings would be weighted in the decision making, and these would emerge hierarchically as dimensions in the analysis. Therefore, the concept of similarity, rather than the semantic baggage of differentials, is employed in this experiment.

Method

Stimuli. Graduate student instrumentalists on alto saxophone, clarinet, flute, oboe, trumpet, violin, French horn, soprano saxophone and a professional bassoonist were recorded playing a Bb major diatonic scale across the regular tessitura of their instrument. The resultant signals were ca. 1.5 seconds in performed length and separated from each other by silence. Recordings were made in a moderately reverberant concert hall (reverberation time = ca. 1.6 sec) using an AKG coincident microphone (Model 422) feeding a matrix box (Audio Engineer Associates Model MS 38) set for a crossed orthogonal figure eight with an axis of 45 degrees to the source. Specific placements of the microphone relative to each seated instrumentalist were made by a professional recording engineer. Signals were transferred digitally to tape and then to computer hard disk. Stereo signals were mixed to monophonic and were equalized for loudness through signal normalization employing the equal loudness contour (Sound Forge, version 6) followed by perceptual adjustment by experienced listeners. (Kendall, Carterette, and Hajda (1999) found no statistical difference in subject responses to stereo or monophonic among a set of similar timbres.)

Pitch chromas of Bb3, F4, and Bb5 were extracted for use in this study. Bb3 is outside of the flute range. For this timbre, the C4 flute was extracted from the McGill University Master Samples (MUMS) compact disc and re-sampled down to Bb4. The pitch Bb5 was outside the playing range of bassoon, alto saxophone, and French horn, so piccolo, muted violin, and a second oboe and clarinet timbre were extracted and edited from the McGill University Master Samples compact disc, equalized in loudness with the other instruments, and included only in the Bb5 scaling.[5] The perceptual experiment, including randomization and decoding of subject responses, was handled by the Music Experiment Development System (MEDS) version 2002 (Kendall 1990–2002).

Subjects. Groups of subjects (N = 14) were solicited for course credit from various music classes open to both music students and nonmusic students. (Kendall and Carterette (1991, 1993a, b) and Kendall, Carterette, and Hajda (1999) found no appreciable differences between musicians and nonmusicians in these MDS similarity tasks with orchestral timbres.) Groups were randomly assigned to one or more experiments with the goal of keeping the total time for a given subject to under an hour. The instrumental timbres were compared to each other at pitch chroma Bb3, F4, Bb4, and Bb5 in separate groups (that is not across chroma).

Subjects heard all possible pairs of instruments (for a total of 45 pairs including identities) and rated them on a scale of *similar–not similar* using a mouse that controlled a graphic slider. When the slider was positioned on the scale at the point chosen by the subject, the subject clicked an OK button. The data, quantized to a range of 100 points, was recorded by the computer, and the next stimulus pair was presented. There was a 500ms silence between each of the stimulus pairs. Subjects first participated in a practice session that spanned the range of the stimuli; the practice set included identities (instruments paired with themselves) and hypothetically distant timbres (oboe vs. French horn, for example).

Results and Discussion

The data sets were subjected to classical multidimensional scaling analysis.[6] Figures 4, 5, and 6 represent the perceived distances between timbres for pitch chroma Bb3, F4, and Bb4 (All statistics were performed in *Statistica* versions 5.5 and 6, Statsoft Corporation.)

Interpretation of multidimensional spaces often requires making connections among several frames of reference. Kendall and Carterette (1993a, 1993b) found that subjects' verbal ratings of continuant (steady-state) natural timbres in terms of *nasality* correlated with the first dimension of perceptual spaces at Bb4. *Nasality* is likely related to the *acute* aspect of phonemes in speech. In Figure 4, the Bb3 timbres appear to

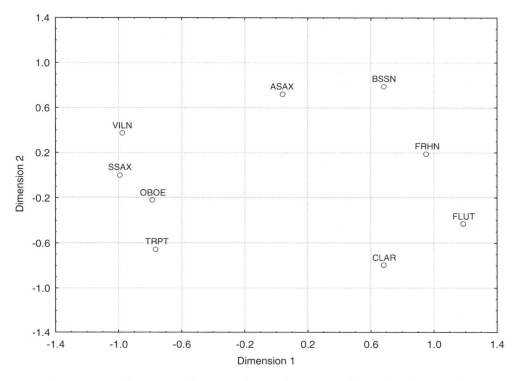

Figure 4. Two dimensional MDS solution for nine orchestral timbres at Bb3.
Stress = .08 (N = 14).

arrange themselves such that *not nasal* timbres are to the right and *more nasal* timbres are to the left. Similarly *less reedy* to *more reedy* timbres spread on the second dimension from bottom to top. This second dimension can also be interpreted relative to perceived vibrato (the attribute *tremulous* in Kendall and Carterette 1999: 353–356). The clarinet in the *chalumeau* register vs. alto sax and bassoon are extremes on this dimension. Such a general interpretation can be seen to apply to the F4 and Bb4 spaces as well. The most variable instrument across this range is the bassoon; as it approaches the very highest tessitura at Bb4 it becomes dramatically *less nasal* and *less reedy/ tremulous*. The alto saxophone, as it moves from its middle register written G4 to G5 becomes less *nasal* and approaches the timbre of the French horn (an instrument for which it often serves as a replacement in school-band scores). The soprano saxophone and oboe remain stable in high *nasality* across this octave range. The violin becomes more *reedy/tremulous* sounding and somewhat less *nasal* as it approaches Bb4. At Bb3 the timbres spread themselves in perceptual space such that a semi-circular arrangement is obtained, although this would be even more apparent if the trumpet, playing an open horn on its C3, was less *nasal*. The second-dimension attributes, unlike nasality, had relatively low correlations with the perceptual spaces (ca. $r = .45$, see Kendall and Carterette 1999: 356) and that responses were highly variable, thus echoing remarks made earlier about the use of verbal rating scales.

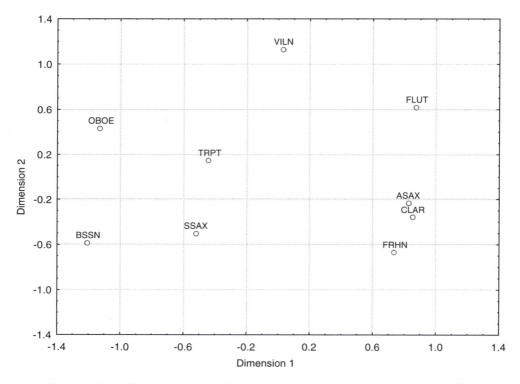

Figure 5. Two dimensional MDS solution for nine orchestral timbres at F4.
Stress = .12 (N = 14).

A less subjective interpretation of the relationship among the perceptual spaces
can be had through quanitificational means. Table 1 presents the correlation among
timbre distances on the first dimension. The relationships are moderately strong, the
weakest being between the F4 scaling and Bb4 scaling. This interval spans the register
change on the clarinet, and the bassoon is on an extremely high note, resulting in shifts
in the timbre space.

The second dimension (see Table 2) has, overall, weaker correlations, the highest
being between the smaller interval of Bb4 to F3. The octave interval and the fourth
produce rather large changes in the perceptual space on the second dimension, one

Table 1
Pearson correlations *r* among first dimension distances

	Bb3 Dim. 1	F4 Dim. 1	Bb4 Dim. 1
Bb3 Dim. 1	1.0		
F4 Dim. 1	.53	1.0	
Bb 4 Dim. 1	.60	.35	1.0

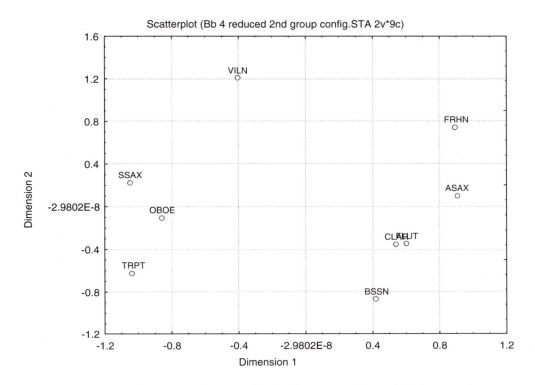

Figure 6. Two dimensional MDS solution for nine orchestral timbres at Bb4.
Stress = .13 (N = 14).

characterized by elements of *tremulousness/reediness*. Again, changes in register result in these variations.

Further quantificational analysis involves linking the perceptual frame of reference to the vibrational (acoustical) frame of reference. The physical variable most commonly thought to connect to timbre is the spectrum, a combination of the frequency and amplitude of the harmonics of a complex signal. What is a single measure of such a multidimensional physical structure?

Consider a teeter-totter with the fulcrum placed in the center. The teeter-totter is in balance. If one adds two individuals of exactly equal weight to the ends of the

Table 2

Pearson correlations *r* among second dimension distances

	Bb3 Dim 2	F4 Dim. 2	Bb4 Dim. 2
Bb3 Dim. 2	1.0		
F4 Dim. 2	.47	1.0	
Bb4 Dim. 2	.23	.28	1.0

system, it will remain in balance. If one adds another individual of half the weight at one end of the system, the fulcrum must be moved towards the additional weight to keep the system in balance.

The spectral-centroid measure is essentially the fulcrum in the balance point of harmonic amplitudes. In the analogy, the frequencies of the spectrum are distances along the teeter-totter and the amplitudes are the weights of the individuals. The balance point for the fulcrum is measured along the frequency scale and provides the spectral-centroid measure. For the purposes of comparing spectra across the diatonic scale, as in this experiment, the measure is normalized through division by the fundamental frequency; it becomes a relative unitless measure.[7]

Figure 7 is the spectrum of the oboe at Bb4. (All spectral analyses were conducted in the Music Experiment Development System (MEDS) 2000–2002, programmed by Roger A. Kendall.) Note the rise in amplitude among the first three harmonics. Figure 8 is the spectrum of the oboe at Bb5. Note that at this frequency, the harmonics descend monotonically and rapidly. The spectral centroid of Figure 7 is considerably higher (3.7) than that of Figure 8 (1.7) because of the amount of amplitude in the first three harmonics of the spectrum for Bb4 relative to the rapidly decreasing pattern in the spectrum of Bb5.

In previous research a strong relationship between spectral centroid and dimensional analysis of timbre perception was found (for example Grey and Gordon 1978, Krimphoff et al. 1994, Kendall and Carterette 1989, 1991, 1999, Kendall 2002, 2003). Additional studies (Kendall and Carterette 1989, 1993c; Sandell 1995) found that combinations of timbres in dyads fused or blended when spectral centroids were close and diffused otherwise. Hajda (1996) found that spectral centroid did not correlate well with time-variant spectra of low redundancy such as that found in impulse

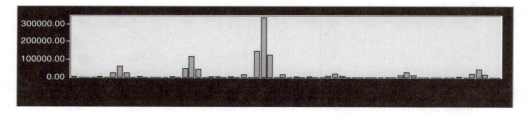

Figure 7. Spectral analysis of oboe Bb4.

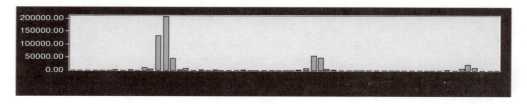

Figure 8. Spectral analysis of oboe Bb5.

instruments such as piano and guitar, but did with continuant instruments, that is, instruments that provide energy to maintain a steady-state condition.[8] I hypothesize that spectral centroid will continue to have a strong correlation with the first dimension of the perceptual spaces across pitch chroma.

Acoustical analysis parameters were as follows: analysis was performed on signals downsampled to 22.05 k samples/sec. Instrument signals were analyzed starting 500ms from the onset to avoid transients. (See Kendall, Carterette, and Hajda 1996: 367–347) for details on attack and signal length parameters and how they do not matter in this type of analysis for continuant timbres.) A ninth-order FFT with Hanning window was performed on 529ms of the steady-state, producing 23 analysis frames, each 23ms in duration. The long-time-average-centroid was calculated as the mean of the centroid across the analysis frames.

Results of Experiment 1, first dimension, correlate with spectral centroid as follows: Bb3, $r = .79$; F4 $r = .76$; Bb 4, $r = .88$. Thus, these moderately high values confirm the continuing strength of the spectral centroid to define perceptual similarity among continuant timbres across a sample of pitch chroma spanning an octave.

Completing the experiment are data from subject similarity ratings at Bb5. At this pitch chroma, only six of the original set of instruments are within their playing range: Trumpet, soprano saxophone, clarinet, oboe, violin, and flute. This scaling includes 1.5 second segments of tones drawn from the Monteral University Music Samples compact disc. The original onsets were retained, and an artificial ramp decay was added to shorten the lengths to match the signals recorded for the previous analyses. Oboe 2, Clarinet 2, muted violin and piccolo were the added timbres. Figure 9 presents the perceptual space based on classical MDS for these timbres.

It is immediately apparent that the violins, followed by piccolo and flute, are separated along the first dimension from the other winds. In particular, the violin timbre is uniquely maximally distant from those winds. Previous research provides a possible clue to the interpretation of this space.

Figure 10 presents a plot of pitch chroma by spectral centroid for five instruments. Three of the instruments (clarinet, oboe, and violin) span two octaves from Bb3 to Bb5. Note the convergence of centroid at Bb5 of oboe and clarinet, and their position in perceptual space in Figure 9. Similarly, the violin spectral centroid remains quite a bit higher than that of oboe and clarinet, and in Figure 9 it is maximally separated in perceptual space. For the winds, the air column becomes increasing shorter, and therefore fewer modes of vibration are available in the spectrum for the higher frequency. Thus their centroids, and timbres, begin to converge.

Conclusion

Over a large number of studies, multidimensional scaling has provided a stable and revealing data set relating timbres to cognitive schemata. Relying on the concept of the similarity of musical objects, rather than their emotional or associative meaning, removes the often variable and difficult task for the subject of connecting semantic schemata with sound schemata. However, there are obvious limitations in the MDS approach. Firstly, the interpretation of the spaces is not automatic. Secondly, the data are descriptive rather than inferential. Thirdly, it is necessary to connect the data to

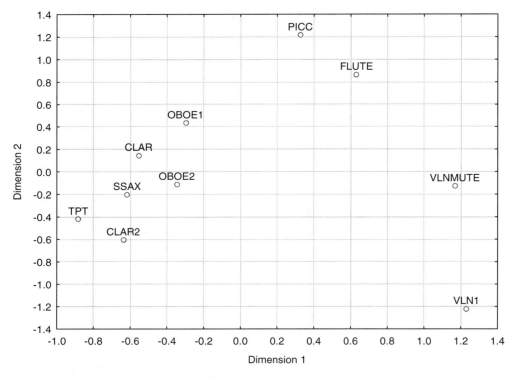

Figure 9. Two-dimensional MDS solution for nine orchestral timbres at Bb5.
Stress = .09 (N = 14).

previous research in other domains or frames of reference, such as the acoustical frame, or the result is simply a pretty set of graphs.

Another approach to timbre without the use of semantic differentials or verbal labels is categorization (Kendall 1986). An expansion of the essence of this technique can be applied to a fairly ineffable aspect of the process of music communication—the performer-generated messages commonly called musical expression, the focus of the next experiment.

Experiment 2: Categorization of Musical Expression

The music communication process (Figure 2) involves the recoding of musical messages among composer, performer, and listener. The performer not only decodes the musical notation provided by the composer, and recodes this into the vibrational frame of reference, but also inserts performer-generated information commonly called "musical expressiveness." A number of studies have assumed that using affective or emotive words to induce the performer to generate musical messages is musically valid. The great majority of music notation does not have detailed expressive information

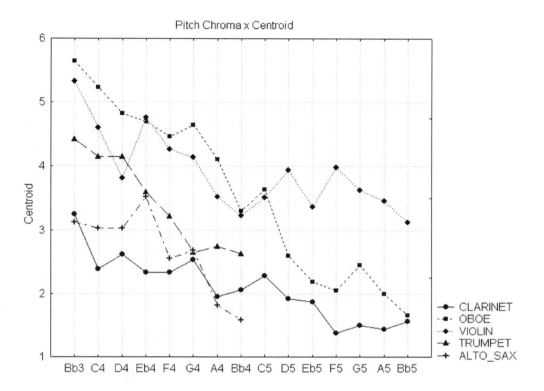

Figure 10. Spectral centroid by pitch chroma for five orchestral instruments.
(Based on Kendall, 2002. Used by permission.)

coded into the score, particularly references to *anger, hate, fashionability*, and so on. A tempo marking such as *Allegro giocoso* is all that might be expected; the specific stylistically correct expressive messages to code 'giocoso' are not notationally specified. The performer's implicit knowledge leads to coding the appropriate message. Unfortunately, the fact is that a large number of empirical studies have forced the performer to generate messages that are in direct conflict with the stylistic elements culturally normative for the music they were to interpret, and I would suggest that tables of acoustic-level and musical parameters said to relate to different induced emotions should be treated with caution if not amazement (see Juslin 2001: 315).

Kendall and Carterette (1990) conducted an experiment based on modeling behavior designed to reduce interference with the normative processes in expressive performance. A virtuoso concert pianist produced three different expressive interpretations of a monophonic musical phrase, and instrumentalists notated their own blank scores and reproduced what they heard using the diverse hardware (instruments) they were trained on. The experimental question was whether the performer intent was communicated to the listener. Subsequent experimental analyses of acoustical signals found that much information was contained in the micro-timing variations and that patternings of expressive nuance among instrumentalists varied greatly by instrument. In addition, the virtuoso performer was able to construct completely new messages among the three examples, whereas the graduate performers appeared to possess a lexicon of patterns that were varied to create different messages.[9]

Method

All recordings took place in UCLA's Schoenberg Hall (reverberation time ca. 1.6 sec) and were digitally recorded by a professional recording engineer. He used a coincident microphone (AKG Model 422) feeding a matrix box (Audio Engineer Associated Model MS 38) set for an orthogonal figure eight with an axis of 45 degrees to the source.

A professional concert pianist performed three renditions of Schubert's *Der Müller und der Bach*. This selection was chosen because it fit the playing ranges of the instruments. It has a phrase structure of A, B, A', thus facilitating analysis of expression between two nearly identical phrases after the intervention of contrasting material, something that had not been done in the previous experiment (Kendall and Carterette 1990). The A and A' phrases differ minimally: the A' phrase begins with an anacrusis (pick-up) whereas the A phrase starts on the downbeat. After the first two beats, the phrases are identical.

One performance rendition was without expression, the second with appropriate expression, and the third with exaggerated expression. Four instrumentalists (oboe, clarinet, violin, trumpet) listened with headphones to the recorded model performances of each of the three levels of expressivness. They listened only one time. They could mark their scores at liberty after which they played the selection at the intended level of expressiveness. Figure 11 is an example of the score markings of the oboist. The note numbers were added later by the experimenter for data analysis.

The recordings were transferred to computer. In order to operationalize the communication of the performer's intent, the categorization paradigm invented in Kendall and Carterette (1990) was employed. Figure 12 shows a representation of the computer screen as seen by a subject. The three boxes at the top of the screen represent the model performances of the pianist randomly ordered. The oboe, clarinet, trumpet and violin performances of the three levels of expressiveness (total = 12) appeared as unlabeled colored boxes at the bottom of the screen. These were the choices; they were also randomly ordered. When the subject right-clicked on a box, the musical performance associated with it played. The task was for the subject to group the choice stimuli under the appropriate model. The subject could left-click and drag the choice box underneath a model box. Subjects could play the stimuli, both choice and model, as often as they wished to review their selections. Subjects could change the position of the choice boxes at will until they felt their groups consisted of homogenous expression.

There were two groups of subjects. Musicians (N = 9) had completed the UCLA music theory sequence and were enrolled as music majors. Nonmusicians (N = 9) had no formal music instruction at the university level.

Results

The results across instruments are presented in Table 3.

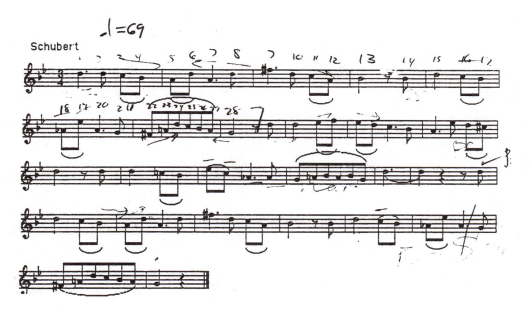

Figure 11. Score of Schubert's *Müller und der Bach*
as annotated by the oboe performer.

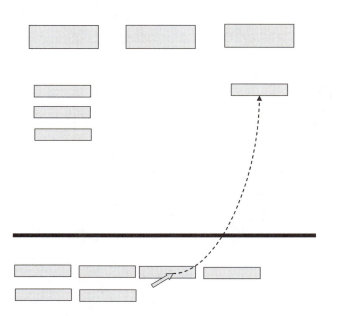

Figure 12. A representation of the computer screen used
for the categorization paradigm.

Table 3a
Schubert phrase 1 non-musicians (54% correct)

	Model 1	Model 2	Model 3
Expressive 1	**21**	7	8
Expressive 2	9	**18**	9
Expressive 3	6	11	**19**
Total	36	36	36

Table 3b
Schubert phrase 2 non-musicians (44% correct)

	Model 1	Model 2	Model 3
Expressive 1	**21**	6	9
Expressive 2	6	**15**	15
Expressive 3	9	15	**12**
Total	36	36	36

Table 3c
Schubert phrase 1 musicians (70% correct)

	Model 1	Model 2	Model 3
Expressive 1	**28**	3	5
Expressive 2	9	**24**	7
Expressive 3	3	9	**24**
Total	36	36	36

Table 3d
Schubert phrase 2 musicians (56% correct)

	Model 1	Model 2	Model 3
Expressive 1	**28**	4	4
Expressive 2	3	**17**	16
Expressive 3	5	15	**16**
Total	36	36	36

Musicians had, over all conditions, more categorization matches (63%) than non-musicians (49%); the total percentage of correct categorizations for all subjects was 56%. Although this is well above chance (33%), there are some striking patterns in the data that indicate subject performance degradation.

Musicians had 78% of their responses correct in the mechanical, without-expression condition, as opposed to 57% and 56% for the appropriate expression and exaggerated expression levels. It is clear from Table 3 that categorization responses were nearly split among the responses for Phrase 2; Phrase 1 responses were much more accurate. One source for the Phrase 2 difference can be found in response matrices for the individual instruments. Table 4 presents the response matrix for clarinet.

For the second phrase, the musicians confused expressive level 2 and 3 for the clarinet. Similar patterns are found for the other instruments, although the tendency is to split approximately evenly the difference between these expressive levels.

The first phrase accuracy levels are similar to those found for the same paradigm using $3^{1}/_{2}$ measures of Purcell's *Thy Hand, Belinda* in Kendall and Carterette (1990). This study also found that there was more confusion among the appropriate and exaggerated expressive levels than with the mechanical, without expression condition. However, the accuracy level change for Phrase 2 in the current experiment was not anticipated.

It is possible that the model performance for the second phrase varied from the first sufficiently that the other instrumentalists found it difficult to emulate. After the intervening B phrase in the ABA structure, the instrumentalists may have been unable to recall sufficient performance detail to retain a distinctive expressive contour at the return of the A phrase. Specifics regarding the source of the changes in the second phrase responses require additional data than that provided here.

Conclusion

There are two competing aspects regarding the usefulness of this approach: (1) the nonverbal approach removes semantic conflict and interference in the

Table 4a
Schubert phrase 1 clarinet: musicians (78% correct)

	Model 1	Model 2	Model 3
Expressive 1	7	1	1
Expressive 2	1	6	2
Expressive 3	0	1	8
Total	8	8	11

Table 4b
Schubert phrase 2 clarinet musicians (48% correct)

	Model 1	Model 2	Model 3
Expressive 1	7	1	1
Expressive 2	1	3	5
Expressive 3	1	5	3
Total	9	9	9

perception of expressive messages; and (2) the data resulting is nonparametric, that is frequency data, which are notoriously difficult to analyze and present other than descriptively. Further, the results of this experiment suggest caution in attempting to work with musical material of moderate length. This is in fact a general problem in empirical work, that is, finding performer and listener tasks that provide some specificity and reliability in the data with durations of more than a few bars.

Experiment 3: Perception of Musical Meaning in Multimedia

One of the most influential writings on meaning for musical empiricists is Leonard Meyer's *Emotion and Meaning in Music* (1956). After providing an outline of issues in music perception and meaning, he went forward to forge a new music theory based on elements of Gestalt psychology connected to the idea of embodied meaning arising from expectations in tandem with the conflict theory of emotion: when a tendency to respond within music is blocked or inhibited, affect occurs. Soon after its publication, musical research began to incorporate elements of information theory (Weaver and Shannon 1949), where chains of notational events were seen to imply expectation through varying degrees of information complexity/redundancy.

A central taxonomy in the first part of *Emotion and Meaning in Music* (Meyer 1956) consists of three categories of meaning. First, referentialism is meaning that is denotative; the musical elements point outside of themselves by arbitrary association. Davies (1978) refers to this aspect of musical meaning as DTPOT—Darling They're Playing Our Tune, the idea that arbitrary associations are made among life events and pieces of music. Other examples of referentialism include national anthems. There is nothing particularly American about the Star-Spangled Banner; however, the tune is associated with the country. Such referential meanings are used to great effect in, for example, the *1812 Overture* and the movie *Cassablanca*. Second, formalism involves meanings arising from explicit knowledge about the structure and context of music. Formalist meanings come from knowing the information commonly attributed to music theory and music history. Third, expressionism includes meanings that arise from the patterns of tension and release within the music itself. Thus, a central idea in Meyer's (1956) writing is this concept of "embodied meaning," an idea whose genesis can be observed in Hanslick (1957 [1854]: 118–119).

Dowling and Harwood (1986: 203–219) provide a taxonomy of meaning based on the writings of Charles Peirce (1931–1935: Volume 2). There are three components of this taxonomy. First, index is a type of associative meaning parallel to Meyer's referentialism. Second, icon is a type of meaning that is partially associative, derived from connecting patterns of music to extra-musical patterns. Dowling and Harwood (1986) tie this concept to patterns of tension and release within the music itself, implying a connection to Meyer (1956). They propose iconic emotion in the manner of Suzanne Langer (1942), a concept that might be called physiognomic emotion: patterns of tension and release within music connect themselves to patterns of tension and release in life itself. Therefore music iconically represents emotion. It is here that the iconic concept is often confused with associative, indexical meanings, often also called emotions, of the type mentioned earlier and exemplified in the work of Hevner and others, namely that major is *happy* and minor is *sad*. Despite these confusions in the literature, musical iconicity is very important in linking musical patterning to visual patterning; patterns of music can suggest rising and falling, moving forward and backward, or becoming larger or smaller (see iconic archetypes, below). Third, symbol is a type of meaning arising from the syntactical relation of a sign to other signs. This is closest to Meyer's (1956) concept of embodied meaning and expressionism.

I believe it is possible to rationalize these two taxonomies into a single model. However, it is important to reject the taxonomic nature of the model in its entirety. Musical meanings flex through time, and iconic and indexical meanings depend on syntactical meanings as a fundamental, source-level of meaning; one must apprehend syntactical relationships before the suggestiveness of iconicity or the associations of indexical meaning can arise.

I suggest as a simple model a *continuum* of referentiality. Musical meanings range from being largely syntactical in the pure patterning of sound events within the music itself, to patterns iconically suggesting connections to visual or emotional meaning elements, to arbitrary associations. This one-dimensional continuum from areferential to referential, passing through iconicity, is "simple" because it is more valid to suggest that index, icon, and syntax related to cognitive schemata are themselves multidimensional.

Consider associational, indexical meanings. Figure 13 presents a hypothetical model based on the research cited earlier involving adjective checklists (Hevner 1935a, 1935b, 1935 and the semantic differential (Osgood et al. 1957).

The three dimensions of the model connect to the main factors in Osgood et al. (1957): The x-axis (left to right) represents the evaluative factor, musically connected to major versus minor and culturally associated with good (left) vs. bad (right). The y axis (top to bottom) represents the potency factor, musically connected to dynamic variables of loud and soft and connected to strong versus weak. The z axis (front to back) is the activity factor musically connected to slow to fast tempo. Verbal labels at the extrema are attached by lines to indicate trajectories through the multidimensional space; music can either gradually or suddenly change among any of these points, or even exist at a middle level of all the variables.

Iconic meanings are partially referential. Iconic meanings in the case of multimedia connect visual to musical patterns. Figure 14 presents a small set of iconic archetypes.

The x axis is time, and the y axis can be any musical variable, such as pitch, loudness, timbre/texture, or tempo. Various camera effects can be connected, including pan (left to right), zoom (front to back) and cut (sudden perspective change), in addition to object or character movements in three dimensions. From left to right in Figure 14, the first two figures in the first line are ramps. This is a very common iconic connection where the increase or decrease in magnitude of a variable is involved. Decending pitch ramps are often connected in cartoons with characters falling off cliffs or shelves or with camera zooms and pans in film. The opening title of *Close Encounters of the Third Kind* (Steven Spielberg, director, music by John Williams, 1977) is an example of a dynamic, textural, and dissonance ramp leading to a burst, at which time the screen changes suddenly from black to white (Collectors DVD edition, Disc 1, Track 1, titled

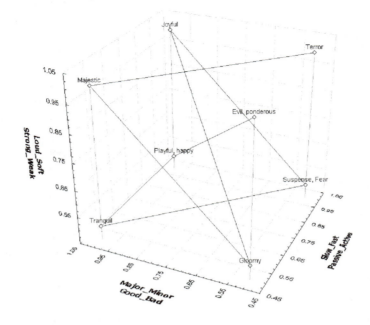

Figure 13. Three-dimensional "mood cube" based on previous research
in musical meaning.

"Start"). The burst icon, sometimes called a "stinger," is shown in Figure 14 as the last
object on the first line. This icon is used to great effect in *Laura* (Otto Preminger, director, music by David Raksin, 1944) in a scene without dialog where the inspector
(McPherson) investigates Laura's apartment. Lights switched on and a cigarette being
put out are accompanied by small burst icons. The second row of Figure 14 illustrates
the arch icon. Musical arches of pitch often accompany visual indications of wind
or water motion, as is used throughout the *By A Waterfall* scene in *Footlight Parade*
(Bacon, dir., music by Fain, Kahal, Warren and Donaldson 1933) and the "color-of-the-
wind" sequence in *Pocohontas* (Gabriel and Goldberg, dirs., music by Alan Menken,
1995). Sometimes a single arch is used in isolation, but most often a sequence of arches
through time suggests the visual motion. The final figure on row three simply indicates
that iconic archetypes can be nested or concatenated. Arches of pitch in the woodwinds nested within a general orchestral ramp series is the architectonic structure of
the dawn sequence which begins Suite Number Two in Ravel's *Daphnis et Chloe* ballet
(1912). The arches are meant to suggest a babbling brook, and the ramp sequences
suggest the sun emerging over the horizon. It is the power of icons to reinforce and dis-
ambiguate visual images that make them very common in multimedia with music.

Syntactical relations involve pure patterning and are best exemplified by music
and dance, gymnastics, and ice skating, although syntactic relations exist in film as

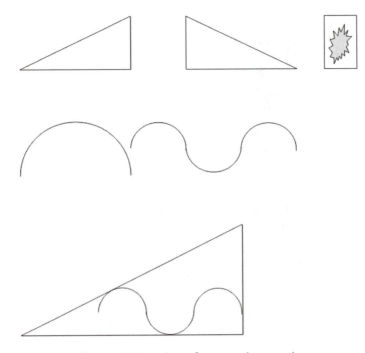

Figure 14. Iconic archetypes (see text).

well. Note the visual/musical accent alignment in the bicycle scene of *ET* (music by John Williams, directed by Steven Spielberg, 1982) and the combination of syntax and referentiality in the music for the bicycle riding of the Wicked Witch of the West in *Wizard of Oz* (music by Harold Arlen, directed by Victor Fleming, 1939).

Method

The present experiment was conducted to see if subjects can use the continuum of referentiality in response to music and visual combinations. Six music and visual combinations were hypothesized to span a continuum from areferential (syntactical) through iconic to referential meanings. Thirty-second excerpts were recorded to VHS videotape in random order. Table 5 details the origin of the stimuli and the hypothesized meaning.

Six volunteer graduate-student ethnomusicology majors participated in the experiment. Subjects read a written explanation of index, icon, and syntax. After each example on the tape, thirty seconds of blue screen provided time for the subject to mark their response by placing an "X" across a scale consisting of a 5-inch line. Underneath the left end of the scale was the label "syntax/areferential," in the middle the label "icon" was placed, and the right end of the scale was labeled "index/referential." Subjects were instructed to use the entire scale in evaluating the music video examples. Data were scored by the experimenter by measuring the position in centimeters of the "X" at the point it crossed the line starting from the left end of the scale.

Table 5
Stimuli for Experiment 3

Title	Description	Hypothesized Meaning	Abbreviation
Footlight Parade (1933)	Shanghai Lil Sequence	Referential (American Patriotic)	REF1
West Side Story (1961)[10]	Cool Dance Sequence	Syntactical (Polyphonic Music and Dance)	SYN1
Ben Hur (1959)[11]	Galley Rowing Sequence	Iconic	ICON1
Close Encounters of the Third Kind (1977)[12]	Inside the Ship (Alternate Ending)[13]	Referential and Iconic	ICREF1
Paul Wyle Olympic Program (1992)[14]	Albertville, France. Music from Henry V.	Iconic and Syntactic	SYNIC1
Fantasia (1940/1990)[15]	Bach Toccata and Fugue in D minor	Iconic and Syntactic	SYNIC2

Results

Figure 15 is a graph of the six means. The y-axis represents the mean marked position on the scale; higher numbers indicate increasing referentiality. The differences among these means, analyzed using Repeated Measures Analysis of Variance (ANOVA), were statistically significant (F (5, 25) = 8.11, $p < .0001$). Post-hoc analysis of the matrix of means indicates that all means are statistically different from one another except for the two syntactic/icon means.

Conclusion

It is apparent that subjects were able to utilize the entire scale of referentiality in judging audio/visual composites. Further research with multiple scales, as well as similarity scaling for multidimensional analysis, would usefully extend these findings. A tracking procedure, where judgments are made throughout a more lengthy sequence, could provide clues as to how imparted meanings dynamically change through time. The study of musical/visual iconicity in terms of archetypes is now underway using original constructions of animations and music. This research should provide details about interactions of ideal to marginal to unacceptable relationships between music and visual patterning.

Coda

The struggle between reliability and validity in empirical research is well known. Empirical studies that are reductionist tend to be highly reliable, but quickly lose their

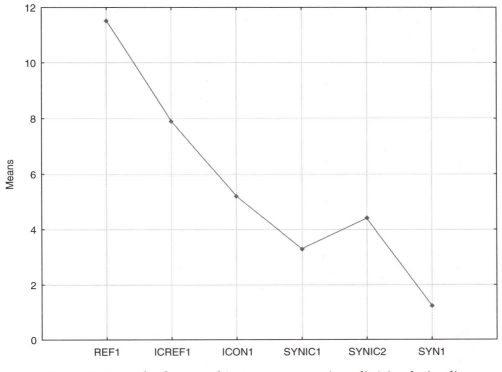

Figure 15. A graph of mean subject responses to six audio/visual stimuli
(see Table 5 for key).

ecological validity. Studies that rely on nonempirical techniques may apparently gain validity, in that they sometimes rather monolithically reference whole pieces of music, but the repeatability of the data is never tested, and thus they suffer in reliability. With the ubiquitous availability of computer sound, and the recent affordability of video processing by computer, empirical studies are on the verge of addressing previously unapproachable domains. What is most needed, at this juncture, is an expansion of the available and proven methods to operationalize these new questions. The field of music cognition has been rather slow to invent new procedures and has relied heavily on emotive and affective rating scales and similar techniques. When the field values the invention and testing of method as much as it values data and results, empirical studies can enter a new era of discovery.

NOTES

1. I have had some scholars lament that their sociological and anthropological approach is very difficult because they, unlike empiricists like me, cannot rely on computers and engineering devices to provide the answers. It should be clear that such devices are inventions themselves, and only provide output dependent on the paradigm they were designed to provide data about. They are, in fact, reflections of the experimental world they were designed for, and provide nothing more than such an interpretation.

2. Those working in the neurophysiological frame of reference might claim special status since their work would appear closer to the source of musical behaviors. However, I would argue that they are engaged in exactly the same process of theory-building as I have described, and much of their work involves the same kind of interpretive invention.

3. A physiognomic emotion is when a pattern or structure in one frame of reference suggests a link to another frame of reference. The example most often given in North America is that of the phrase "weeping willow" for the tree with descending, arched branches (see Davies 1978: 34–37).

4. Multidimensional scaling of musical pitch by Shepard (1965) led to the famous and ubiquitous pitch spiral; it demonstrated that, cognitively, pitch is not a continuum from low to high, but rather a spiral containing elements of pitch chroma (the position of a tone relative to the diatonic system) versus pitch height (the high vs. low aspect of pitch). It is worth noting, as an aside, that the scientific basis for the metaphorical consideration of pitch as *high* versus *low* has not been ascertained, nor has the source of the near-universal concept of the octave (which is necessary for the data reduction of the auditory bandwidth of frequencies to a set of pitch elements amendable to storage in cognitive schemata of limited information channel capacity).

5. The six original instruments whose tessitura included Bb5 were deemed insufficient to produce a workable dimensional solution, hence the inclusion of other timbres.

6. Similarity ratings produce triangular data sets. With the one-directional order used for the present experiment, a lower triangle is produced. The diagonal (hypotenuse) of the ratings matrix is similarity of identical instruments, that is, oboe with oboe. If a given subject's ratings of identities were large, found by taking the mean of this diagonal, they were flagged for consideration as outlying subjects. The subject data was also subjected to hierarchical cluster analysis by subject. Combining data from these two procedures allowed data from the original 16 to be removed from the final matrix.

7. The formula used was:

$$\text{spectral centroid} = \frac{\displaystyle\sum_{n=1}^{p} f_n A_n}{f_1 \displaystyle\sum_{n=1}^{p} A_n}$$

where p is the number of partials (harmonics), n is the nth partial, f is the frequency of the nth component, and A is the amplitude of the nth component.

8. In fact, impulse instruments such as the piano that do not have a true steady-state are unidentifiable when their signals (thus spectra) and played backwards. Continuant steady-state instrument played backwards are often recognizable (see Hajda 1996).

9. Clynes (1983) believed that "composer pulses," patterns of dynamic and temporal variation, could be painted on the music of given composers to provide musical expressiveness. This formulaic approach was challenged scientifically and successfully by Repp (1989, 1990). Kendall and Carterrette (1990) argued that musical structure is not invariant, but is a dynamically flexing set of unit boundaries through time. As such, musical expressiveness cannot be tied to something as definite as "the" musical structure.

10. Leonard Bernstein, music, Jerome Robbins, choreography and director.

11. Miklos Rosza (sic.), music, William Wyler, director

12. John Williams, music, Steven Spielberg, director.

13. This scene was deleted in the DVD release *Collectors Edition*, but is included on Disc 2 as an extra. The referential meaning arises from associations elicited with an interpolation of the song "When You Wish Upon a Star."

14. Patrick Doyle, music (his first film score).

15. J. S. Bach, music, Stokowski, orchestral arrangement, Disney studios, Samuel Armstrong, director. 1990 restoration used here.

REFERENCES

Asada, M. and Ohgushi, K.
1991   "Perceptual analysis of Ravel's *Bolero*." *Music Perception* 8: 241–250.

Bartlett, F.C.
1932   *Remembering*. Cambridge: Cambridge University Press.

Berger, K.
1964   "Some factors in the recognition of timbre." *Journal of the Acoustical Society of America* 36 (10): 1888–1891.

Bismarck, G. von
1974a   "Timbre of steady sounds: A factorial investigation of its verbal attributes." *Acustica* 30: 146–159.
1974b   "Sharpness as an attributes of the timbre of steady sounds." *Acustica* 30: 159–192.

Campbell, W. C. and Heller, J. J.
1981   "Psychomusicology & psycholinguistics: Parallel paths or separate ways." *Psychomusicology* 1(2): 3–14.

Caputo, J.
1987   *Radical Hermenutics*. Indianapolis: Indiana University Press.

Clynes, M.
1983   "Expressive microstructure linked to living qualities." In J. Sundberg, ed., *Publications of the Royal Swedish Academy of Music* 39: 76–181.

Crowder, R. G.
1984   "Perception of the major/minor distinction: I. Historical and theoretical foundations." *Psychomusicology* 4: 3–10.
            "Perception of the major/minor distinction: II. Experimental investigations." *Psychomusicology* 5: 3–24.

Davies, J. B.
1978   *The Psychology of Music*. Stanford: Stanford University Press.

Dowling, W. and Harwood, D.
1986   *Music Cognition*. New York: Academic Press.

Flew, A.
1984   *A Dictionary of Philosophy*. Revised Second Edition. New York: St. Martin's Press.

Gabrielsson, A. and Lindstrom, E.
2001   "The influence of musical structure on emotional expression." In P. Juslin and J. Slobada, eds., *Music and Emotion*. Oxford: Oxford University Press: 223–248.

Grey, J.
1975   An Exploration of Musical Timbre. Doctoral dissertation, Stanford University. [Department of Music Report STAN-M-2]. Stanford, CA: Center for Research in Computer Applications in Music and Acoustics.

1977   "Multidimensional perceptual scaling of musical timbres." *Journal of the Acoustical Society of America* 61 (5): 1260–1277.

Grey, J. and Gordon, J.
1978   "Perception of spectral modifications on orchestral instrument tones. *Computer Music Journal* 11: 24–31.

Hajda, J.
1996   "The effect of reverse playback partitioning on the identification of percussive and nonpercussive musical tones." In B. Pennycook and E. Costa-Giomi, eds., *Proceedings of the Fourth International Conference on Music Perception and Cognition*. Montreal: McGill University, 25–30.

Hajda, J M., Kendall, R. A., Carterette, E. C. and Harshberger, M. L.
1997   "Methodological issues in timbre research." In I. Deliège and J. Sloboda, eds., *The Perception and Cognition of Music*. London: L Erlbaum, 253–306.

Handel, S.
1989   *Listening*. Cambridge, Massachusetts: The MIT Press.

Hanslick, E.
1957 [1854]   *The Beautiful in Music*. Translated by Gustav Cohen, edited by Morris Weitz. New York: Liberal Arts Press.

Heisenberg
1971   *Physics and Beyond*. Translated by Arnold J. Pomerans. New York: Harper.

Helmholtz, H. von
1954 [1863]   *On The Sensations of Tone*. New York: Dover.

Hevner, K.
1935a   "The affective character of the major and minor modes in music." *American Journal of Psychology* 47: 113–118.
1935b   "Expression in music: A discussion of experimental studies and theories." *Psychological Review* 47: 186–204.
1936   "Experimental studies of the elements of expression in music." *American Journal of Psychology* 48: 246–268.
1937   "The affective value of pitch and tempo in music." *American Journal of Psychology* 49: 621–630.

Juslin, P.
2001   "Communicating emotion in music performance." In P. Juslin and J. Sloboda, eds., *Music and Emotion*. Oxford: Oxford University Press, 309–337.

Juslin, P.N. and Sloboda, J.A.
2001   *Music and Emotion*. Oxford: Oxford University Press.

Kendall, R.
1986   "The role of acoustic signal partitions in listener categorization of musical phrases." *Music Perception* 4: 185–214.
1990–2002   *Music Experiment Development System*. Public domain software.
2002   "Musical timbre beyond a single note (II)." In C. Stevens, D. Burnham, G. McPherson, E. Schubert, and J. Renwick, eds., *Proceedings of the 7th International Converence on Music Perception & Cognition*. Adelaide: Causal Productions. (CD ROM, ISBN: 1876346396).
2003   "Extending timbre research." Invited Paper. Society for Music Perception and Cognition. Las Vegas: University of Nevada, June 18, 2003.

Kendall, R. and Carterette, E.

1989   "Perceptual, verbal, and acoustical attributes of wind instrument dyads." In *Proceedings of the First International Conference on Music Perception and Cognition*. Kyoto Japan: Japanese Society of Music Perception and Cognition, 365–370.

1990   "The communication of musical expression." *Music Perception* 8 (2): 129–163.

1991   "Perceptual scaling of simultaneous wind instrument timbres." *Music Perception* 8: 129–162.

1993a   "Verbal attributes of simultaneous wind instrument timbres: I. von Bismarck's Adjectives." *Music Perception* 10 (4): 445–467.

1993b   "Verbal attributes of simultaneous wind instrument timbres: II. Adjectives induced from Piston's *Orchestration*." *Music Perception* 10 (4): 469–499.

1999   Perceptual and acoustical features of natural and synthetic orchestral instrument tones. *Music Perception* 16: 327–364.

Krimphoff, J. McAdams, S. and Winsberg, S.

1994   "Caractérisation du timbre des sons complexes. II. Analyses acoustiques et quantification psychophysique." *Journal de Physique IV*, Colloque C5, supplément au Journal de Physique III, 4: 625–628.

Kuhn, T. S.

1962   *The Structure of Scientific Revolutions*. Chicago: University of Chicago Press.

Langer, S. K.

1942   *Philosophy in a New Key*. Cambridge, MA: Harvard University Press.

Lipscomb, S. and Kendall, R.

1994   "Perceptual judgment of the relationship between musical and visual components in film." *Psychomusicology* 13: 60–98.

Marshall, S. and Cohen, A.

1988   "Effects of musical soundtracks on attitudes to geometric figures." *Music Perception* 6: 95–112.

Maslow, A.

1968   *Toward a Psychology of Being*. 2nd ed. New York: Van Nostrand Reinhold.

Meyer, L.

1956   *Emotion and Meaning in Music*. Chicago: University of Chicago Press.

Miller, J. R. and Carterette, E. C.

1975   Perceptual space for musical structures. *Journal of the Acoustical Society of America* 27: 337–352.

Mursell, J.

1937   *Psychology of Music*. New York: W. W. Norton.

Namba, S., Kuwano, S., Hatoh, T., and Kato, M.

1991   "Assessment of musical performance by using the method of continuous judgment by selected description." *Music Perception* 8: 251–276.

Neisser, U.

1976   *Cognition and Reality*. San Francisco: Freeman.

Osgood, C., Suci, G., and Tannenbaum, P.

1957   *The Measurement of Meaning*. Urbana, Ill.: University of Illinois Press.

Peirce, C.
    1931–1935   *Collected Papers* Vols. 1–6. C. Hartshorne and P. Weiss, eds., Cambridge, MA:
                 Harvard University Press.

Pinochot, M. and Crowder, R.
    1990   "Perception of the major/minor distinction: IV. Emotional connotations in
                 young children." *Music Perception* 8 (2): 189–202.

Repp, B.
    1989   "Expressive microstructure in music: Preliminary perceptual assessment of
                 four composer's 'pulses.'" *Music Perception* 6 (3): 243–274.
    1990   "Further perceptual evaluations of pulse microstructure in computer per-
                 formances of classical music." *Music Perception* 8 (1): 1–33.

Saldanha, E. and Corso, J.
    1964   "Timbre cues and the identification of musical instruments." *Journal of the
                 Acoustical Society of America* 68 (3): 858–875.

Sandell, G.
    1995   "Roles for spectral centroid and other factors in determining "blended"
                 instrument pairings in orchestration." *Music Perception* 13: 209–246.

Scherer, K. R.
    2001   "Foreword." In P. Juslin and J. Sloboda, eds., *Music and Emotion*. Oxford:
                 Oxford University Press, p. x.

Scherer, K. R. and Oshinsky, J. S.
    1977   "Cue utilization in emotion attribution from auditory stimuli." *Motivation
                 and Emotion* 1: 331–346.

Seashore, C.
    1938   *Psychology of Music*. New York: Dover reprint.

Senju, M. and Ohgushi, K.
    1987   "How are the player's ideas conveyed to the audience?" *Music Perception* **4**:
                 311–323.

Weaver, W. and Shannon, C.
    1949   *The Mathematical Theory of Communication*. Urbana: University of Illinois
                 Press. Republished in paperback 1963.

Wedin, L. and Goude, G.
    1972   "Dimension analysis of the perception of instrumental timbre." *Scandina-
                 vian Journal of Psychology* 13 (3): 228–240.

Subjective Evaluation of Tuning Systems for Piano

HARUKA SHIMOSAKO

National Institute of Advanced Industrial Science and Technology

KENGO OHGUSHI

Department of Music, Kyoto City University of Arts

Most pianos nowadays are tuned in equal temperament and we generally accept equal temperament naturally. The acceptance of equal temperament is not universal, however. For example, Hirashima (1983) and Takahashi (1992) have both refused equal temperament and expressed a preference for unequal temperaments, such as Werckmeister temperament and Kirnberger temperament. These dissenting voices represent a serious problem, for if they were objectively valid, it would be necessary to re-evaluate the current practice of tuning pianos to equal temperament. Thus, we investigated the evaluation of intonations performed in subjective listening experiments. The results showed that Werckmeister and Kirnberger temperaments were never rated higher than equal temperament. Generally, although just intonation would seem to be desirable for harmonic phrases, for melodic phrases Pythagorean tuning would seem to be preferable. However, as most pieces of music include both harmonic and melodic factors, the highest ratings for equal temperament are probably because this represents a good compromise as a middle position between Pythagorean tuning and just intonation. Thus, we could not find objective support for the suggestions from Hirashima and Takahashi.

1. Introduction

Although there are a number of tuning systems for piano, we usually hear piano performances in equal temperament, because most pianos today are tuned in equal temperament.[1] As each of twelve semitones is represented by an equal frequency ratio in equal temperament, it is possible to play in all keys. Equal temperament is generally accepted as being natural, and its use is rarely questioned.

However, acceptance of equal temperament is not universal. Hirashima (1983) criticized equal temperament, saying that it was painful for him to play a piano tuned in equal temperament. He supported Werckmeister temperament and Kirnberger temperament. Takahashi (1992) also supported his opinion. Their criticisms of equal temperament, however, are based on their personal preferences, rather than being based on the results of a perceptual listening experiment. It is therefore necessary to conduct some perceptual experiments in order to investigate whether or not these criticisms are valid.

There seems to be no published study in which a number of listeners evaluated the acceptability of a variety of tuning systems, such as equal, Werckmeister, and Kirnberger temperaments, in piano performances. In the present study, we examined the subjective acceptability of five tuning systems in piano performances: Pythagorean tuning, just intonation, Werckmeister temperament, Kirnberger temperament and equal temperament. Using several piano pieces in several keys as well as an atonal piece, we investigated whether the acceptability of each tuning system would vary according to the kind of piano piece.

2. The Tuning Systems Used in this Experiment

2.1 The Variety of Tuning Systems

In this study, we used equal temperament, Werckmeister's first temperament, and Kirnberger's third temperament. In addition, Pythagorean tuning in C major and just intonation in C major were also used for references. Werckmeister's first temperament and Kirnberger's third temperament are, according to Barbour (1972 [1951]), the well-known temperaments.

2.2 An Outline of Each Tuning System

In the following descriptions of the five tuning systems, the frequency ratio of an octave is 2:1 for all.

2.2.1 Pythagorean Tuning

Pythagorean tuning is the oldest tuning and has played an important role from ancient to modern times. It is a tuning system based on the octave (2:1) and the perfect fifth (3:2). It is possible to tune all the notes of the diatonic scale in a succession of the perfect fifths and octaves. However, such a procedure causes a tuning error called the Pythagorean comma, which is an interval between twelve perfect fifths and seven octaves, and its interval is 23.46 cents. Therefore, one perfect fifth should be narrower than the other eleven perfect fifths by 23.46 cents. It is not possible for a pianist to play all keys perceptually naturally by using this tuning. In this experiment, the perfect fifth between G# and Eb was narrowed by 23.46 cents.

2.2.2 Just Intonation

Just intonation is a system of tuning based on the octave (2:1), the perfect fifth (3:2) and the major third (5:4). In other words, the tonic, dominant, and subdominant triads (do, mi, sol; sol, ti, re; and fa, la, do, respectively) are all tuned in the exact frequency ratios of 4:5:6, which gives the three major triads great consonance. However, there is also a tuning error associated with the intonation, called a syntonic comma (22 cents). Moreover, there are two values for a whole tone, a large whole tone (8:9) and a narrow whole tone (9:10). Again, it is not possible to play all keys perceptually naturally by using this tuning. In this experiment, we chose the tuning system by narrowing the interval between D and A by 22 cents, which means the tuning for C major.

2.2.3 Werckmeister's First Temperament

There have been a number of proposals for correcting the Pythagorean comma, but Werckmeister's first temperament is one of the most famous of those. In this tuning, the Pythagorean comma is divided equally into four perfect fifths (C-G, G-D, D-A, B-F#). These four perfect fifths (696.1 cents) are narrower than the exact perfect fifth by 5.9 cents.

2.2.4 Kirnberger's Third Temperament

Kirnberger's third temperament is another modified temperament, but here the Pythagorean comma is divided unequally into five perfect fifths (C-G, G-D, D-A, A-E and F#-C#). The first four perfect fifths (696.6 cents) are 5.4 cents narrower than the exact perfect fifth and the last perfect fifth is 700 cents.

2.2.5 Equal Temperament

In equal temperament, the Pythagorean comma is divided into 12 perfect fifths equally, so that all perfect fifths are 700 cents. In other words, each of the twelve semitones has the same frequency ratio $12\sqrt{2}$ (=1.059463). The octave is divided into twelve logarithmically equal steps. The musical intervals are constant in all keys. In the tuning systems other than equal temperament, the frequency ratio of the musical intervals within a scale change with each key.

Table 1 and Figure 1 show the differences in interval sizes for the five tuning systems in terms of cent differences for a tonic. Pythagorean tuning and just intonation were tuned in C as a tonic.

2.2.6 The Musical Intervals of Each Tuning System

There are major differences between equal temperament and the other four tuning systems, apart from Pythagorean tuning and just intonation in C# major. The major differences are found in the interval sizes from a tonic to the major third, the major sixth, and the major seventh. Explanations of the relationships between the five tuning systems with respect to these three intervals are given below.

For C major: The major third, the major sixth, and the major seventh in Pythagorean tuning are larger than in equal temperament. In contrast the major third, the major sixth, and the major seventh are smaller in just intonation than in equal temperament. This means that Pythagorean tuning and just intonation differ in opposite directions from equal temperament. The major third, the major sixth, and the major seventh are smaller in Werckmeister and Kirnberger than in equal temperament and are close to just intonation.

For E major: Pythagorean, with tuned C as a tonic, has, apart from the smaller seventh, similar interval sizes to those in Pythagorean tuning in C major. Just

Table 1(a)

Musical intervals in each tuning system used in the experiment: C Major
(expressed in cents where a cent is a unit of interval measure equaling
the 1200th part of an octave, a semitone in equal temperament is 100 cents)

	Pythagorean	Just Intonation	Werckmeister	Kirnberger	Equal Temperament
C	0.0	0.0	0.0	0.0	0.0
D	203.9	203.9	192.2	193.2	200.0
E	407.8	386.3	390.2	386.3	400.0
F	498.0	498.0	498.0	498.0	500.0
G	702.0	702.0	696.1	696.6	700.0
A	905.9	884.4	888.3	889.7	900.0
B	1109.8	1088.3	1092.2	1088.3	1100.0

Table 1(b)

Musical intervals in each tuning system used in the experiment: E Major

	Pythagorean	Just Intonation	Werckmeister	Kirnberger	Equal Temperament
E(C)	0.0	0.0	0.0	0.0	0.0
F#(D)	203.9	203.9	198.1	203.9	200.0
G#(E)	407.8	386.3	402.0	405.9	400.0
A(F)	498.1	498.1	498.1	503.4	500.0
B(G)	702.0	702.0	702.0	702.0	700.0
C#(A)	905.9	884.4	900.0	903.9	900.0
Eb(B)	1086.3	1129.3	1103.9	1107.8	1100.0

Table 1(c)

Musical intervals in each tuning system used in the experiment: C# Major

	Pythagorean	Just Intonation	Werckmeister	Kirnberger	Equal Temperament
C#(C)	0.0	0.0	0.0	0.0	0.0
Eb(D)	180.4	244.9	203.9	203.9	200.0
F(E)	384.3	427.3	407.8	407.8	400.0
F#(F)	498.0	519.5	498.0	500.0	500.0
G#(G)	702.0	702.0	702.0	702.0	700.0
Bb(A)	882.4	946.9	905.9	905.9	900.0
C(B)	1086.3	1129.3	1109.8	1109.8	1100.0

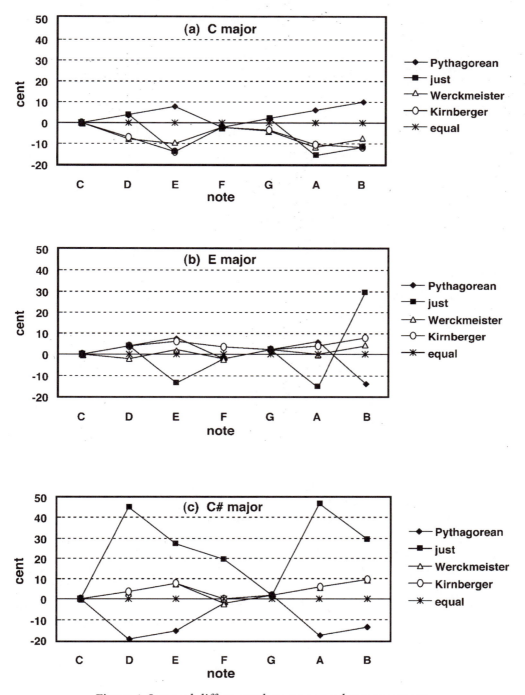

Figure 1. Interval differences between equal temperament
and the other four tuning systems.

intonation, with tuned C as a tonic, also has similar interval sizes to those in just intonation in C major, except that the larger seventh is 29 cents larger than that in equal
temperament. The major third, the major sixth, and the major seventh in Werckmeister
and Kirnberger are, in contrast to C major, larger than those in equal temperament.
Thus, these three interval sizes are close to just intonation in the case of C major, but
for E major, the intervals are middle sizes between equal temperament and
Pythagorean tuning.

For C# major: The major third, the major sixth, and the major seventh in Werckmeister and Kirnberger are larger than those in equal temperament. Comparing these
two temperaments and Pythagorean tuning in C major, all the interval sizes on a diatonic scale are very similar to each other. In Kirnberger, all the interval sizes are the
same as Pythagorean, except for the major fourth. As Pythagorean tuning and just
intonation are tuned according to C major, there are large differences in the interval
sizes compared with equal temperament.

3. Experiment 1

The first experiment examined general preference for each tuning system. The
listeners were university students, not majoring in music and who had received no formal music education. The same musical excerpts in five tuning systems were paired
and presented randomly through two loudspeakers. Listeners were required to judge
which of the paired tuning systems was more acceptable.

3.1 Method

Listeners: Thirteen university students not majoring in music participated in the
experiment. None had ever studied music formally.

Stimulus materials: The beginning twelve measures of the first movement in
Mozart's piano sonata (K.545) were used as a stimulus. This piece is in C major and
is composed of notes in the diatonic scale of C major apart from one extra note.
Performances of this piece were recorded in five tuning systems: Pythagorean tuning, just intonation, Werckmeister temperament, Kirnberger temperament, and equal
temperament.

A pianist played the pieces on an electronic piano (Roland HP-2800) using a
piano voice. The pieces were recorded as MIDI data on a computer (Power Macintosh
7100/66AV) using the sequencer software "Vision." The same electronic piano was
used for all performances, which were varied by changing the intonations as explained
above. A recorded performance was then transferred to digital audio tape in the above
five tuning systems.

Procedure: In a trial session, the differences among the five tuning systems were
explained to the listeners. First, to allow the listeners to experience the differences
among the five tuning systems, performances of Mozart's sonata in each tuning system
were presented once to the listeners through two loudspeakers. After that, the listeners
were required to judge all possible pair combinations of the five tuning systems,
although no tuning system was paired with itself. In all, they listened to twenty stimulus pairs, and, without being told which tuning systems were involved, they judged

which of the paired pieces was the more acceptable. The presentation order of the stimulus pairs was randomized to prevent possible order effects.

3.2 Results and Discussion

Evaluations of tuning systems were scored, with two points for tuning systems judged as "more acceptable" and one point for tuning systems judged as "no difference." Figure 2 shows the total scores for each tuning system. Each letter under the horizontal axis indicates the first letter of each tuning system: "P" represents Pythagorean tuning, "J" represents just intonation, "W" represents Werckmeister temperament, "K" represents Kirnberger temperament, and "E" represents equal temperament.

Of the five tuning systems, equal temperament was rated the highest, with Pythagorean tuning next. After these two tuning systems, Kirnberger and Werckmeister temperaments were also rated highly. Just intonation was rated the lowest.

This data was analyzed by Scheffe's paired comparison test, which indicated that equal temperament and Pythagorean tuning were rated significantly higher than just intonation ($p<.01$), and that Kirnberger temperament was also rated significantly higher than just intonation ($p<.05$). Thus, there were significant differences between just intonation and the other tuning systems apart from the Werckmeister temperament.

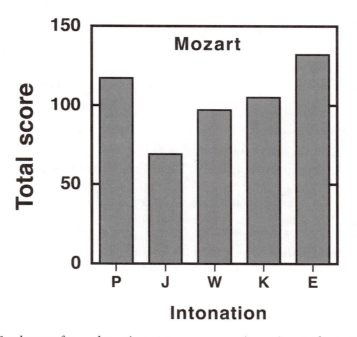

Figure 2. Total score for each tuning system: nonmusic-major students. Each letter under the horizontal axis indicates the first letter of each tuning system: "P" = Pythagorean tuning, "J" = just intonation, "W" = Werckmeister temperament, "K" = Kirnberger temperament, and "E" = equal temperament.

4. Experiment 2

This experiment examined whether the preference for each tuning system would be influenced by musical experience. The listeners were university students majoring in western classical music. Adopting the same procedure used in Experiment 1, we compared the results of Experiment 1 and 2 to discuss whether musical experience influenced preference judgments for tuning systems.

4.1 Method

Listeners: Seven students majoring in music participated in the experiment. They had formally studied western classical music at the Kyoto City University of Arts.

Stimulus materials were:

1. The first twelve measures of the first movement of Mozart's piano sonata (K.545) in C major.
2. The second theme from the first movement of Beethoven's piano sonata (Op.53) in E major.
3. The first four measures from the first piece in Schoenberg's sixth short composition (Op.19), atonal.

Mozart's sonata and Beethoven's sonata are composed of notes from the diatonic scale of C major and E major respectively, with one extra note. Beethoven's excerpt is actually in E major, but this part is modulated from C major. Schoenberg's piece is composed from all twelve notes of the chromatic scale. The three pieces were performed in the five tuning systems and recorded on digital audio tape in pairs. The order of the stimuli was randomized for each piece.

Procedure: The procedure was the same as that used for Experiment 1, except that the stimuli pieces were increased to three. All tuning pairings for Mozart's sonata were presented first, followed by all the pairings for Beethoven's sonata and finally Schoenberg's piece.

4.2 Results and Discussion

Evaluations for the tuning systems were scored in the same way as in Experiment 1, and the results are shown in Figure 3. The data were analyzed by Scheffe's paired comparison test.

For Mozart's sonata, just intonation was rated significantly lower than the other intonations ($p<.01$). This result is similar to the ratings of the students not majoring in music (Experiment 1), but just intonation was rated much lower. Similarly, for the music-major students, there were no significant differences among the four other tuning systems. Irrespective of musical experience, the ratings obtained in Experiments 1 and 2 are similar for the piece in C major.

For Beethoven's sonata, Pythagorean tuning and just intonation were rated much lower. This is clear to see in Figure 1(b), which shows the large deviations of just intonation and Pythagorean tuning from equal temperament. All differences were significant ($p<.01$), except for the difference between Werckmeister and Kirnberger

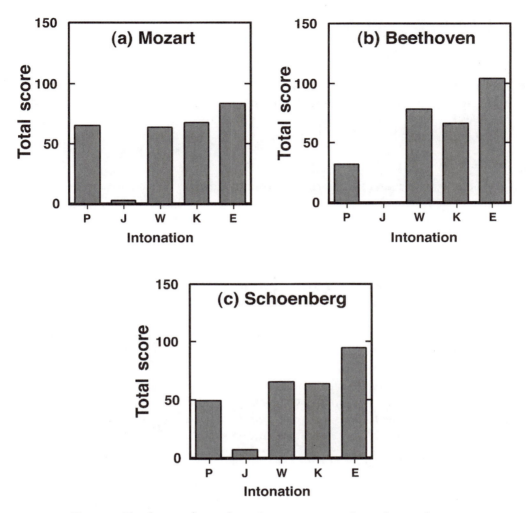

Figure 3. Total score for each tuning system: music-major students.
(a) Mozart, (b) Beethoven, (c) Schoenberg. Each letter under the
horizontal axis indicates the first letter of each tuning system.

temperaments. Equal temperament was rated the highest. Werckmeister and Kirnberger temperaments were rated lower than equal temperament ($p < .01$).

For Schoenberg's composition, equal temperament was also rated the highest and
just intonation was also rated the lowest. These two tuning systems differed significantly from the other three tunings ($p < .01$). No significant differences were found
between Werckmeister temperament, Kirnberger temperament and Pythagorean tuning. The pattern of preference for the five tuning systems for an atonal piece is similar
to that for the piece in C major.

5. Experiment 3

The method of paired comparison used in Experiment 1 and 2 is quite reliable. However, only seven listeners participated in the experiments. In order, therefore, to examine whether the results of Experiment 1 and 2 are general or not, we adopted a rating-scale method in Experiment 3 and asked more listeners to participate. Four pieces were used in this experiment: Mozart's sonata, Beethoven's sonata, Schoenberg's composition, and a composition by Bach.

5.1 Method

Listeners: 55 students majoring in western classical music participated and listened to the three pieces excluding the composition by Bach. A week later, the same participants listened again to the same stimulus pieces but in a different order. For the composition by Bach, 59 different students majoring in music participated on another day.

Stimulus materials: In addition to the three pieces used in Experiment 2, the first sixteen bars of the Prelude from Bach's *Well-tempered Clavier* (BWV 848) in C# major were also used. This is composed of notes from the diatonic scale in C# major, with three extra tones.

Procedure: The performances were presented to the listeners through two loudspeakers. The listeners were required to rate their subjective acceptability on a five-point scale (5: very acceptable–1: unacceptable). In the first session, the five tuning systems for the three stimuli pieces were presented in the same order as in Experiment 2. In the second session one week later, the order of the stimulus pieces was the same but the order of the tunings was changed. Bach's composition was presented on another day. These experiments were performed in a quiet room.

5.2 Results and Discussion

For the ratings of Mozart, Beethoven, and Schoenberg, we calculated the correlation coefficient for the data obtained for the first session and the data for the second session. As the correlation coefficients for all three pieces were high ($r > .8$), the ratings from both sessions were combined. The mean ratings for the five tuning systems for the three pieces are shown in Figure 4 (a)–(c). For Bach's composition, the mean ratings from 59 sets of data are shown in Figure 4 (d).

Generally, equal temperament was rated highly, with low ratings for just intonation. This tendency is similar to the results of the paired-comparison tests used in Experiments 1 and 2.

5.2.1 Evaluation of the Five Tuning Systems for Each Piece of Music

The data were analyzed in a one-way analysis of variance for each piece. For all pieces, there was a significant main effect of tuning system (Mozart: $F[4,108] = 171.17$, $p<.01$, Beethoven: $F[4,108] = 225.81$, $p<.01$, Schoenberg: $F[4,108] = 132.89$, $p<.01$, Bach: $F[4,58] = 68.57, p<.01$). In the multiple comparison technique, Tukey's HSD test was used.

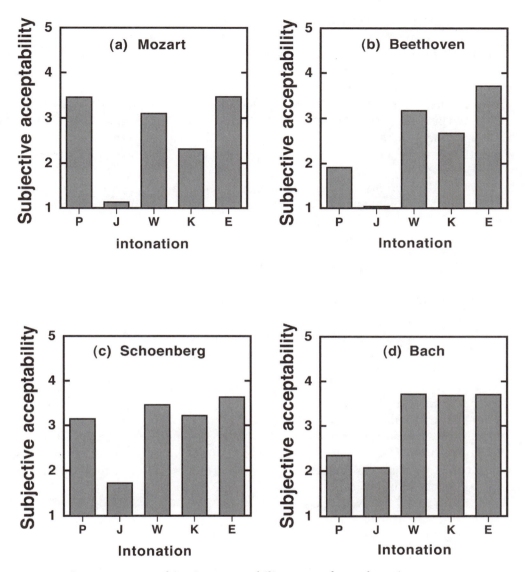

Figure 4. Mean subjective acceptability scores for each tuning system:
(a) Mozart, (b) Beethoven, (c) Schoenberg, (d) Bach. Each letter under
the horizontal axis indicates the first letter of each tuning system.

Mozart's sonata: Equal temperament was rated the highest, followed in descending order by Pythagorean tuning, Werckmeister temperament, Kirnberger temperament, and just intonation. Although the difference between equal temperament and Pythagorean tuning was not significant, the differences between other tunings were all significant ($p<.01$).

Beethoven's sonata: Equal temperament was rated the highest, followed by Werckmeister temperament, Kirnberger temperament, Pythagorean tuning, and just intonation, and all differences between the tunings were significant ($p<.01$).

Schoenberg's composition: Equal temperament was rated the highest, followed by Werckmeister temperament, Kirnberger temperament, Pythagorean tuning, and just intonation. This order is the same as that for Beethoven's sonata. However, the differences between equal temperament and Werckmeister temperament, Werckmeister temperament and Kirnberger temperament, Kirnberger temperament and Pythagorean tuning were not significant for this piece, although all other differences were significant ($p<.01$).

Bach's Well-tempered Clavier: Werckmeister temperament, equal temperament, and Kirnberger temperament were rated high, and there were no significant differences among these tuning systems. Pythagorean tuning and just intonation were rated low, and there was no significant difference between these two tunings. However, the three highly rated tuning systems were significantly different from the two low-rated tunings ($p<.01$).

5.2.2 Homogeneity of the Evaluations for Each Tuning System

In order to examine, for each intonation, whether the evaluations for the five kinds of tuning systems were homogeneous among the four pieces of music, we performed a test for the homogeneity of the proportions for each tuning system.

In the ratings for Pythagorean tuning, we found homogeneity between the ratings of Mozart and those of Schoenberg. Atonal music was rated as high as the music in C major. Otherwise, all the ratings were significantly different ($p<.01$). When the excerpt was not in C major, the rating was lower.

In the ratings for just intonation, we found homogeneity between the ratings of Mozart and those of Beethoven, but Schoenberg's atonal composition was rated significantly differently from the other excerpts ($p<.01$). Thus, the ratings for just intonation were high for the atonal piece.

In the ratings for Werckmeister and Kirnberger, we found no homogeneity between the ratings of Mozart and those of Bach, and the ratings of Beethoven and those of Bach respectively ($p<.01$). That is, the ratings for pieces in a nonrelative key were higher than for pieces in a relative key.

In contrast to the four tuning systems above, the ratings for equal temperament were homogeneous among all excerpts, except between the Mozart and the Schoenberg ($p<.05$). Among the five tuning systems, only equal temperament was always rated high, regardless of the excerpt.

5.2.3 Difference According to the Listener's Major

To examine the influence of the listener's major on the evaluations, the data were analyzed in a one-way analysis of variance for each tuning system for each piece of music. The listeners were either students of the piano, string instrument, wind instrument, or vocal music. The results showed that there were only significant differences for Bach's excerpt in Pythagorean tuning (F [5, 53] $=10.30$, $p<.01$). The ratings from piano students were lower than those of vocal students. However, all listeners rated the

Bach in Pythagorean tuning as quite low. The mean evaluation never reached 3 point (the acceptable level) in all cases. Otherwise, there were no significant differences, suggesting that the listener's major did not greatly affect their ratings of each tuning system. Furthermore, there was no listener who rated equal temperament higher than the other tuning systems for all pieces.

6. Discussion

6.1 The Problem of Familiarity with Equal Temperament

The results of the present study show that equal temperament was rated the highest by both students majoring in music and those not majoring in music. Currently, most pianos used in both compulsory education (7–15 years old) and professional education in Japan are tuned in equal temperament. We should examine whether the prime cause of the high ratings is simply familiarity with equal temperament.

Ohgushi (1994) reported that music students listening to a simple melody (diatonic scale) rated Pythagorean tuning higher than equal temperament. This result is interesting, because they were exposed to equal temperament from infancy.

However, the results of some other experiments suggest that this might be natural. Experimental research has been reported concerning the musical intervals for string instruments determined in actual performance. Cornu and Mercadier (1869) investigated major-third intervals performed both melodically and harmonically. They found that, in harmonic performances, the frequency ratio was 4:5 (that is, 386 cents, equal to the major third in just intonation), but in melodic performances, the ratio was greater and moved towards equal temperament and Pythagorean tuning. However, the interval sizes were scattered, making these findings inconclusive. Greene (1937) also investigated the performances of six violinists, measuring the fundamental frequency. He found that the ratio of the melodic major second and the major third were not close to just intonation and equal temperament, but were closer to Pythagorean tuning. In addition, Loosen (1993) analyzed the C major diatonic scale played by eight violinists and found that the scale was close to the mid-point between equal temperament and Pythagorean tuning.

These results suggest that when violinists play melodic phrases without accompaniment, the intonation is closer to Pythagorean tuning and equal temperament, rather than just intonation. It is possible that equal temperament is preferred not because of familiarity, but because of other reasons.

Using a computer, Loosen (1995) generated, for one octave in C major, ascending and descending diatonic scales, which were tuned in Pythagorean tuning, equal temperament, and just intonation. Seven violinists, seven pianists, and ten nonmusicians were presented with the scales and asked to judge which intonation was most accurately tuned. The results showed that violinists preferred Pythagorean tuning, and that pianists preferred equal temperament, while the nonmusicians failed to show any preference among the three intonations. The listeners were also required to indicate whether paired intonations were the same or not. When the identical scales were presented as stimulus pairs, 42% of the violinists, 50% of the pianists and 54% of the nonmusicians judged they were not identical. Thus, approximately half of the listeners failed to recognize identical scales as being the same, even though Pythagorean, equal temperament, and just intonation were markedly different from each other. As the differences among equal, Werckmeister, and Kirnberger temperaments are smaller than the differences among equal temperament, Pythagorean tuning, and just intonation, it unlikely that the familiarity with equal temperament is a factor.

6.2 Equal Temperament: A Compromise Between Pythagorean Tuning and Just Intonation

It seems that when playing without accompaniment string- and wind-instrument performers instinctively choose Pythagorean tuning for melodic phrases and just intonation for harmonic phrases. Heman (1964) noted that there are linear intonation and harmonic intonation in string instrument performances, pointing out that the players should use the former in melodic performances and the latter in harmonic performances. Thus, players must make the major third and the major sixth narrower and the minor third and the minor sixth wider for harmonic performances. In contrast, for melodic performances, players should make the major third and the major sixth wider and the minor third and the minor sixth narrower. That is, harmonic phrases should be played in an intonation close to just intonation, and melodic phrases should be played with an intonation close to Pythagorean tuning. The suggestion in the case of harmonic phrases is acoustically well established, for players need to have a simple frequency ratio in harmony to maintain a minimum number of beats.

The stimuli used in the present experiments included both melodic and harmonic factors, so it is possible that the preference for equal temperament is the result of a compromise, being in the middle between just intonation and Pythagorean tuning.

6.3 Concerning the Suggestions from Hirashima and Takahashi

In the results of this series of experiments, the Werckmeister and Kirnberger temperaments recommended by Hirashima and Takahashi were never rated higher than equal temperament. Both Werckmeister and Kirnberger temperaments are close to just intonation in C major, but are also close to equal temperament in C# major. This suggests that a key with few sharps and flats, such as C major, is desirable for harmonic pieces, and that a key with many sharps and flats, such as C# major, is preferable for melodic pieces.

However, harmonic pieces are not always in C major and melodic pieces are not always in C# major. As most pieces of music generally include both harmonic phrases and melodic phrases in any key, the preference found in the ratings from the present study for equal temperament would appear natural, for equal temperament represents the middle characteristic between Pythagorean and just intonation. Thus, it is difficult to say that the suggestions from Hirashima and Takahashi are objectively valid.

7. Summary

Most pianos nowadays are tuned in equal temperament and we generally accept equal temperament naturally. The acceptance of equal temperament is not universal, however. For example, Hirashima (1983) and Takahashi (1992) have both refused equal temperament and expressed a preference for unequal temperaments, such as Werckmeister temperament and Kirnberger temperament. These dissenting voices represent a serious problem, for if they were objectively valid, it would be necessary to re-evaluate the current practice of tuning pianos to equal temperament. Thus, we investigated the evaluation of intonations performed in subjective listening experiments. The results showed that Werckmeister and Kirnberger temperaments were never rated higher than equal temperament. Generally, although just intonation would seem to be desirable for harmonic phrases, for melodic phrases Pythagorean tuning would seem to be preferable. However, as most pieces of music include both harmonic and melodic factors, the highest ratings for equal temperament are probably because this represents a good compromise as a middle position between Pythagorean tuning and just intonation. Thus, we could not find objective support for the suggestions from Hirashima and Takahashi.

In this experiment, we investigated the evaluation of the five tuning systems for piano performances. However, it is possible that for organ tones, which have long duration, harmony would be more important. Clearly, further studies are needed to consider differences in timbre characteristics, such as organ tones

NOTES

1. We wish to express our gratitude to Ms. Eri Matsumoto, who played the piano for our experiments, and to Professors Ichiro Fujinaga, Dr. Peter Desain, and Ms. Karen Burland for valuable comments. This study was supported by a Grant-in-Aid from the Ministry of Education of Japan, for Science Research 06610079 (1994–1995). Portions of this paper were published in the Journal of the Musicological Society of Japan, vol. 41, no. 2 (1995) in Japanese. This publication is with permission of the Musicological Society of Japan.

REFERENCES

Barbour, J. M.
     1972 [1951]   *Tuning and Temperament.* New York: Da Capo Press.

Cornu, A. and Mercadier, E.
     1869   "Sur les intervalles musicauz." *Comptes Rendus des Seances de l'Academie des Sciences* 68: 301–308, 424–427.

Greene, P. C.
     1937   "Violin intonation." *Journal of Acoustical Society of America* 9: 43–44.

Heman, C.
     1964   *Intonation auf Streichinstrumenten.* Baerenreiter-Verlag.

Hirashima, T.
     1983   *Rediscovery of zero beat.* Tokyo: Ongakusha. In Japanese.

Loosen, F.
     1993   "Intonation of solo violin performance with reference to equally tempered, Pythagorean, and just intonations." *Journal of Acoustical Society of America* 93: 525–539.
     1995   "The effect of musical experience on the conception of accurate tuning." *Music Perception* 12: 291–306.

Auditory Roughness as a Means
of Musical Expression

PANTELIS N. VASSILAKIS
DePaul University

This study argues that auditory roughness (rattling sound associated with certain types of signals) is an important sonic aspect of music, one that musical aesthetic judgments around the world are often based on. Within the Western tradition there is a strong link between roughness and annoyance, manifested in the assumption that rough sounds are inherently bad or unpleasant and are therefore to be avoided. Instrument construction and performance practices outside the Western art musical tradition, however, indicate that the sensation of roughness can be an important factor in the production of musical sound. Manipulating the roughness parameters helps create a buzzing or rattling sonic canvas that becomes the backdrop for further musical elaboration. It permits the creation of timbral or even rhythmic variations (through changes among roughness degrees), contributing to a musical tradition's menu of expressive tools. The potential usefulness of a proposed roughness estimation model to musicological research is discussed, drawing on previous and new empirical studies that link dissonance and roughness ratings of harmonic intervals within the Western chromatic scale. It is argued that, within the Western musical tradition, clear presence or absence of roughness dominates dissonance ratings. In most other cases, decisions on dissonance seem to ignore roughness and be culturally and historically mediated.

1. Introduction

Years of ethnomusicological research have shown that aesthetic judgments on pieces of music are culture dependent, with no fixed, cross-culturally accepted aesthetic criteria. At the same time, such judgments are not arbitrarily imposed on pieces of music by musical traditions, and aesthetic criteria are not, in general, invented out of thin air. Rather, they are based on how each different tradition chooses to interpret and value contextual, functional, performance, formal, and (more importantly for the present study) sonic aspects of musical pieces, with aesthetic differentiation going hand in hand with, if not preceding, aesthetic judgment. Interpretive choices and value judgments, which are at the center of all musical experience, have both cognitive and cultural bases and, like all choices, are essentially historical in their reliance on past experiences and in their power to configure future ones. History is understood here in the Gadamerian sense (Gadamer 1989: 265–300), while the notions of past, present, and future are informed by Ricoeur's (1984: 52–87) theory of mimesis. The present study argues that auditory roughness is an important sonic aspect of music, an aspect that aesthetic judgments are often based on.[1] The study examines ways in which roughness provides means of aesthetic differentiation, and how it is utilized and judged within different musical traditions.[2]

The term *roughness* describes an aural sensation and was introduced in the acoustics and psychoacoustics literature by Helmholtz (end of the nineteenth century) to label harsh, raspy, hoarse sounds. It refers to a harshness perceived when sound signals with an amplitude fluctuation rate between ~20 and ~75–150 fluctuations per second (depending on pitch register) reach the ear. Figure 1a shows an example of a signal with steady amplitude over time, while Figure 1b shows a signal whose amplitude fluctuates over time.

If the rate of fluctuation is within the previously mentioned range, the signal will correspond to a rough sound. A familiar example of a signal corresponding to a rough sound would be the signal of a harmonic minor second performed, for instance, on two flutes. Although a harmonic minor second will sound rough regardless of the sound sources involved, steady state sources such as singing voice, bowed strings, and winds (as opposed to impulse sources such as percussion and plucked strings) result in more salient roughness sensations (von Bèckèsy 1960; Terhardt 1974). At relatively low registers, wider intervals such as major seconds and minor thirds can also sound rough and, within the Western musical tradition, are avoided as dissonant. For example, the general practice in Western art music orchestration of spacing out harmonic intervals more at low registers than at high registers has its basis on roughness considerations.

The reason signals of all harmonic intervals other than unisons exhibit amplitude fluctuations is physical and is related to the phenomenon of interference. The reason why the signals of some of these intervals correspond to rough sounds is physiological and has to do mainly with the mechanical properties of the inner ear. The following section examines briefly the above issues by addressing the physical, physiological, and

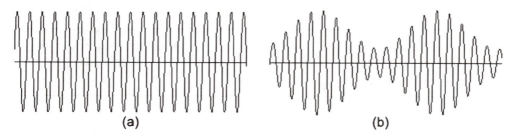

Figure 1. Illustration of a sound signal with (a) steady amplitude and
(b) amplitude that fluctuates over time.

perceptual properties of signals with amplitude fluctuations (also often referred to as "modulated signals").

2. Physical and Physiological Correlates of the Roughness Sensation

The present study approaches roughness as one of the perceptual manifestations of the energy content of amplitude fluctuation and one aspect of timbre. Amplitude fluctuations describe variations in the maximum value (amplitude) of sound signals relative to a reference point and are the result of wave interference. The interference principle states that the combined amplitude of two or more vibrations (waves) at any given time may be larger (constructive interference) or smaller (destructive interference) than the amplitude of the individual vibrations (waves), depending on their phase relationship. In the case of two or more waves with different frequencies, their periodically changing phase relationship results in periodic alterations between constructive and destructive interference, giving rise to the phenomenon of amplitude fluctuations.

Amplitude fluctuations can be placed in three overlapping perceptual categories related to the rate of fluctuation. Slow amplitude fluctuations ($\approx\leq20$ per second) are perceived as loudness fluctuations referred to as beating. As the rate of fluctuation is increased, the loudness appears to be constant and the fluctuations are perceived as "fluttering" or *roughness*. As the amplitude fluctuation rate is increased further, the roughness reaches a maximum strength and then gradually diminishes until it disappears ($\approx\geq75$–150 fluctuations per second, depending on the frequency of the interfering tones).

Assuming the ear performs a frequency analysis on incoming signals, as indicated by Ohm's acoustical law (see Helmholtz 1885; Plomp 1964), the above perceptual categories can be related directly to the bandwidth of the hypothetical analysis-filters (Zwicker *et al.* 1957; Zwicker 1961). For example, in the simplest case of amplitude fluctuations resulting from the addition of two sine signals with frequencies f_1 and f_2, the fluctuation rate is equal to the frequency difference between the two sines $|f_1\text{-}f_2|$, and the following statements represent the general consensus:[3]

a) If the fluctuation rate is smaller than the filter-bandwidth, then a single tone is perceived either with fluctuating loudness (beating) or with roughness.

b) If the fluctuation rate is larger than the filter-bandwidth, then a complex tone is perceived, to which one or more pitches can be assigned but which, in general, exhibits no beating or roughness.[4]

Along with amplitude fluctuation rate, the second most important signal parameter related to roughness is the degree of a signal's amplitude fluctuation, that is, the level difference between peaks and valleys in a signal such as the one in Figure 1b (Terhardt 1974; Vassilakis 2001: Chapter 3). The degree of amplitude fluctuation depends on the relative amplitudes of the components in the signal's spectrum, with interfering tones of equal amplitudes resulting in the highest fluctuation degree and therefore in the highest roughness degree.

For fluctuation rates comparable to the auditory filter-bandwidth, the degree, rate, and shape of a complex signal's amplitude fluctuations are variables that, as it will be shown, are manipulated by musicians of various cultures to exploit the beating and roughness sensations, making amplitude fluctuation a significant expressive tool in the production of musical sound.[5] Otherwise, when there is no pronounced beating or roughness, the degree, rate, and shape of a complex signal's amplitude fluctuations are variables that continue to be important through their interaction with the signal's spectral components. This interaction is manifested perceptually in terms of pitch or timbre variations, linked to the introduction of combination tones.[6]

Similarly to beating, the roughness sensation associated with certain complex signals is therefore usually understood in terms of sine-component interaction within the same frequency band of the hypothesized auditory filter, called *critical band*. The term *critical band*, introduced by Fletcher in the 1940s, referred to the frequency bandwidth of the then-loosely-defined auditory filter. Since von Békésy's studies (1960), the term also refers literally to the specific area on the basilar membrane (an elongated thin sheet of fibers located in the inner ear, inside the cochlea) that goes into vibration in resonance to an incoming sine wave. Its length depends on the elastic properties of the membrane and on active feedback mechanisms operating within the hearing organ. Converging psychophysical and psychophysiological experiments indicate that the average length of the critical band is ~1mm. Psycho-physiologically, the roughness sensation can thus be linked to the inability of the auditory frequency-analysis mechanism to resolve inputs whose frequency difference is smaller than the critical bandwidth and to the resulting instability or periodic "tickling" (Campbell and Greated 1987:61) of the mechanical system (basilar membrane) that resonates in response to such inputs.

3. Western Musical Aesthetics and Roughness

Within the Western musical tradition, auditory roughness has often been linked to the concepts of consonance and dissonance, whether those have been understood as aesthetically loaded, as is most often the case, (Rameau in Carlton 1990, Kameoka and Kuriyagawa 1969a, Terhardt 1984, and others) or not (Helmholtz 1885, Hindemith 1945, von Békésy 1960, Plomp and Levelt 1965, and others). Studies addressing this sensation have occasionally been too keen to establish a definite and universally acceptable justification of the "natural inevitability" and "aesthetic superiority" of Western music theory (for example, Stumpf 1890, in von Békésy 1960: 348; Vogel 1993). This has prevented them from seriously examining the physical and physiological correlates of roughness, an important but certainly not the only perceptual dimension of dissonance. On the contrary, Helmholtz (1885: 234–235), the first researcher to examine roughness theoretically and experimentally as an important attribute of auditory sensation, concluded:

Whether one combination [*of tones*] is rougher or smoother than another depends solely on the anatomical structure of the ear, and has nothing to do with psychological motives. But what degree of roughness a hearer is inclined to . . . as a means of musical expression depends on taste and habit; hence the boundary between consonances and dissonances has frequently changed . . . and will still further change.

Other researchers (for example, Ortmann 1922), as early as the beginning of the twentieth century, have gone even further to suggest that the most important factor in the enjoyment of music is nonauditory, with roughness being much less important than the listener's associations when it comes to music evaluation and appreciation.

After Helmholtz's work, the roughness sensation got little attention in psychoacoustics until the 1960s when studies by von Békésy, Terhardt, Plomp, and others acknowledged roughness as one of the main attributes of timbre.[7] Since then, further studies have demonstrated that this sensation plays an important role in several aspects of sound evaluation, both musical and nonmusical. Within several traditions, the consonance or "absence of annoyance" in nonmusical sounds has also been shown to depend on roughness. For example, studies indicate that listeners judge background noise that is rough as more annoying than "smooth" background noise (for example, Vos and Smoorenburg 1985, Hashimoto and Hatano 1994). (See Imaizumi 1986 for applications of roughness evaluation in voice pathology). More relevantly to the present study, Pressnitzer *et al.* (2000) confirmed that, as the perceptual salience of other sonic attributes such as pitch and tonal character is reduced, the correlation between nontonal tension and roughness increases.

This strong link between roughness and annoyance within the Western musical tradition has resulted in avoiding sound-combinations that sound rough (other than to signify that something horrible is going on) and has been accompanied by the unjustified assumption that rough sounds are inherently bad and unpleasant.[8] The present study treats the sensation of roughness as a perceptual manifestation of the energy content of amplitude fluctuation, which can be manipulated by controlling the fluctuation rate and degree to provide means of sonic variation and musical expression. As the following section will demonstrate, sound variations involving the roughness sensation often constitute a significant and valued expressive tool in the production of musical sound around the world, having both sonic and cultural significance.

4. Roughness as a Means of Musical Expression

4.1 Introduction

The sensation of roughness has been exploited more than any other perceptual manifestations of amplitude fluctuation and by numerous musical traditions, a practice that has not yet been well documented or researched. Manipulating the degree and rate of amplitude fluctuation helps create the buzzing sound of the Indian *tambura* drone and the rattling effect of Bosnian *ganga* singing, resulting in a sonic canvas that becomes the backdrop for further musical elaboration. It permits the creation of timbral variations (as, for example, in Middle Eastern *mijwiz* playing) and rhythmic contrasts (as, for example, in *ganga* singing) through gradual or abrupt changes among roughness degrees. Whether such variations are explicitly sought after, as in *ganga* singing and *mijwiz* playing, or are introduced more subtly and gradually, as may be the case in the typical chord progressions/modulations of Western music, they form an important part of a musical tradition's expressive vocabulary.

Important clues regarding the ways a musical culture approaches the roughness sensation can be identified through an examination of musical instrument construction, performance practice, and the different choices among musical traditions with regards to vertical sonorities such as harmonic intervals and chords. The following sections provide three examples of musical traditions that utilize the expressive possibilities of the roughness sensation. Other similar examples can be found in Quechua Haraui songs of Peru, with their frequent use of narrow harmonic intervals, and in the performance of the *taqara* flutes of the Xingu river in Brazil, where sonic effects similar to those produced with the *mizwij* are produced by two or more simultaneous performers.

4.2 *The Middle Eastern* Mijwiz

The *mijwiz* is an aerophone made out of two identical cylindrical cane pipes, each with a single reed, bound together and played simultaneously (Figure 2). Paired reed-pipes are found all across the Mediterranean. Their considerable cross-cultural and historical consistency with regards to playing technique, musical style, and even musical symbolism has often been attributed to their peculiar acoustical properties (Racy 1994: 38).

The *mijwiz* has a stepped shape. Each of the two pipes is made by joining together three cane tubes of increasing diameter: one that has the vibrating reed, one that acts as a junction, and one that carries the tone-holes. This construction gives the instrument acoustical characteristics that resemble those of conical rather than cylindrical

Figure 2. Ali Jihad Racy (University of California, Los Angeles, Ethnomusicology Department) performing on the *mijwiz*. Circular breathing is a technique used often by accomplished performers to ensure uninterrupted sound with no dynamic variation.

tubes, regarding register (an octave higher than a cylinder of the same dimensions) and spectral composition (denser, richer spectra) of the produced tones. Additionally, the discontinuities of the *mijwiz's* stepped design support a complex mode distribution that results in slightly inharmonic spectral components, as is the case with all compound horns (Fletcher and Rossing 1998: 217). The stepped design helps the instrument speak better because it allows for the use of a smaller reed system, as Racy has noted (1994: 42), but also because it provides better impedance matching between the inside and the outside of the instrument than a cylindrical tube (Nederveen 1998: 59–60). Nonetheless, since the effective cone-angle is very small, as is the diameter of the bore and of the tone holes, the resulting impedance matching is still weak. As a consequence, a large amount of pressure is required before the necessary standing waves can build up inside the tube and transfer energy outside the instrument, a pressure that must stay relatively constant if it is to sustain the free-reed vibrations and a steady tone.

The constant high pressure results not only in a constantly *nasal* tone, rich in upper components, but also in an extremely limited dynamic range. In addition, the equally narrow melodic range (~a fifth), the fact that the two reeds are activated just by air pressure (with no manipulation possible from the lips or tongue, as would be the case for a clarinet-like instrument, where reed manipulation by the lips/tongue permits timbral variation), and the frequent use of the circular-breathing playing technique (which further limits the possibilities for sonic variation by inhibiting any interplay between sound and silence), result in an instrument that has developed a celebrated expressive power without relying on any of the usual sonic expressive tools.[9] For its expressive power, the *mijwiz*, like most double-pipes throughout history, relies mainly on the manipulation and exploration of amplitude fluctuation rates.

The slight detuning between the two, otherwise identical, cane pipes (achieved through slight displacement of the tone-holes) means that when played together, they produce tones that beat constantly and at slightly shifting rates, giving the instrument a rich tonal quality. The shifting beating rates are owed to the slight inharmonicity of the upper components (due to the stepped design), and may be behind the "chorus effect" noted by Racy (1994: 44). The amplitude fluctuation rate is explored further by occasionally increasing the detuning of the near-unisons through partial stopping or by temporarily abandoning the unisons and using one pipe as a high drone while performing a lower melody on the other. With a functional range of approximately a fifth and no possibility of line crossing, this motion between unison, detuned unison, and minor second to minor third harmonic intervals represents a manipulation of roughness degrees rather than a form of polyphony. In its construction and performance practice, the *mijwiz* is an example of an instrument that makes explicit use of the perceptual richness of amplitude fluctuation, through creative exploration of the roughness sensation.

4.3 *The North Indian* Tambura

The structural and symbolic importance of the interaction between drone and melody, exemplified by the role of the *tambura* in Indian musical ensembles, is indicative of the musical significance of sonic contrasts involving the roughness sensation. The *tambura* is an unfretted, long-necked lute with four or five strings (tuned to octaves and a fifth, a fourth, or a seventh, depending on tuning set), used to provide the drone accompaniment for one or more melodic instruments (Figure 3). A cotton thread (*juari*, often referred to as "life giving thread") is inserted between the bridge and the strings, giving the modulation of the string-length (as the string wraps/ unwraps around the bridge) a discontinuous character and resulting in the characteristic, buzzing sound of the instrument. The buzzing is accentuated by the fact that high-frequency waves (associated with the abrupt changes in string slope and the "whipping" of the bridge) propagate on the string faster than lower-frequency waves (dispersion due to string stiffness), reinforcing the energy shift to upper components and increasing the "brilliance" of the buzz.

The buzzing sound of the *tambura* strings provides a dynamic drone of up to four tones that interact with each other and with the melodic line they support. This interaction between background (drone) and foreground (melodic line) results in roughness variations that outline the function of each note within a *rāg* (scale) and provide a point of reference for measuring the relationships among the intervals used. These relationships are responsible for the dynamic quality of a note within a melody, describing a note's degree of instability/tension. They set up patterns of tension and release within a piece of music, governed by the degree of roughness experienced in relation to the first *tambura* drone, and complicated further by the introduction of a second or third drone (Jairazbhoy 1995: 65–69).

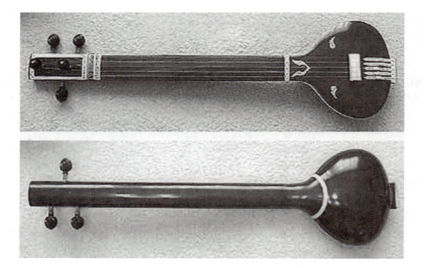

Figure 3. The front and back of a five-string North Indian *tambura*.
(From the Ethnomusicology Department's instrument collection,
University of California, Los Angeles.)

Contemporary North Indian classical music theory links sound to emotion (*rasa*), color, the Hindu deities, and more. The concept of rāg is partly based on the idea that certain note-patterns evoke a heightened state of emotion (Jairazbhoy 1995: 28). It has its roots in the second half of the seventeenth century and is a direct descendent of the ancient court tradition, where the patronage system created a highly competitive atmosphere (Jairazbhoy 1995: 21, 27). Virtuosity, invention, and showmanship have therefore always played an important role, with the sonic effect of a musical performance holding special significance. This effect is mainly based on contrasts between states of tension and release or, as Jairazbhoy puts it (1995: 70), on contrasts of energy levels. The roughness sensation is at the root of these energy-level contrasts, with the *tambura's* buzzing sound often considered the life of a musical piece (Carterette *et al.* 1989: 87).

4.4 Bosnian Ganga *Songs*

Ganga is a style of singing common in Bosnia-Herzegovina and the Dalmatian Zagora regions of the Balkans. *Ganga* songs consist of two alternating sections, one sung by a soloist and one by a soloist and a chorus (three to five singers). The melodic range rarely exceeds a fourth while, in the choral sections, voices sing at minor/major second harmonic intervals that may or may not alternate with unison passages. People in the region consider these intervals consonant and the resulting sound pleasant and desirable. Singing *ganga* provokes a feeling of corporate unity among singers and (initiated) listeners (Petrović 1977: 336), and good performances have a strong emotional impact. People in the specified regions generally associate the *ganga* sound with extreme joy. In contrast, the majority of listeners outside the region find the *ganga* sound annoying and even offensive.

The length and content of the lyrics vary greatly among performances. The singers are relatively free in their choice of words, which are often just vocalizations (Petrović 1977: 144), indicating that words are of far less importance to this genre than to most other types of folk songs. Within its geographical territory, *ganga* is often valued for its distinct sonic effect rather than its semantic content. As it was argued in the case of *mizwij* playing, this effect relies mainly on the manipulation of and contrast between roughness degrees through (often rhythmic) alterations of solo, unison, and minor/major second passages.

The *ganga* style was initially approached by scholars as representing an inability to sing "correctly" (Marić 1933, in Petrović 1977: 73). Further research revealed an explicit musical system, characterized by specific rules of musical creation and performance, and surprisingly fine (considering the narrow pitch and dynamic ranges employed) distinctions between substyles and good and bad songs and performances (Rihtman 1951, in Petrović 1977: 76; Petrović 1977). Except for some stylized improvisation, *ganga* melodies are thoroughly composed and the principle structural feature of the songs is the contrast between solo and choral sections. This is simulated on a smaller scale in the choral passages through alterations among unisons and minor and major seconds.

The clear intention to achieve expressive goals through explicit use of sounds involving the roughness sensation is illustrated through the *ganga* rules governing a good song or performance:

   a) Singers must sing loudly and maintain uniform strength between each other and through time (Petrović 1977: 45, 101). Combining sound-waves of high and steady intensities results in signals with pronounced amplitude fluctuations and rougher sound.

   b) The melodic range must not exceed a major third while harmonic intervals must not exceed a major second (Petrović 1977: 326). Narrow harmonic intervals give amplitude fluctuation rates within the range corresponding to rougher sounds. The few regions that have increased their range to include wider harmonic intervals produce songs that are considered "impure" and are referred to, with a negative connotation, as "widely sung" (Petrović 1977: 260).

   c) The voices must be as identical as possible, nasal, and without vibrato so that they blend. Perfect blending of voices is a characteristic insisted upon heavily, requiring from the ensemble to "sound as one person" (Petrović 1977: 308–309). Similar vocal timbres with no vibrato correspond to signals with similar and steady spectral envelopes. This similarity ensures that the resulting degree of amplitude fluctuation and the associated roughness will be maximal. At the same time, nasal timbres correspond to spectra with more energy at the frequency region that human hearing is most sensitive and to more salient roughness sensation.

These loudness and timbral requirements are accompanied by very specific performance arrangements. Singers never move or dance while singing. They stand very tightly together, in an arch, turned slightly towards each other so that their voices will "collide" at the right point (Figure 4). For waves interfering in three dimensions (as is the case with sound waves in air), the geometric condition for maximum interference is collinearity (that is, waves moving along the same line; Westervelt 1957, in Beyer, 1999: 317). This condition is always satisfied for sound waves originating in the same source. For more than one source, such as a choral ensemble, a performance arrangement such as the one found in *ganga* singing does satisfy the collinearity requirement. If the above conditions are not fulfilled "the *ganga* will not be good" (Petrović 1977: 113). Performers refuse to sing under different conditions or to perform individual parts from the choral sections (when asked by researchers) since, when stripped from their perceptually rough intervals, these lines apparently "make no sense" (Petrović 1977: 117). In other words, *ganga* represents a rare folk vocal genre where the sense of a song is related more to its sound than to its lyrics. Moreover, the conditions for a good song that makes sense are also conditions that guarantee the perceptual salience of amplitude fluctuations and of the roughness sensation. This relationship is illustrated further by the three types of choral sections found in *ganga* songs:

   a) Two to three voice parts sing in minor and major seconds with periodic insertions of unisons, always resolving on a major second. The unisons are not inserted randomly. Their function is to create specific rhythmic effects through the sudden contrast between perceptual roughness and smoothness.

Figure 4. Members of the Balkan Music Ensemble
(University of California, Los Angeles,
Ethnomusicology Department)
performing a *ganga* song.

Petrović (1977: 288–294) includes a list of such rhythmic effects that are relatively consistent across the *ganga* territory.

b) Voices move in parallel seconds without unison insertions.

c) The leading (lower) part may cross the accompaniment and move a major second above it rather than remain, as is more often the case, below it. There are no cases of voices in contrary motion.

Although most songs start with a solo passage, performers refer to the entry of the choral section as the beginning of the song, and the importance of this section is closely related to its potential for roughness variations.

Ganga singing provides a striking example of a musical tradition that has developed performance techniques and practices that highly correspond to perceptual roughness considerations. This genre's expressive musical vocabulary relies heavily on the sonic effects produced through the manipulation of roughness degrees, and its aesthetic attitudes towards the roughness sensation are in sharp contrast to those of the Western art musical tradition. Along with the other examples cited, it indicates that auditory roughness and its study have musical significance that extends far beyond Western tradition's concern with consonance and dissonance.

5. Roughness Estimation Models

5.1 Existing Models Quantifying Roughness and Their Drawbacks

Having established the musical significance of the roughness sensation, one way to proceed is to devise a model that would systematically quantify the roughness degree of a given sound, permitting the empirical testing of hypotheses that link roughness to musical variables. For example, a roughness estimation model would permit the empirical examination of claims linking a) roughness to dissonance within the Western musical tradition, b) roughness profiles to patterns of tension and release in Near Eastern or North Indian musical pieces (as intended by performers and/or perceived by listeners), or c) to rhythmic effects found in Balkan folk songs.

The two principal studies that have systematically examined the sensation of roughness (von Békésy 1960: 344–354; Terhardt 1974) have, to a large extent, been ignored by existing models quantifying auditory roughness of complex spectra. Numerous such models have been proposed over the last ~100 years (for example. Helmholtz 1885; Plomp and Levelt 1965; Kameoka and Kuriyagawa, 1969a, b; Hutchinson and Knopoff 1978; Sethares 1998). They have been employed in later studies that mainly link roughness to sensory consonance[10] (for example, Bigand *et al.* 1996; Vos 1986; Dibben 1999), demonstrating a relatively low degree of agreement between predicted and experimental data.

All the above models misrepresent the contribution of the amplitudes of the interfering sines (and therefore of the degree of amplitude fluctuation of the resulting complex signal) to the degree of roughness.[11] Usually, the roughness estimation function for a sine-pair (with amplitudes A_1 and A_2) is multiplied by the product of the two amplitudes $(A_1{}^*A_2)$, ensuring minimum roughness if either of the amplitudes approaches zero. This, however, severely overestimates the increase in roughness with increasing amplitudes and, most importantly, fails to capture the relationship between the amplitude difference of two sines close in frequency and the salience of the resulting beats/roughness.

Correct estimation of the roughness degree of a pair of sines or of any arbitrary spectrum is necessary before some claimed link between roughness and an acoustic, perceptual, or musical variable can be systematically tested.

5.2 A New Roughness Estimation Model for Complex Spectra

Existing roughness estimation models do not adequately account for the roughness contribution of amplitude fluctuation, they often fail to capture reliably the effect of pitch register on roughness, and demonstrate a relatively low degree of agreement between predicted and observed roughness levels (for details see Vassilakis 2001, Section 5.3). Based on the roughness-estimation model introduced by Sethares (1998), a new model that includes a term to account for the contribution of the amplitudes of interfering sines to the roughness of a sine-pair has been proposed (Vassilakis 2001, Section 6.4.1).[12] This new term is based on existing experimental results (von Békésy 1960; Terhardt 1974), adjusted to account for the quantitative difference between amplitude modulation depth and degree of amplitude fluctuation (Vassilakis 2001, Chapter 3). The model estimates the roughness of complex spectra with more than two sine components by adding the roughness of the individual sine-pairs. Although it has been argued that the total roughness can be less than the sum of the roughness of each sine-pair (von Békésy 1960: 350–351), pilot experiments indicated otherwise confirming results from previous studies (Terhardt 1974; Lin and Hartmann 1995). The proposed model does not account for the influence of phase on roughness

(Pressnitzer and McAdams 1999) and is not fit to handle continuous spectra. For more details on this and earlier roughness models and for improvement suggestions, see Vassilakis 2001 (Sections 5.3, 6.4.1, & 6.4.2).

6. Roughness Degrees and Harmonic Interval Dissonance Ratings in the Western Musical Tradition

6.1 Introduction

Roughness estimation models have to date been applied mainly to address issues of consonance/dissonance within the Western musical tradition. For comparison purposes, the proposed model was also applied to the issue of consonance, testing the following hypothesis:

> For musicians within the Western musical tradition, roughness ratings of harmonic intervals agree with the roughness degrees estimated using the proposed roughness estimation model (Vassilakis 2001, Section 6.4.1) and correlate with the dissonance degrees suggested by Western music theory. Additionally, dissonance ratings correlate with roughness degrees indicating that, in the Western musical tradition where sensory roughness is in general avoided as dissonant, the consonance hierarchy of harmonic intervals corresponds mainly to variations in roughness degrees (Vassilakis 2001, Section 6.4.3).

Helmholtz (1885), Pratt (1921), and others conducted somewhat similar experiments that compared roughness-model estimations or roughness ratings to music-theory claims. Vassilakis (2001) was the first to examine simultaneously the relationship among roughness model estimations, roughness ratings, dissonance ratings, and Western music theory claims.

6.2 Methods

The thirteen harmonic intervals of the chromatic scale, starting on middle C (C4; fundamental frequency: 256Hz; equal temperament), served as experiment stimuli. The intervals where constructed using digitally synthesized complex tones with slightly detuned sawtooth spectra ($A_n = A_1/n$; A_n: amplitude of the nth component) and six components each.

Along with the predictions of the proposed model, the predictions of two earlier roughness estimation models (Helmholtz 1885: 332; Hutchinson and Knopoff 1978: 17–23) were examined for comparison purposes. All models assume sawtooth spectra and the same starting note, C4. Both earlier models assume ten- rather than six-component complex tones. The Hutchinson and Knopoff model is based on Helmholtz's model, modified to reflect the results by Plomp and Levelt (1965) regarding the effect of pitch register on roughness. Plomp and Levelt examined this effect using six-component complex tones. Therefore, Vassilakis (2001) opted for the use of six- rather than ten-component complex tones.

Intervals were presented randomly to two groups of ten subjects through headphones (same signal in both ears). The first group of subjects was asked to rate the stimuli in terms of roughness, on a scale outlined by the labels: *Not rough–Rough*. The second group of subjects was asked to rate the stimuli in terms of dissonance, on a scale outlined by the labels: *Not dissonant–Dissonant*. Subjects were able to familiarize themselves with the stimuli in a practice experiment. In addition, they demonstrated their understanding of *roughness* in training sessions that included amplitude-modulated sines as stimuli, at various modulation rates and depths and various roughness degrees.

Response scales ranged from 0 (Not Rough/Not Dissonant) to 42 (Rough/Dissonant). The range (0–42) was based on the roughness of the stimuli calculated using a computer implementation of the proposed model. The predictions of the two comparison models were scaled to fit this range. The experiment was designed and conducted using *MEDS* (Music Experiment Development System) by Kendall (2001). Experiment implementation was automated and experimenter interaction with the subjects was limited to offering initial instructions and administrating training sessions. Subjects entered their responses by moving a scroll bar along the relevant response scales and the scroll-bar starting position was random.

6.4 Results and Discussion

Figure 5 displays the estimated roughness for the thirteen harmonic intervals used in the experiment, based on three roughness estimation models.

The roughness estimates of the proposed model correlate better with the estimates of the Hutchinson and Knopoff model ($r = 0.86$) than with those of the

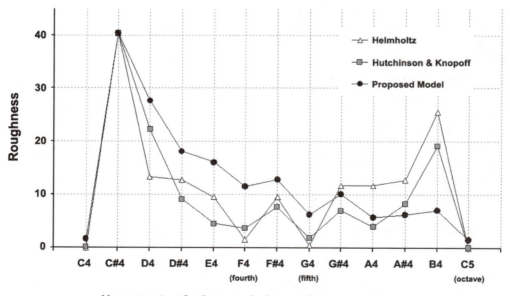

Figure 5. Estimated roughness for all 13 intervals in the chromatic scale starting at C4. Values were estimated using the proposed model and two earlier roughness estimation models by Helmholtz (1885) and Hutchinson and Knopoff (1978).

Helmholtz model ($r = 0.72$). ("Perfect" correlation corresponds to $|r| = 1.0$.) The main reason for this difference is that the Hutchinson and Knopoff model accounts for the effect of pitch register on roughness while the Helmholtz model does not.

Based on Figure 5, a number of differences among the roughness predictions of the three models can be identified:

a) The proposed model predicts a much lower roughness level for the major-seventh interval (C4–B4) than the other two models.

b) The Helmholtz and the Hutchinson and Knopoff models predict lower roughness levels than the proposed model for the intervals between major second (C4–D4) and fifth (C4–G4).

c) Contrary to the earlier models, the proposed model predicts the augmented-fourth interval (C4–F#4) to be smoother than the major third (C4–E4).

d) The proposed model results in a relatively linear roughness curve between the minor second (C4–C#4) and octave (C4–C5) intervals, without the pronounced contrasts found in the roughness curves of the other models.

e) Lastly, the proposed model predicts slightly higher roughness levels for the unison (C4–C4) and octave (C4–C5) intervals than the other models.

The slightly higher roughness levels predicted for the unison and octave intervals by the proposed model are due to the slight detuning applied to the experimental stimuli. The Helmholtz and the Hutchinson and Knopoff models assume perfectly harmonic spectra that bring the roughness levels of unisons and octaves very close to zero.

All other differences (including the difference in the roughness ranking of the augmented fourth [C4–F#4] among the three models) can be explained in terms of the different assumptions each model makes regarding the contributions of degree of amplitude fluctuation and of sound pressure level to roughness. The Helmholtz and the Hutchinson and Knopoff models overestimate the contribution of sound-pressure level and underestimate the contribution of amplitude-fluctuation degree (Vassilakis 2001). This results in overestimating the roughness contribution of some sine-pairs, while underestimating the roughness contribution of others. The higher roughness of the fourth interval relative to the major seventh, predicted by the proposed model, is consistent with experiments indicating that fourths are less likely to be perceived as single tones (less prone to tonal fusion) than major sevenths (DeWitt and Crowder 1987, in Huron 1991: 136).[13] The somewhat linear shape of the proposed model's roughness curve is due to the progressive decrease in *AF-degree* for the sine-pairs that contribute the most to the roughness of each interval, as intervals widen. As the intervals get wider, the amplitude difference of the closely interacting sine components gets larger and the *AF-degree* gets smaller.

Figure 6 displays the mean responses and standard deviations of the subject-groups rating the stimuli in terms of roughness and dissonance.

Dissonance responses correlated well with roughness responses ($r = 0.94$), indicating that changes in dissonance among the thirteen intervals corresponded to changes in roughness. This suggests that the presence of roughness provides an important clue for dissonance judgments of isolated harmonic intervals.

Analysis of variance suggested that subjects rating dissonance used slightly different criteria than subjects rating roughness (analyses were performed using *Statistica*

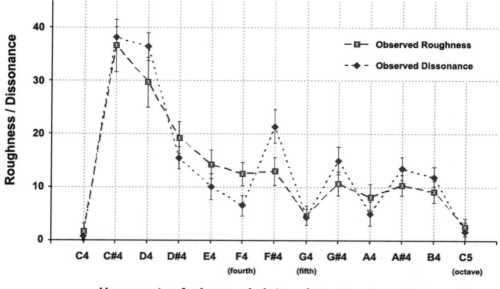

Figure 6. Mean observed roughness and dissonance for
all thirteen intervals in the chromatic scale starting at C4
(10 subjects per group—error bars: ± 1 standard deviation).

5.5 for Windows, StatSoft, Inc., 2000). Post-hoc analysis indicated that this difference
was manifested the strongest in the ratings of the augmented-fourth, the perfect-
fourth, and the minor-sixth intervals. The perfect-fourth interval was judged more
rough than dissonant while the augmented-fourth and minor-sixth intervals were
judged more dissonant than rough.

To investigate further the observed differences, two separate analyses were performed on the means obtained from the "roughness" and the "dissonance" subject-
groups, organizing the intervals into the roughness and dissonance categories
displayed in Table 1.

Table 1 indicates similarities as well as differences between the roughness and dissonance ratings of the thirteen harmonic intervals, and will be examined in some
detail. When subjects make dissonance judgments they do not necessarily rely on
strictly acoustical criteria. Cultural conditioning has been introduced as an explanation to the consonance/dissonance concept since the 1940s (for example, Cazden
1945, in Sethares 1998: 78–79). At the same time, the historical tension between sedi-
mentation and innovation within a musical tradition has supported what Helmholtz
recognized as continuously changing attitudes towards consonance and dissonance
(Helmholtz 1885: 84–85). Therefore, historical and cultural criteria must be included
along with physical, physiological, and psychological ones when trying to explain dissonance judgments.

Table 1

Mean roughness and dissonance ratings grouped according to
statistical significance by Tukey HSD post-hoc comparisons

Roughness			Dissonance		
Category	Interval	Mean Roughness	Category	Interval	Mean Dissonance
1	Unison	1.7	1	Unison	0.8
1	Octave	2.5	1 - 2	Octave	1.7
1 - 2	Perfect Fifth	4.7	2 - 3	Perfect Fifth	4.4
2 - 3	Major Sixth	8.2	3	Major Sixth	5.1
3 - 4	Major Seventh	9.2	3	Perfect Fourth	6.6
3 - 4 - 5	Minor Seventh	10.4	4	Major Third	10.1
3 - 4 - 5	Minor Sixth	10.7	4 - 5	Major Seventh	12
4 - 5	Perfect Fourth	12.5	5 - 6	Minor Seventh	13.5
4 - 5	Aug. Fourth	13	5 - 6	Minor Sixth	15
5	Major Third	14.3	6	Minor Third	15.5
6	Minor Third	19.2	7	Aug. Fourth	21.4
7	Major Second	29.7	8	Major Second	36.4
8	Minor Second	36.6	8	Minor Second	38.2

As a first observation, the intervals in Table 1 are grouped into eight roughness and eight dissonance categories. However, there is less overlap in the dissonance categories, indicating that subjects rated dissonance with more confidence than they rated roughness. As opposed to the short history of the concept of roughness, limited within areas outside the mainstream music disciplines, the concept of dissonance has had a long tradition in Western music discourse (Hutchinson and Knopoff 1978: 1; Sethares 1998: 73–80). It should therefore be expected that subjects would be more familiar with the concept of dissonance than with the concept of roughness and would make dissonance ratings with more confidence. The experiment results support this suggestion and show signs of categorical perception for dissonance, while roughness ratings seem to have been made along a continuum.

The extremes of the two rating scales in Table 1 are occupied by the same intervals, indicating that the clear presence or absence of roughness dominates dissonance decisions. At the same time, the roughness differences among these harmonic intervals are larger than their dissonance differences. This reduced resolution in the dissonance ratings at the extremes of the scale is consistent with Western culture's preference for smooth sounds over rough ones, offers one more indication of categorical perception for dissonance, and suggests a possible difference-threshold for the dissonance/annoyance level of roughness that needs to be systematically examined in a future study.

For intervals located closer to the middle of the rating scale, roughness ratings become increasingly ambiguous (increasing overlap among roughness categories). Dissonance ratings, on the other hand, become increasingly categorical, demonstrating differences larger than those found in the roughness ratings (for example, see the relationship among the augmented-fourth, perfect-fourth, major-third, and minor-third intervals). When the roughness of an interval is neither very large nor very small, dissonance decisions appear to be based on clues additional to roughness, occasionally ignoring roughness altogether (for example, see the relationship between the augmented-fourth and perfect-fourth intervals).

The high dissonance rating of the augmented-fourth interval (in spite of its low roughness level compared to the major third) and the overall higher dissonance ratings of minor over major intervals (regardless of their roughness ratings) indicate that, when there is no clear presence/absence of roughness, dissonance decisions are not based on acoustical cues. Rather, they may be culturally and historically mediated. The augmented fourth is the only interval within the chromatic scale that is not found in the harmonic series and cannot be arrived at through integer divisions of a string. The mathematical impossibility of the augmented-fourth interval, along with the long-standing link between mathematics and music, may have provided the original basis for the unfavorable aura that has followed this interval for centuries. The clear separation between major and minor intervals in the dissonance ratings along with the strong Western-based association of dissonance with unpleasantness reflect a dislike for minor sonorities so ingrained within the Western tradition that is already present in pre-language children (Kastner and Crowder 1990). The culture-specific nature of this attitude, however, is indicated by the increase in the distinction between major and minor with age (that is, minor becomes increasingly "negative" the longer one is exposed to a "pro-major" tradition) and is fully exposed through encounters with musical traditions where minor harmonies are considered joyful, as is the case with the music of the Andean highlands of Peru (Turino 1993: 43–58).

The results, therefore, indicate that roughness constitutes a significant but not the sole factor guiding listeners in their dissonance judgments. In terms of existing theoretical models, the dissonance ranking of the intervals obtained from the experiment agrees best with Stumpf's ranking (1898, in Davies 1978: 158) except for the major-seventh interval, which was rated less dissonant than predicted by all models other than the proposed model. Stumpf's dissonance ranking was based on his concept of *fusion*. The fusion hypothesis was excluded from the present study because it is based on a large number of interacting and hard-to-quantify variables and does not provide a readily measurable physical correlate for dissonance.

For a more detailed examination of the three models addressed in this study, Figures 7, 8, and 9 compare the observed roughness and dissonance levels to the roughness values estimated by each model (for details on the statistical analysis of the data see Vassilakis 2001, Section 6.4.3).

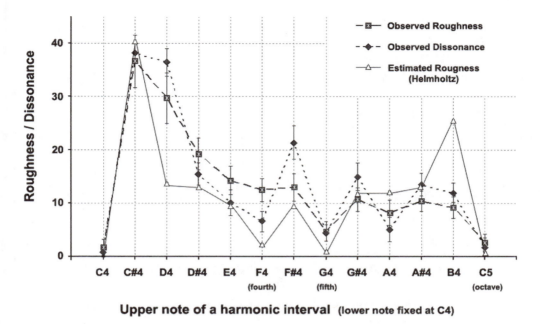

Figure 7. Estimated roughness (Helmholtz 1885) versus observed roughness and observed dissonance for all thirteen intervals in the chromatic scale starting at C4.

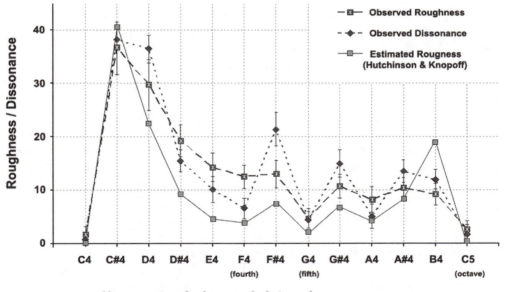

Figure 8. Estimated roughness (Hutchinson and Knopoff 1978) versus observed roughness and observed dissonance for all thirteen intervals in the chromatic scale starting at C4.

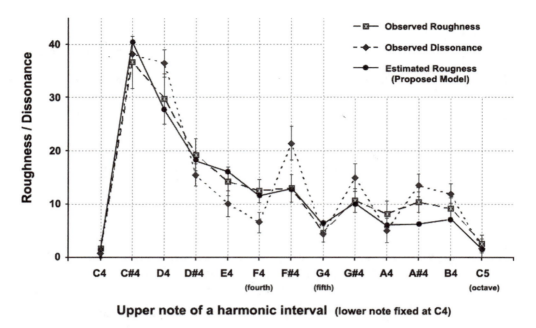

Figure 9. Estimated roughness (proposed model) versus observed roughness and observed dissonance for all thirteen intervals in the chromatic scale starting at C4.

The proposed model demonstrates the best agreement between estimated and observed roughness ($r = 0.98$) as well as between estimated roughness and observed dissonance ($r = 0.91$). With the exemptions discussed previously, observed dissonance also correlates well with observed roughness ($r = 0.94$).

The results support the claim that, in the Western musical tradition where sensory roughness is avoided as dissonant, the consonance hierarchy of isolated harmonic intervals corresponds mainly to variations in roughness degrees, with subtle roughness variations being, in general, ignored. As the presence/absence of roughness become less pronounced, sensory dissonance/consonance gives way to alternative criteria for dissonance judgments. Tenney (1988, in Sethares 1998: 73–76) discusses five distinct ways in which the consonance and dissonance concept has been understood in music, none of which makes any direct reference to the cultural or the historical dimension of dissonance. The results of the present study suggest that in the absence of strong sensory cues, dissonance judgments of isolated harmonic intervals appear to be culturally and historically mediated. Such a conclusion is consistent with the highly varied attitudes around the world towards the roughness sensation, presented in this study. As has been demonstrated, roughness may in some cases even be considered "consonant," with roughness variations being credited as responsible for sonic, structural, semantic, and expressive aspects of musical pieces. The proposed roughness estimation model provides the means to examine empirically such claims, offering opportunities for further study.

7. Summary and Conclusions

Examination of musical instrument construction and performance practices from around the world illustrates the musical relevance of the roughness sensation and indicates that sound variations involving this sensation are found in many musical traditions. The use of rough sounds helps create a buzzing (Indian *tambura* drone) or rattling (Bosnian *ganga* singing) sonic canvas that becomes the backdrop for further musical elaboration. It permits the creation of timbral variations (Middle Eastern *mijwiz* playing) and rhythmic variations (*ganga* singing) through gradual or abrupt changes among roughness degrees. Whether such variations are explicitly sought after (as in *ganga* singing and *mijwiz* playing) or are introduced more subtly and gradually (as may be the case in the typical chord progressions/modulations of Western music), they appear to form an important part of a musical tradition's expressive vocabulary.

Models estimating the roughness degree of musical sounds have been developing since the end of the nineteenth century. Existing roughness estimation models, however, do not account for the roughness contribution of amplitude fluctuation, they often fail to capture reliably the effect of pitch register on roughness, and demonstrate a relatively low degree of agreement between predicted and observed roughness levels. It is argued that a new roughness estimation model (Vassilakis 2001) better represents the theoretical knowledge and experimental results on sensory roughness and is better fit to test hypotheses linking the roughness sensation to musical variables than are existing models.

The proposed model is compared to two earlier roughness estimation models (Helmholtz 1885; Hutchinson and Knopoff 1978), indicating several differences in prediction. For example, the proposed model estimates much lower roughness values than the other models for the major seventh and the augmented fourth intervals. The majority of differences in the predictions of the three models can be explained in terms of the different assumptions each model makes regarding the contributions of degree of amplitude fluctuation and of sound pressure level to roughness.

An experiment (Vassilakis 2001, Section 6.4.3) rating isolated harmonic intervals in terms of roughness and dissonance is discussed and the results are compared against the predictions of the three models. The proposed model demonstrates the best agreement between estimated and observed roughness, as well as between estimated roughness and observed dissonance. The results indicate that, within the Western musical tradition, the clear presence or absence of roughness in the sound of an interval dominates dissonance ratings. When the roughness is neither very large nor very small, decisions on dissonance often ignore roughness and appear to be culturally and historically mediated. Overall, dissonance ratings correlate well with roughness ratings, indicating that, in the case of isolated harmonic intervals, the sensation of roughness is the primary cue guiding dissonance judgments. The results also support the hypothesis that, in the Western musical tradition where sensory roughness is in general avoided as dissonant, the consonance hierarchy of harmonic intervals corresponds to variations in roughness degrees. Further study should include cross-cultural empirical investigations.

NOTES

1. Portions of this work were presented at the 142nd meeting of the Acoustical Society of America.

2. The author would like to thank Professors R. A. Kendall, R. W. H. Savage, A. J. Racy, and N. A. Jairazbhoy (University of California, Los Angeles, Department of Ethnomusicology) for reading early versions of this manuscript and offering valuable suggestions.

3. A *sine signal* is a signal with a sinusoidal shape. Such a signal represents the simplest type of vibration, called simple harmonic motion (similar to a free pendular motion). The wave originating from a simple harmonic motion is also represented by a sine signal and is called *sine wave*. When a sine wave with frequency and amplitude values within the auditory limits reaches the ear, it gives rise to the sensation of a *pure tone* (that is, a tone similar to the sound produced by a tuning fork or an electric sine-wave generator).

4. The term *complex tone* refers to the sensation arising from sound waves represented by complex signals. Any signal that does not have a sinusoidal shape is called *complex*. Fourier (early 1800s) proved that complex signals can be analyzed mathematically into the sum of a set of sine signals. These are called the Fourier or spectral components of a given complex signal and make up the complex signal's *spectrum*. Analysis of a complex signal into sine components is called Fourier analysis, while the reverse process, constructing a complex signal out of a set of sines, is called Fourier synthesis. For periodic signals (such as the signals corresponding to most musical sounds), the lowest frequency component is called the fundamental and all components have frequencies that are integer multiples of the frequency of the fundamental. That is, if the fundamental has frequency f, then the components have frequencies $1f, 2f, 3f, 4f$, and so forth. Such complex signals are also called harmonic; all other signals are called inharmonic. The pitch of a harmonic signal matches in frequency the frequency of the fundamental (whether or not the fundamental component is actually present in the signal's spectrum).

5. The roughness sensation is not necessarily linked to the addition of two or more tones. It can also arise from the interference among the components of a single complex tone or from performance practices in monophonic music (for example, fast vibrato, reed rattling in woodwinds, and vocal techniques). The only condition is that the resulting complex signal exhibits amplitude fluctuations within the specified range of fluctuation rates.

6. The term *combination tones* was introduced by Helmholtz in the late 1800s to describe tones that can be traced not in a vibrating source but in the combination of two or more waves originating in independent vibrating sources. A specific combination tone, the difference tone, is one of the perceptual manifestations of amplitude fluctuation. Combination tones are the products of wave interference and have significant physical origins along with physiological, neurological, and cognitive ones. The physical origins of combination tones can be attributed to the transfer characteristics of the wave propagation medium. For sound waves propagating in air, the physical origin of combination tones is based on the following asymmetry: *effective propagation velocity* (c_{ef}) > *velocity of sound in air* (c_0) in condensations and $c_{ef} < c_0$ in rarefactions (noted in 1808 by Poisson and in 1860 by Riemann, and cited in Beyer 1999: 40 and 148–149, respectively).

7. Kendall *et al.* (1999) have argued that the degree of a sound's "nasality" constitutes the primary dimension of timbre. They quantify "nasality" in terms of *spectral centroid*, a measure of the energy distribution and time-variancy in the spectrum of a complex signal. The present study considers roughness another important dimension of timbre and references an appropriate roughness measure.

8. This attitude dates back to the ancient Greeks and the Pythagorean conception of harmony. To date, no study has systematically examined the origin and history of Western tradition's deep dislike towards rough sounds.

9. Loaded with festive and ecstatic connotations, the *mijwiz* is hailed for inspiring "strong passions and exerting compelling powers and energies" (Racy 1994: 50). The buzzing, rough sound of another double-pipe, the ancient Greek *aulos*, was prominent in cult rituals (Marcuse 1975: 56).

10. The term *sensory consonance* was introduced by Plomp and Levelt (1965) to refer to consonance understood specifically as absence of roughness. In more general terms, the concept of consonance has been loaded with all kinds of associations/connotations. Similarly to timbre, consonance seems to have been a wastebasket of aesthetic and evaluative judgments in music, as well as the source of justification arguments regarding general stylistic trends or specific compositional decisions. The term "wastebasket" is used as a reference to Bergman's (1990: 93) assessment that timbre seems to be the wastebasket of all sound characteristics that cannot be placed under the labels of pitch or loudness.

11. If two sines with different frequencies f_1, f_2, ($|f_1 + f_2|/2 \gg |f_1 - f_2|/2$) and amplitudes A_1, A_2 ($A_1 \geq A_2$) are added together, the amplitude of the resulting signal will fluctuate between a maximum ($A_{max} = A_1 + A_2$) and a minimum ($A_{min} = A_1 - A_2$) value. The degree of amplitude fluctuation (AF_{degree}) is defined as the difference between the maximum and minimum amplitude values relative to the maximum amplitude value. So, $AF_{degree} = (A_{max} - A_{min})/A_{max} = 2A_2/(A_1 + A_2)$. Degree of amplitude fluctuation, therefore, depends less on the absolute and more on the relative amplitudes of interfering sines.

12. According to the proposed model, the roughness **R** of pairs of sines with frequencies f_1 & f_2 ($f_2 \geq f_1$), amplitudes A_1 & A_2 ($A_1 \geq A_2$) and equal initial phases is: $R = X^{0.1} * Y^{3.11} * Z$. $X = A_1 * A_2$, represents the dependence of roughness on intensity (amplitude of the added sines); $Y = 2A_2/(A_1 + A_2)$, represents the dependence of roughness on amplitude fluctuation degree (amplitude difference of the added sines); $Z = e^{-b1s(f2-f1)} - e^{-b2s(f2-f1)}$, represents the dependence of roughness on amplitude fluctuation rate (frequency difference of the added sines) and register (average frequency of the added sines), with $b_1 = 3.5$, $b_2 = 5.75$, $s = 0.24/(s_1 f_1 + s_2)$, $s_1 = 0.0207$, & $s_2 = 18.96$. For more details see Vassilakis (2001, Sections 6.4.1 and 6.4.2).

13. The fusion of two simultaneous tones is proportional to the degree to which the tones are heard as a single perceptual unit. According to Stumpf, fusion is the basis of consonance (Stumpf 1898 in Sethares 1998: 77).

REFERENCES

Békésy, G. von
    1960 [1989]   *Experiments in Hearing.* New York: Acoustical Society of America Press.

Bergman, A.
    1990   *Auditory Scene Analysis.* Cambridge, MA: MIT Press.

Beyer, R. T.
    1999   *Sounds of Our Times. Two Hundred Years of Acoustics.* New York: AIP Press; Springer-Verlag.

Bigand, E., Parncutt, R., and Lerdahl, F.
    1996   "Perception of musical tension in short chord sequences: The influence of harmonic function, sensory dissonance, horizontal motion, and musical training." *Perception and Psychophysics* 58: 125–141.

Campbell, M. and Greated, C.
1987   *The Musician's Guide to Acoustics*. New York: Schirmer Books.

Carlton Maley, V. Jr.
1990   *The Theory of Beats and Combination Tones, 1700–1863*. [Harvard Disserta-
                tions in the History of Science. O. Gingerich, editor]. New York: Garland
                Publishing.

Carterette, E. C., Vaughn, K., and Jairazbhoy, N. A.
1989   "Perceptual, acoustical, and musical aspects of the Tambura drone." *Music
                Perception* 7(2): 75–108.

Davies, J. B.
1978   *The Psychology of Music*. Stanford: Stanford University Press.

Dibben, N.
1999   "The perception of structural stability in atonal music: The influence of
                salience, stability, horizontal motion, pitch commonality, and dissonance."
                Music Perception 16(3): 265–294.

Fletcher, N. H. and Rossing, T. D.
1998   *The Physics of Musical Instruments*. 2nd ed. New York: Springer-Verlag.

Gadamer, H. G.
1989 [1960]   *Truth and Method*. 2nd edition. New York: Continuum. [*Wahrheit und
                Methode*, 1960. Tubingen, trans. J. Weinshamer and D. Marshall.]

Hashimoto, T. and Hatano, S.
1994   "Roughness level as a measure for estimating unpleasantness: Modification
                of roughness level by modulation frequencies." *Proceedings of the Inter-Noise
                94 Conference*. Yokohama, Japan, pp. 887-892.

Helmholtz, H. L. F.
1885 [1954]   *On the Sensations of Tone as a Physiological Basis for the Theory of Music*.
                2nd English edition. New York: Dover Publications. [*Die Lehre von den Ton-
                empfindungen*, 1877. 4th German edition, trans. A. J. Ellis.].

Hindemith, P.
1945   *The Craft of Musical Composition*. New York: Associated Music Publishers
                Inc. [4th edition,trans. A. Mendel.]

Huron, D.
1991   "Tonal consonance versus tonal fusion in polyphonic sonorities." *Music Per-
                ception* 9(2): 135–154.

Hutchinson, W. and Knopoff, L.
1978   "The acoustic component of Western consonance." *Interface* 7: 1–29.

Imaizumi, S.
1986   "Acoustic measures of roughness in pathological voice." *Journal of Phonetics*
                14 (3/4): 457–462.

Jairazbhoy, N. A.
1995   *The Rāgs of North Indian Music. Their Structure and Evolution*. 2nd ed. Bom-
                bay, India: Popular Prakashan.

Kameoka, A. and Kuriyagawa, M.
1969a   "Consonance theory, part I: Consonance of dyads." *Journal of the Acoustical
                Society of America* 45(6): 1451–1459.

1969b "Consonance theory, part II: Consonance of complex tones and its calculation method." *Journal of the Acoustical Society of America* 45(6): 1460–1469.

Kastner, M. P. and Crowder, R. G.
1990 "Perception of the major/minor distinction: IV. Emotional connotations in young children." *Music Perception* 8: 189–201.

Kendall, R. A.
2001 "Music Experiment Development System (MEDS) 2001B for Windows." Los Angeles: University of California Los Angeles, Department of Ethnomusicology, Program in Systematic Musicology.

Kendall, R. A., Carterette, E. C., and Hajda, J. M.
1999 "Perceptual and acoustical features of natural and synthetic orchestral instrument tones." *Music Perception* 16(3): 327–363.

Lin J. Y. and Hartmann, W. M.
1995 "Roughness and the critical bandwidth at low frequency." *Journal of the Acoustical Society of America* 97(5/2): 3274.

Marcuse, S.
1975 *A Survey of Musical Instruments.* New York: Harper and Row.

Nederveen, C. J.
1998 *Acoustical Aspects of Woodwind Instruments.* 2nd ed. DeKalb: Northern Illinois University Press.

Ortmann, O.
1922 "The sensorial basis of music appreciation." *Journal of Comparative Psychology* 2: 227–256.

Petroviç, A.
1977 "Ganga: A Form of Traditional Rural Singing in Yugoslavia." Unpublished Dissertation. Belfast: University of Belfast; Department of Social Anthropology.

Plomp, R.
1964 "The ear as a frequency analyzer." *Journal of the Acoustical Society of America* 36(9): 1628–1636.

Plomp, R. and Levelt, W. J. M.
1965 "Tonal consonance and critical bandwidth." *Journal of the Acoustical Society of America* 38(4): 548–560.

Pratt, C. C.
1921 "Some Qualitative Aspects of Bitonal Complexes." *American Journal of Psychology* 32: 490–515.

Pressnitzer D. and McAdams, S.
1999 "Two phase effects in roughness perception." *Journal of the Acoustical Society of America* 105(5): 2773–2782.

Pressnitzer, D., McAdams, S., Winsberg, S., and Fineberg, J.
2000 "Perception of musical tension for nontonal orchestral timbres and its relation to psychoacoustic roughness." *Perception and Psychophysics* 62 (1): 66–80.

Racy, A. J.
    1994   "A dialectical perspective on musical instruments: the East Mediterranean
                   Mijwiz." *Ethnomusicology* 38(1): 37–58.
Ricoeur, P.
    1984   *Time and Narrative, Vol. #1*. Chicago: The University of Chicago Press.
                   [Trans. K. McLaughlin & D. Pellauer.]
Sethares, W. A.
    1998   *Tuning, Timbre, Spectrum, Scale*. London: Springer-Verlag.
StatSoft, Inc.
    2000   "Statistica 5.5 for Windows." Tulsa, Oklahoma: StatSoft, Inc.
Terhardt, E.
    1974   "On the perception of periodic sound fluctuations (roughness)." *Acustica*
                   30(4): 201–213.
    1984   "The concept of musical consonance: A link between music and psychoa-
                   coustics." *Music Perception* 1(3): 276–295.
Turino, T.
    1993   *Moving Away from Silence: Music of the Peruvian Altiplano and the Experi-
                   ence of Urban Migration*. Chicago: The University of Chicago Press.
Vassilakis, P.
    2001   "Perceptual and Physical Properties of Amplitude Fluctuation and their
                   Musical Significance." Doctoral Dissertation. Los Angeles: University of Cal-
                   ifornia, Los Angeles; Systematic Musicology.
Vogel, M.
    1993   *On the Relations of Tone*. Bonn: Verlag für systematische Musikwissenschaft,
                   GmbH [Lehre von den Tonbeziehungen, 1975. Bonn, trans. V. J. Kisselbach].
Vos, J.
    1986   "Purity ratings of tempered fifths and major thirds." *Music Perception* 3(3):
                   221–258.
Vos, J. and Smoorenburg, G. F.
    1985   "Penalty for impulse noise, derived from annoyance ratings for impulse and
                   road-traffic sounds." *Journal of the Acoustical Society of America* 77(1):
                   193–201.
Zwicker, E.
    1961   "Subdivision of the audible frequency into critical bands." *Journal of the
                   Acoustical Society of America* 33(2): 248–249.
Zwicker, E., Flottorp, G., and Stevens, S. S.
    1957   "Critical band-width in loudness summation." *Journal of the Acoustical Soci-
                   ety of America* 29(5): 548–557.

Reflections on the Nature of Music Learning

FRANK HEUSER

University of California, Los Angeles

This paper presents the position that the ability to understand and perform music is not a mystifying endeavor available only to the talented, but is instead a collection of cognitive skills that may be developed to lesser or greater degrees in all people. Drawing an analogy between the von Neumann model of computer architecture and human cognition, the paper suggests that music learning might be regarded as having two distinct yet interconnected components that can be identified as: (1) the acquisition of musical information; and (2) the acquisition of the cognitive processes that permit effective use of information. This paradigm might prove useful for analyzing and informing instructional practices in music. This view suggests that the purpose of a musical education is to help individuals acquire the cognitive structures allowing a variety of interactions with music. The acquisition of such cognitive structures will enable individuals to make meaningful evaluations and decisions regarding their own involvement with music.

Members of concert and opera audiences marvel at the feats of flawless virtuosity demonstrated by world-class performing musicians. For many listeners however, the process through which the skills central to decoding, performing, and interpreting musical materials are acquired seems magical. Somehow, the process of interacting with numerous pieces of music and practicing a seemingly endless array of scales, etudes, and other technical exercises provides individuals with the ability to decode musical notation, construct the motor patterns necessary to make a composer's intentions audible, and elucidate musical meaning from the pieces performed. No wonder that the process of learning music seems mysterious. The position taken in this paper is that the ability to understand and perform music is not a mystifying endeavor that is available only to the talented, but is instead a collection of cognitive skills that can be developed to lesser or greater degrees in all people. In this view, the purpose of a musical education is to help individuals acquire the cognitive structures that will allow a variety of interactions with music. The acquisition of such cognitive structures will allow individuals to make meaningful evaluations and decisions regarding their own involvement with music.

Purpose

The purpose of this paper is to explore aspects of the multifaceted nature of music learning and present a paradigm that might be useful for analyzing and informing instructional practices in music. In this exploration, parallels are drawn between an artificial-intelligence approach to the understanding of human cognition and the processes involved in music learning and functioning. In particular, the paper makes a loose analogy between the processes involved in music learning and the von Neumann model of computer architecture. In this model, a computer uses the same random access memory to hold both data and the encoded instructions for processing that data (Stillings et. al. 1996: 22). In other words, both information (data) and the instructions to use that information (programs) are accessible to the same memory system. Although a variety of paradigms for understanding human cognition and learning are available, the von Neumann model offers a useful way of reducing the variables that frequently accompany discussions of learning into two basic components: information and the processes that allow individuals to use that information. Drawing an analogy between the von Neumann model of computer architecture and human cognition suggests that music learning might be regarded as having two distinct yet interconnected components that can be identified as: (1) the acquisition of musical information, and (2) the acquisition of the cognitive processes that permit effective use of information. For the purposes of this paper, the von Neumann model provides an entry point with which to comprehend and explain the basic processes underlying musical behavior.

This information-processing approach to understanding the nature of music learning allows those involved in music education to value the acquisition of fundamental musical knowledge as well as the development of the sophisticated processes that allows musical information to be used for a large variety of purposes and goals. If, as Elliot (1995: 56) has suggested, "our musical thinking and knowing are in our musical doing and making," then a goal of the learning process should be to provide students with the cognitive information and processes central to thinking, knowing, doing, and making. The information-processing approach to cognition adopted in this paper suggests that the efficacy of any given pedagogical vision rests with the ability of that vision to provide students with strongly stored mental representations of musical information and processes. The reason that students acquire and become adept at using these mental representations is so that they might become proficient at making decisions about music and therefore able to determine their own future musical involvement and values. By considering both the knowledge necessary for, and the processes underlying, a wide range of human musical behaviors, a view of music learning can be developed that reflects the totality of musical experiences and encourages students to mature into musically literate citizens. This paper will explore the representational nature of music learning, provide examples of how mental representations are used in music, examine the traditional categorization of knowledge into separate domains, and present a framework statement regarding music learning.

The Representational Foundations of Musical Responsiveness

Insightful musical awareness, whether expressed through thoughtful performance, aesthetic responsiveness, or critical evaluation, is the direct result of activity in the human cognitive system. Sophisticated cognitive processes in any area of expertise are dependent on an individual's ability to access a rich library of discipline-specific information (Ericsson et al. 1991: 363–406). In music, highly developed thinking and performance skills require immediate and fluent functional access to a large variety of mental representations regarding musical patterns, relationships, understandings, and actions (Sloboda 1985: 3–5). Although a precise definition is difficult (Guttenplan 1994: 441), mental representations are defined in this paper as the abstractions one develops of information and actions that are stored in long-term memory in the cognitive system and available for immediate and future use.

Rudimentary mental representations of musical information are acquired through the process of enculturation, that is, the everyday encounters an individual has with music. These representations can be refined, strengthened, and enhanced through formal education. The instructional process allows previously acquired musical knowledge to be assessed and representations already stored in memory to be refined. It also provides opportunities to strengthen and to expand a person's library of the mental representations central to music making and understanding. Formal instruction will acquaint students with previously unknown musical materials and help them create mental representations of this information.

An example of how musical functioning develops in the absence of formal refinement as well as an indication of how instruction might aid this process comes from the work of Davidson (1994). He found that in musically untrained children between the ages of three and six, tonal structures are represented in the form of contour schemes rather than through scales, as happens in students with formal musically training. These contour schemes are seemingly associated with age, and they function as framing intervals within which children sing songs. The framing intervals increase from approximately the interval of a third at the age of three to the interval of a sixth at age six. Adults without formal training tend to continue using contour schemes rather than developing and employing an internalized representation of tonal space. This is evidenced by the inability of many adults to negotiate the octave leap in "Happy Birthday." This implies that the process of acquiring, refining, and strengthening mental representations of tonal information occurs through carefully constructed and repeated instructional engagements with musical materials rather than simple exposure to music.

Types of Mental Representations in Music

The information required for informed interactions with music is stored in the cognitive system as mental representations of musical structures, styles, actions, events, and contexts. Meaningful instruction will provide individuals with abstractions of musical information in each of these categories of knowledge. However, the depth to which such information is represented will vary from student to student. For those whose primary interaction with music will be as listeners, learning to recognize basic musical structures and styles might be a reasonable goal. Others, such as those with professional aspirations in music, will acquire the ability to aurally identify and label complex tonal structures, develop increasingly sophisticated levels of musical discrimination, and make the refined movements necessary for performance. Regardless of the level of sophistication, meaningful interactions and involvement with music require the acquisition and refinement of mental representations of musical information and processes. For those concerned with the process of music instruction, an understanding of possible meanings of the terms musical structures, styles, actions, events, and contexts is essential.

Mental representations of musical structures include, of course, the tonal and rhythmic building blocks central to a culturally specific music system. However, the concept of musical structures should not be limited to tonal and rhythmic materials. This concept of musical structures is in essence multi-dimensional and should include a wide range of sonic configurations. These might include, for example, traditional and innovative combinations of instrumental timbres and different or unique tuning systems. An example of how the concept of structure might be expanded is provided by tuba player Roger Bobo (1961), who describes implied differences in the function of the low brass section in two symphonies of Tchaikovsky. The primary role of the trombones and tuba in the Fourth Symphony is to reinforce low strings and provide a massive wall of dark, round, supporting sound. In contrast, the Sixth Symphony often requires these players to function in the capacity of a quartet that at one moment serves in a solo capacity and at another blends subtly with other voices. The ability of musicians to realize such fine nuances in their performance and of listeners to make discriminations of this nature and recognize deeper meanings in repeated hearings of a work is dependent on a rich supply of multidimensional structural mental representations.

Information regarding musical styles includes both general and specific mental representations about particular stylistic periods, genres, composers, and artists. The strongly represented abstractions of a specific composer's style allows one to recognize a previously unheard work as being of that composer, or allows a performer to successfully improvise in the style of a great creative artist. In *The Classical Style*, Charles Rosen (1972) eloquently reminds us that the distinctions between structure and style are frequently blurred in the creative work of outstanding composers. Developing the ability to recognize both the basic nature as well as the interrelatedness of these concepts is fundamental to the task of insightful music teaching. The strength and depth to which a wide variety of structural and stylistic representations are acquired, developed, stored, and made readily available to individuals will, in large part, determine their future sophistication and flexibility in musical settings.

Actions, events, and contexts are also terms that are interrelated and carry a variety of meanings. The degree to which each is developed depends on the aspirations of the students one is teaching. Actions that might be developed in all students may be as simple as learning to maintain a pulse and sense differences between strong and weak beats so that the recognition of meter is facilitated. Actions may also refer to the full range of fine motor skills and motor programs required to manipulate artistically the voice or an instrument. Individuals aspiring to perform at high levels must develop strong representations of the entire range of motor actions required for artistic and insightful performance. Strong representation is necessary so that the cognitive system can instantly access abstractions of physical motions, thereby constructing and adjusting motor programs in real time during the process of music making. Although the term "events" might initially suggest musical presentations of varying types, in this framework it is expanded to include all aspects of the musical experience, including practice, drill, lessons, and analytical study. Developing abstractions by applying drill in a mindful rather than mindless manner (Howard 1991) or using the lessons of analysis to help clarify musical structure during performance are two examples of an expanded understanding of this term. Mental representations of the many contexts—historical, cultural, and social—that become attached to various aspects of the musical process allow individuals to understand and value the variety of roles that music might play in any given society. In short, the terms actions, events, and contexts guide the acquisition of representations surrounding the entire realm of possible musical activities.

The Cognitive, Affective, and Psychomotor Domains

Although attempts are regularly made to categorize intelligent behavior into separate spheres of knowledge, the cognitive, affective, and psychomotor domains of human understanding are interrelated. Because the experiences and decisions made in one realm will influence the knowledge and understandings available in the others, we must approach the term "cognitive activity" with caution. Rather than restrict our understanding of this term to highly intellectual linear thought and verbal understandings, cognitive activity or thought processes should be interpreted in a much broader manner. Even though we may use verbal information to enhance our understanding of music, it is essential to realize that cognitive activity in music takes place in the medium of music. The nonverbal essence of musical thought rests in the process of pattern comparison (Fiske 1993). This universal aspect of music cognition allows us to assess if a given musical pattern is the same as, a variation of, or different from another pattern. In this regard, the process of music learning should improve efficiency at making increasingly refined comparisons in the nonverbal thought patterns of music by equipping individuals with a rich mental library of musical information and cognitive processing tools. Although verbal descriptions and understandings might enhance aspects of music cognition, recognizing that the evaluation and decision-making process takes place in the medium of music acknowledges the value and nonverbal nature of the art form.

Understanding that meaningful affective responses depend on learned cognitive information and processes provides insight into the role education can play in this area of musical understanding. The culturally relevant affective meanings that accompany a wide variety of musics must be learned in order to make increasingly subtle and sophisticated responses. A reminder of how appropriate affective responses are dependent upon learned cognitive information is provided by Sloboda (1985: 2), who describes how the uninformed listener might mistake a desperately sad Greek folk song for a jolly melody because of its presentation in the major mode. Guidance and experience in developing culturally appropriate affective responses to a large variety of musics provides students with models of how to evaluate musical materials and make appropriate decisions.

Psychomotor evaluations and decisions are dependent on a strongly represented library of musical as well as motor skill information. An individual must have a clear mental concept of an intended musical outcome before the motor plans permitting performance can be constructed and executed by the cognitive system (Halsband et al. 1994). During performance, subtle inflections in the communicative intent of the musician are made possible through the ability to rapidly evaluate musical structures. Conversely, the extent to which musicians develop the capacity to make rapid evaluations and decisions concerning musical structures and styles affects their ability to perform in a musically convincing manner. Moreover, the refinement of psychomotor skills also affects the understanding of cognitive and affective issues in the music with which one is interacting. The mastering of a new position on the cello not only expands one's technical proficiency, but in fact demands new ways of thinking about music previously learned and expands one's understanding of the affective possibilities of any given piece (Davidson 1994). Competence at making synthesized cognitive, affective, and psychomotor evaluations and decisions concerning musical information is dependent on the ability to access functionally a stored mental library of musical information. The educational process should create and reinforce mental representations of musical information and processes to such a depth that both can be rapidly accessed and synthesized for a variety of purposes when an individual engages in musical activities. Teachers must be aware that differing personal inclinations and aspirations mean that students will acquire, refine, and strengthen their abstractions of musical information to varying degrees of depth. For example, the musical needs of someone who listens to, rather than performs, music might require that tonal information only be developed to a depth that allows the individual to recognize and label the major or minor modality of a triad. A performer, on the other hand, might need to represent that information to a depth that allows sophisticated decisions be made regarding the exact placement of the third within the interval of a perfect fifth in different tuning situations. In this scenario, tonal information interacts with strongly developed psychomotor processes so that the fine adjustments necessary for in-tune performance become highly proceduralized, and the evaluation and decision-making process is instantaneous.

This example illustrating the interconnectedness of tonal and motor skill information is a reminder that the cognitive, affective, and psychomotor domains of musical understanding are not mutually exclusive. Instead, these domains can be viewed as realms of knowledge that are constantly changing in content and often fluctuating in meaning. Various portions of these realms frequently overlap, thereby influencing each other's content. Viewing these domains in such a manner permits teachers to make curricular modifications based on the educational needs and aspirations of the learner. Instructional strategies will be adopted for their ability to provide students with strength and depth in their mental abstractions of musical information and processes. In this view, music education is neither static nor prescribed. Emphasis is placed on helping individuals acquire the necessary information to refine their evaluation and decision-making skills to become active participants in shaping their own musical understandings and values.

A Framework Defining the Nature of Music Learning

The forgoing suggests that music learning is representational in nature. The paper presents an information-processing perspective on human cognition that values both the musical information and the processes necessary to manipulate meaningfully and understand that information. Additionally, the paper explores the multifaceted nature as well as the interconnectedness and complexity of the components of music learning and suggests that the acquisition, refinement, and development of mental representations of musical information and processes are the central concern of the music-learning process. The potential complexity of the mental representations required for musical functioning and the sophisticated nature of the relationships between those various representations becomes evident in the following statement defining a representational framework of music education.

Music learning involves the process of acquiring, refining, and strengthening an individual's mental representations of musical structures, styles, actions, events, and contexts so that the individual is able to access functionally those representations, thereby becoming increasingly adept at synthesizing cognitive, affective, and psychomotor information and thus facilitating a variety of evaluations and decisions concerning musical involvement and values.

The statement delineates relationships between specific types of information and the mental processes (accessing, synthesizing, evaluating, and deciding) that are developed and refined through education. This can serve as a framework for guiding instruction and designing curricula. Careful application of this framework allows each component to be isolated and emphasized during the learning process, yet remain interrelated to the others. This representational framework of music learning values equally the process of knowledge acquisition, the skills required to use that knowledge, and the refinement of evaluation and decision-making abilities. Like all frameworks, this statement requires thoughtful application to avoid a narrow and uninformed interpretation that could result in abuses. However, by regarding the terms used, as well as the relationships between the components in the framework, in the most comprehensive ways possible, this statement might allow for a better understanding of the process of music learning.

The framework reminds us that the cognitive, affective, and psychomotor information central to musical understandings is interrelated and that music instruction must be structured so that students develop their abilities to access functionally and synthesize this information and thereby become increasingly adept at making meaningful musical decisions. By suggesting that the underpinnings of diverse musical understandings are representational in nature, the framework implies that the efficacy of any given pedagogical vision is related to the ability of that vision to help individuals acquire and develop strongly represented abstractions of musical information and processes. By exploring the question, "What information and cognitive processes does a person need to know in order to be aesthetically responsive, to evaluate music criti-cally, or to perform insightfully," teachers will become better equipped to provide their students with the various types of mental representations required for insightful musi-cal responsiveness.

Identification of the specific types of mental representations that underlie and form the foundation for meaningful musical decision making will directly affect the decisions teachers make regarding curricula. When issues of foundational knowledge are considered, the selection of specific instructional materials and techniques might be guided by some of the following questions:

1. What musical information and processes are necessary to produce the identi-fied educational outcome in students?
2. Which musical materials will most effectively develop the identified mental representations in students?
3. To what extent will the mental representations of the selected information and processes be developed?
4. Which teaching methods will most efficiently develop an individual's func-tional access to those representations?
5. What learning environment will encourage individuals to practice accessing acquired mental representations for a variety of purposes?
6. How do the different aspirations and backgrounds of individual students affect the selection of pedagogical materials and setting of educational goals?

The suggested representational framework of music learning provides guidance for instruction, offers both focus and flexibility, and allows music teachers to make highly reasoned curricular decisions.

This view emphasizing the acquisition of information and processes should not be confused with educational philosophies that emphasize teaching a carefully pre-scribed core curriculum for the purpose of promoting universal common values (Hirsch 1988). Although emphasizing an individual's need to develop access to specific forms of information, a representational view of music education differs from core-value curricula in that there is no predefined list of essential musical information that all students must assimilate. In this representational framework, consideration is given to the differing aspirations, backgrounds, and needs of individual students, and the process of music learning becomes generative rather than prescriptive. Of course, in order to teach in this manner, music educators must have extremely rich backgrounds and be acutely aware of the nature of music instruction. They must also be capable of designing instructional programs that allow for individual differences and encourage development of multiple meanings. In this representation view of learning, the concept of sequential instruction changes from that of a rigidly predefined order of events and actions to the generatively constructed preparation of the student for lifelong learning. This is also a departure from teaching a canon, Western or otherwise, in that emphasis is on acquisition of fundamental knowledge and processes rather than on acquiring a rigidly prescribed body of information. A representational perspective can provide students with the skills required to access knowledge so that they become capable of intelligently exploring a variety of views about the nature and value of music as well as the variety of meanings possible from musical experiences.

This paper also suggests that a major outcome of music instruction is the development of an individual's ability to make meaningful evaluations and decisions regarding his or her own interactions with music. There are, of course, a number of other very desirable outcomes of music learning that might guide instruction and curriculum development. However, by acknowledging the relationships between fundamental components of musical understanding, this representational framework may offer insight as to why music is an essential component of the human psyche and must be taught in our schools. In this model, music is seen as an area of activity in which many modes of human cognition intersect in a variety of ways. In music, verbal and nonverbal modes of knowing directly and actively reinforce one another as they are called upon to examine and express the many ineffable aspects of human understanding. This juxtaposition and interaction of the analytical, affective, and psychomotor aspects of human knowing and doing might be one of the reasons music is such a powerful mode of cognition and so essential to the human spirit.

The presented information-processing model and representational framework of music learning emphasize acquiring the specific information and the cognitive processing skills that will allow for musical independence, aesthetic responsiveness, and the development of critical evaluation skills. Such a framework for evaluating the instructional process is seemingly simple, as it reduces music learning to two fundamental issues: the acquisition of information and the refinement of cognitive processes. The simplicity of this framework allows teachers to examine the extent to which any given educational methodology or philosophy helps students acquire essential information and processes. Additionally, the framework does not offer an instructional vision based on a single characteristic of music that might be most worth knowing. Instead, it suggests that the purpose of education is to provide students with a rich supply of strongly represented abstractions of musical information and processes so that individuals become capable of exploring for themselves what might be most worth knowing in music. The final outcome will be an individual capable of accessing musical information in a variety of ways for a variety of multiple outcomes. Such an individual will be empowered to make informed and intelligent decisions regarding their own musical future and values.

REFERENCES

Bobo, Roger
    1961   "Tuba: A Word of Many Meanings." *Instrumentalist* 16 (April): 73–76.

Davidson, Lyle
    1994   "Songsinging by Young and Old: A Developmental Approach to Music." In Rita Aiello and John Sloboda, eds., *Musical Perceptions.* New York: Oxford University Press, pp. 99–130.

Elliot, David J.
    1995   *Music Matters: A New Philosophy of Music Education.* New York: Oxford University Press.

Ericsson, K. A., Krampe, R. T., and Tesch-Romer, C.
    1991   "The Role of Deliberate Practice in the Acquisition of Expert Performance." *Psychological Review* 100: 363–406.

Aesthetic and Philosophical Perspectives

Aesthetic and Philosophical Perspectives in Systematic Musicology

ROGER W. H. SAVAGE

University of California, Los Angeles

From a contemporary vantage point, systematic musicology appears as an arcane designation for a research field dispersed across multiple scholarly disciplines. In the nineteenth century, the term "systematic" was intended to distinguish this field from historical musicology's methods and subject matter. Ensuing debates over systematic musicology's identity, coherence, and disciplinary integrity pitted systematic principles against historical ones. This debate defined systematic musicology's intellectual reach in opposition to historical inquiry. The disciplinary umbrella uniting disparate disciplines ranging from the sociology and psychology of music to philosophical aesthetics derived its legitimacy from the field's attempts to define its common methods and procedures. As a result, the concern to identify systematic musicology's "systematic" nature eclipsed its dependence upon the history through which it attained its disciplinary autonomy.

The situation in which we currently find ourselves calls into question the distinction between systematic and historical inquiry, which Guido Adler codified in the nineteenth century. Postmodern deconstructions of meta-theory shatter the pretence of unifying systematic musicology's multiple disciplines under a single methodological or epistemological rubric. More critically still, by acknowledging the insight advanced through phenomenological hermeneutics, namely that the methods we use to extend the boundaries of our knowledge are themselves historically conditioned, we foreground the reliance of research upon the scholarly and intellectual traditions to which it contributes. This insight confronts the social and human sciences with their role in contributing to our understanding of who we are as social beings, political agents, and historical actors. The reflexive relation between advances in our knowledge and the cultivation of our self-understanding gains a new purchase on thought with postmodernity's receding political, intellectual and institutional hold. Recognizing this relation situates knowledge and reason on the cusp of a historical interlude whose "postpostmodern" designation marks the passing of postmodernity. However, this moment is not without risk. In the aftermath of postmodern destructions of meta-theory, the retrenchment of objective ideals blocks the path of reflection on our relation to our subject matter. Conversely, the hermeneutical path indicated by this reflection on the condition of our knowledge renounces all methodological certitude and instead acknowledges that the histories that affect our understanding inform the questions that we ask. This hermeneutical rehabilitation of the human sciences transfigures systematic musicology's traditional underpinnings. In an age of hermeneutical reason, systematic musicology's separation from historical musicology is the trace of a struggle to legitimate a field of research whose autonomy and disciplinary integrity depended upon its fictitious suprahistorical [*überhistorische*] nature.

The turn toward hermeneutically informed research distinguishes systematic musicology's contemporary philosophical arm from the quest for an epistemologically unified field. This philosophical arm intersects the field's historic concerns with fundamental issues of music's meaning, its power to communicate, and the social and cultural circumstances surrounding its production and reception. Yet, its reflexive relation to the history affecting it proscribes the search for ultimate foundations. This reflexive relation illuminates the limit of systematic inquiry within the field's philosophical purview. Bound to the history of the questions and methods that condition it, systematic research is as much an inquiry into the hidden presuppositions that inform these questions and methods as it is research that pushes back the boundaries of our knowledge. Because such knowledge corresponds to the situation of every researcher who finds that the disciplinary methods and perspectives she or he inherited are no longer adequate, this knowledge is invariably partial and incomplete. This historical condition and contingency attests to the impossibility of a system-building enterprise that would be perfectly complete. Attuned to this insight, systematic musicology's philosophical reach stretches toward understanding music's significance as a human phenomenon in the light of a received history of answers and questions.

Philosophical research's reflexive relation to this received history evinces a correlative feature that brings systematic musicology's hermeneutical dimension to the fore. The explanations we give of music's meaning, its culturally embedded significance, and its critical and social value also affect our understanding of ourselves and of the traditions that comprise our subject matter. The practice of reflexivity in ethnomusicology and anthropology verifies the fundamental problem affecting all human and social sciences. For these sciences, there is no methodological objectivity comparable to that of the natural sciences. Every explanation is at the same time an interpretation that adds to the intellectual and practical traditions on which it draws and to which it refers. The crisis of representation, which anthropology and ethnomusicology encountered in the 1980s, intensified the paradox that the ethnographer confronts when, in representing others, she or he is involved with her or his subjects through asymmetrical power relations. By foregrounding the role power plays in different social formations, anthropology's engagement with this crisis illumines critical deficiencies within traditional ethnographic modes of representation. This crisis therefore opens a path for reflecting not only upon ethnography's dependence upon the representations a culture gives itself through its signs and works, but also upon interpretation's role in the formation and handing down of traditions. Systematic musicology's practical interest in music's power as a cultural work intersects with ethnography at the point where the latter encounters the hermeneutical condition evinced by the crisis that calls ethnography to the task of self-reflection.

The concern with music's cultural power is a centrifugal force that extends across the field's transdisciplinary researches. By transecting the nebula of aesthetic, social, and political issues and positions that stem from critical social theory and cultural studies, the themes of music's cultural efficacy and its mode of being contribute to developing a systematic approach. The critique of music's aesthetic autonomy stands at the center of this nebula. Contemporary music criticism shares ethnomusicology's suspicion of the formalist dogma that music is a self-contained entity free of the social or cultural meanings that bind it to real-life contexts and conditions. However, this suspicion occludes the effects of Kant's subjectivization of aesthetics in separating art from reality. Music criticism and ethnomusicology accede to these effects when, in contesting the musical work's isolation from reality, they transpose the aesthetic doctrine of imitation onto the social plane. This transposition operates within the schema that Kant's subjectivization of aesthetics inaugurated. The paradox that aesthetics might serve emancipatory as well as ideological interests confounds this reversal by identifying music's opposition to reality as both productive and dissembling. In view of this paradox, the question of music's political significance therefore emerges only at the end of the detour through a critique of the phenomenon of ideology and of Kant's subjectivization of aesthetics.

The papers in the part of this volume devoted to systematic musicology's critical reach extend the field's boundaries by drawing upon different critical, historical, aesthetic, and philosophical resources. In her article, Angeles Sancho-Velázquez confronts critiques of musical formalism with the history of the work's aesthetic autonomy. For her, the formalist concept of the work that has come under attack impoverishes the Romantic heritage of the work's temporally dynamic character. Early nineteenth-century musical practice and aesthetic ideas evince proto-phenomenological understandings that conflict with formalist precepts. These precepts subordinate the Romantic legacy to a formalist concept of the work that ratifies the *Werktreue* principle of compliance with the score. By recovering the richness of Romantic understandings, Sancho-Velázquez advances a more nuanced concept of a work's autonomy in which music's distance from reality is also the condition of its socially and culturally productive character. In this way, she confronts the impasse of reducing aesthetics to ideology with precedents that prefigure the hermeneutical recovery of music's social and cultural efficacy.

Lillis Ó Laoire's article on Gaelic music and song aesthetics among Gaelic-speaking Tory Islanders examines the metaphoricity of the world disclosed by the language the Islanders use to describe and evaluate sung performances. By drawing upon Hans-Georg Gadamer's insight that language discloses the significance of a work's metaphorical usage in advance of conceptual analyses' abstractions, Ó Laoire reflects upon how the Islander's use of their Irish language reveals a world where dance and song attest to the people's will to endure. Preparations for the dance reflect the desire [*dúil*] to achieve a big night by keeping up the heat [*teas*]. This heat's metaphorical significance extends to close relations among people who, by assuming "responsibility for each other's well being are considered to be 'warm to one another' [*te dá chéile*]." Consequently, the physical heat created by the number of the dance's participants is a symbolic representation of an ideal community that celebrates the mutual responsibility and interdependence of its individual members. For Tory Islanders, a song's right [*ceart*] performance achieves the proper "shape" [*cuma*] and "skin" or "finish" [*craiceann*] for expressing feelings that unite the communities in shared remembrances and expectations. By uncovering a matrix of metaphorical understandings, Ó Laoire's ethnography uncovers abundantly nuanced meanings within cultural practices that embody this community's self-affirmation within a changing world.

Brana Mijatovic's study of popular music in the former Yugoslavia examines the contested political terrain of Serbian history under the Milosevic regime. By identifying two competing appropriations of Serbian traditions, she demonstrates how turbo-folk and the singer-songwriter Djordje Balasevic's pop music by turn supported and subverted Milosevic's nationalist political agenda. Mijatovic relates turbo-folk's and this pop music's social and cultural significance within the former Yugoslavia to Gadamer's insight into the effects of tradition and history on a community's self-understanding. Turbo-folk, which advanced the regime's aims by glamorizing violence and nationalist extremism, promoted an understanding of Serbian supremacy. Conversely, Mijatovic demonstrates how Balasevic's music served as a catalyst for political opposition through creating a community of resistance. Through examining turbo-folk's and Balasevic's cultivation of conflicting allegiances, moral ideals, and feelings of solidarity, Mijatovic reveals the intimate relation between popular music's meaning and the occasions of its performance.

Paul Attinello explores the aesthetic and cultural implications of graphic notation. In his reflections on the hieroglyphic features of Bussotti's *pièces de chair II*, Attinello questions the precept that notation offers a transparent medium for musical communication. Through challenging the conventional wisdom of music histories and theories that graphic scores are peripheral to mainstream compositional practices, he argues that postmodern conditions favor the return of hieroglyphs and ideograms. Bussotti's theatrical *pièces de chair II* deconstructs modernist precepts by foregrounding intensely physical, erotic elements. By transgressing modernist proscriptions, this graphic score erases the difference between musical and extramusical elements. Attinello argues that by expanding a musical code that has been impoverished through its use as a notational tool, hieroglyphic gestures augment conventional musical signs with visual supplements. Consequently, hieroglyphic writing inscribes music's seductive sensuality in the margins of traditional notion.

My contribution to this volume confronts postmodern musicology's renunciation of formalist aesthetics with the effective history of Kant's subjectivization of aesthetics. Kant's transcendental justification of taste inaugurated the schema of art's separation from reality by reducing the sense of reality shared by a historical community [*sensus communis*] to a subjective principle. Hence he denied taste any importance as a mode of knowledge by divorcing aesthetic judgments from their surrounding cultural ethos. Critical musicology's rejection of formalist aesthetics neglects the effects of the history stemming from Kant's radical subjectivization of aesthetics. In my article, I argue that Theodor Adorno's two-fold concept of art foregrounds the impossibility of overcoming the opposition between music and social reality without confronting this history. Adorno's concept of art as an aesthetically autonomous entity and a social fact runs aground on the performative contradiction of an art whose truth depends on the work's antithetical relation to social reality. Yet, by identifying music's distance from reality as the condition of its truth, Adorno's critical theory sets music criticism on the path toward a hermeneutics of the musical work.

These articles' explorations into the history of the idea of music's aesthetic autonomy, hieroglyphic notation, conflicting appropriations of tradition, and metaphorical evaluations of song performance push back the boundaries of music analysis, criticism, and ethnography. Each responds to theoretical, critical, and interpretative challenges arising from the confluence of multidisciplinary discourses. Hence each in its own way augments systematic musicology's transdisciplinary inquiries. These inquiries are no longer constrained by institutional borders that separate musicology from music theory, or that divide systematic musicology and ethnomusicology. Research that transgresses disciplinary boundaries in order to understand better how the music we describe, analyze, and critique affects our world is systematic in its philosophical stance. This research, which is both reflexive and critical, enlarges both our knowledge of our subject matter and our knowledge of ourselves.

The Roots of Autonomous Music: Rethinking Autonomy Before and After Formalism

ANGELES SANCHO-VELÁZQUEZ
California State University, Fullerton

The idea that musical works are autonomous wholes detached from social and cultural contexts has been under criticism for some time now (McClary 1991, Goehr 1992, Small 1998). Autonomy has been identified with the formalist reduction of music to self-enclosed objects, and with the concurrent aestheticist tenet that the meaning and value of a work of art lies exclusively in itself. The attack on this formalist concept of autonomy constitutes an important development that has helped to unveil the ideological and practical trappings of formalist and aestheticist positions. First, the claim that musical works are absolutely autonomous, and hence have universal and absolute value, disguised the fact that music can embody ideological contents. Second, the identification of the autonomy of music with total detachment from social and cultural contexts resulted in a notion of art as exclusively decorative and ultimately irrelevant. The critique of the absolute autonomy of music has thus opened up avenues to argue for the cultural and social relevance of music.

This critique, however, has also made any concept of autonomy suspect, with the ironic consequence of putting at risk the very cultural and social significance of music. This is so, because a radical elimination of the idea of autonomy invariably leads to theoretical stances from which it is impossible to argue for the significance of music, and art in general, beyond the mere task of imitating reality. Thus, the present essay partakes of criticisms of the idea of the absolute autonomy of music, but it also proposes the recovery of some sense of autonomy with respect to a social context without loosing sight of music's necessary ties to this context. This recovery, I argue, would prevent the problematic conflation of two distinct areas of inquiry—aesthetics and ideology critique. If a musical work is conceived of as absolutely autonomous, it is implied that the work has no ties to social and cultural contexts; but if it is thought of as absolutely dependent on these realities, then it follows that music could not add anything to them, or challenge them in any meaningful way. A radical critique of autonomy, therefore, in the end reproduces basic problems introduced by the idea of total autonomy: these two opposed positions eliminate the possibility of thinking about music as a creative activity able both to enrich and contest the world from within which it emerged.

In order to escape this theoretical impasse, it is necessary first to extricate the concept of autonomy from a formalist concept of the work with which it has generally been identified. Can music be "autonomous" and, at the same time, culturally significant? Can music be, to a certain extent, independent from its social context and, nevertheless, have links to it? Twentieth-century philosophers working within the Continental tradition have offered theories of art that lay the foundation for elaborating such a possibility. Theories such as those of Theodor Adorno (1989, 1997) and Paul Ricoeur (1984, 1985, 1988) propose nonformalist approaches to art that establish art's cultural roots and that, at the same time, defend the concept of the autonomy of the aesthetic. But my aim here is not to discuss these theoretical positions or suggest how they could be applied to contemporary music scholarship. Instead, I want to argue that these approaches, though introducing crucial theoretical innovations, have important precedents in the history of Western aesthetic ideas and performance practice. The Western musical tradition is much more diverse and richer than the notions of it that we have inherited from the late nineteenth century. Recovering some of the richness of past aesthetic ideas and musical practices may prove to be a powerful means to open up the scope of contemporary reflection on music.

The aesthetic ideas and musical practices of the early nineteenth century show an understanding of music that is grounded in a sense of autonomy, but that does not relegate art to an isolated sphere of the aesthetic. In order to make this point I will discuss three aspects of the early Romantic period that, in my view, have been obscured by accounts of Romanticism that do not differentiate between different stylistic and aesthetic phases within nineteenth-century music. These three aspects are: (1) the nonformalist, phenomenological musical aesthetics of idealist philosophers and Romantic authors; (2) the open, flexible approaches to performance practice in the Romantic period; and (3) the critical and utopian significance of the organicist aesthetics of Romanticism.[1]

In entitling this article "The Roots of Autonomous Music," I have sought to refer both to the historical roots of the term around the turn of the nineteenth century, and to the social and cultural roots of autonomous music in the moment of its inception. My overall aim is to show that the idea of autonomous music was not originally associated with formalist musical aesthetics, rigid performance practices, or aestheticist views of art and life. These were later developments associated with autonomous music, but not derivative of it. The Romantic concept of autonomous art was grounded on an organicist model, according to which works of art were independent in the sense of being self-regulated. This self-regulation, however, did not amount to isolation, since the organicist model also depended on the Romantic metaphysical tenet of the unity of all organisms. Organicist theories of art, furthermore, were a response to the threats of the rapidly advancing mechanization of the means of production. The autonomy of organicist art was, I will argue, a form of resistance to new social realities perceived as oppressive, and it had, therefore, a critical and utopian function.

The contemporary challenges to formalism and the project of analyzing musical works from perspectives of ideology critique need not renounce a certain sense of autonomy—a "phenomenological autonomy," as we will see. In the end, it is this sense of autonomy what gives its full force to the idea that music is culturally and socially relevant.

"Not Merely a Work of Art": A Romantic Phenomenological Understanding of Autonomous Music

> The resulting work of art has a quite peculiar attraction, because we have present before us not merely a work of art, but the actual production of one.
>
> G. F. W. Hegel

Lydia Goehr (1992) has argued that around the turn of the nineteenth century there emerged a new concept of music as autonomous creation with respect to its social context. According to Goehr, after centuries of a performance-oriented musical practice, perfectly completed works became, around 1800, the focus of musical activity. Music, now regarded as a fine art, was increasingly understood in terms of finished compositions whose significance was exclusively aesthetic and not attached to social function. Musical works, Goehr claims, aspired to the status of artifacts produced in the other fine arts, which were beginning to be displayed in museums for the sole purpose of aesthetic contemplation. In music, this meant the emergence of fixed compositions and of the performance ideal of *Werktreue*, or perfect compliance with the score.

As Goehr shows, the emphasis in the nineteenth century on the "work-concept" was inseparable from the process of formation of the Western canon and the idea of "serious" or classical music. Goehr has thus identified an important phenomenon brought about by the process of formalization of Western music: the nineteenth-century reduction of the broad category of "music" to the narrow formalist category of "works"—that is to say, static, self-contained structures—and the concomitant performance ideal of *Werktreue*. But in arguing that these developments coalesced around 1800, Goehr has downplayed the significance of a period in which the concept of autonomy was compatible with an open and flexible approach to the interpretation of works, and, consistent with this, with a concept of work that was more phenomenological than formalist. The turn towards formalism and *Werktreue* did not occur until later in the century with the collapse of Romanticism, decades after musical works had began to be considered autonomous creations.[2]

The relationship between the Romantic concept of autonomy and the formalist tenet that musical value lies exclusively in the musical structures might at first seem obvious. Goehr herself associates the emergence of the concept of autonomy around 1800 with the rise of formalism. She cites Hegel and Schelling to illustrate the formalist view that music, now independent from social function, is "intelligible not because it refers to something outside of itself, but because it has an internal structural coherence" (Goehr 1992: 155). Hegel's and Schelling's ideas of form, however, had little to do with the musical formalism that developed in the second half of the nineteenth century, exemplified in its early stages by Eduard Hanslick's ideas. For Hanslick, "form" referred to a static structure that is permanent in music.[3] Hegel, on the contrary, associated "form" with the idea of a dynamic and developing force whose relevance lies not in its permanence, but rather in its function of giving shape to the fleeting life of spirit.

For Hegel, the most important role of music was to express the inner free life of the soul. "Music," he wrote in the *Aesthetics*, "takes as its subject-matter the subjective inner life itself, with the aim of presenting itself, not as an external shape or as an objectively existing work, but as that inner life" (Hegel 1991 [1835], vol. 2: 909). Hegel's definition of the aim of music as the expression of inner life in its freedom and as something clearly distinct from the presentation of "an objectively existing work," illustrates the difference between the concept of aesthetic autonomy underlying early nineteenth-century aesthetics and the later emphasis on the work as object and on the ideal of objective performance associated with it. For Hegel, in other words, the autonomy of music was not associated with a finished product (the formalist notion of "form"), but with the act of giving shape to the artist's inner life (the phenomenological notion of "forming").

The correct aesthetic attitude toward music was also for Hegel quite different from the detached contemplation of a beautiful object-like piece associated with formalist positions. In fact, Hegel privileged the experience of witnessing the production of a work of art over the contemplation of a finished, static product. When the musical interpreter has "true genius," he wrote, he can offer the listener the opportunity to witness not "merely a work of art but the actual production of one" (quoted above, Hegel 1991 [1835], vol. 2: 957). This statement expresses a conception of music radically different from the formalist views of music that are still prevalent as Christopher Small (1998: 4) has recently denounced: "what is valued is not the action of art, not the act of creating, and even less that of perceiving and responding, but the created art object itself."

Hegel's emphasis on the musical activity of forming over the final result, as well as on the idea that sound, like inner life itself, is an eminently temporal phenomenon, makes his musical aesthetics exemplary of a proto-phenomenological approach to music that preceded the advent of musical formalism. Hegel's phenomenological stance allows him to consider improvised flights from the written work an acceptable musical practice. He writes: "the self-reposing soul of the executant artist abandons itself to its outpouring and in it he displays his inventive genius, his heart's deep feeling, his mastery in execution and, so long as he proceeds with spirit, skill, and grace, he may even interrupt the melody with jokes, caprices, and virtuosity, and surrender to the modes and suggestions of the moment" (Hegel 1991 [1835], vol. 2: 957). These improvised interruptions that would be considered artistic aberrations by formalist critics have room in Hegel's appraisal of music because for him the concept of musical form was fundamentally temporal. Because Hegel did not understand musical form as static structure but as a forming *process*, the artistic inclusion of an improvised passage meant to him not the disruption of a fixed whole, but rather, a creative addition to an unfolding whole.

Far from Hegelian aesthetics, music scholars have often treated musical works as spatial wholes. This confusion is understandable because the sense of completeness signified by the concept of "whole" is much more easily grasped when a spatial form is invoked. Spatial categories are thus a common departure point for discussions on wholeness and unity because they provide a clear—albeit ultimately misleading—mental picture of the topic at hand. Hegel himself, despite his emphasis on temporality, wrote: "we may compare melody, as an essentially self-contained and self-supported whole, to plastic sculpture; in the more detailed characterization of painting we shall find an analogous type to that of musical declamation" (in Lippman 1988: 154). But he soon restricted the import of his comparison by adding that "what constitutes the essential principle of music is the ideality of the soul-life" (ibid.), which is the characteristic that for him enables the musical art to "annihilate the conditions of Space entirely" (Hegel 1991 [1835], vol. 1: 87).

Although Hegel's philosophy in general had an enormous impact on Western thought, his ideas on music exerted a very limited influence on the tradition of music scholarship since its institutionalization in the second half of the nineteenth century. Hanslick's formalist aesthetics, on the contrary, have exerted a great influence on this tradition, arguably to the present.[4]

Hegel's musical aesthetics, however, did not constitute an isolated or uncharacteristic position in the early nineteenth century. His phenomenological orientation was in step with basic Romantic attitudes toward art. In this regard Tilottama Rajan (1995: 161) has written: "Romantic theory is broadly phenomenological in approaching genres as modes of consciousness rather than analyzing their mechanical features. It is also phenomenological in being concerned with processes rather than products: both the process (individual or cultural) from which the artwork emerges and the process it stimulates in the reader."

The Romantic focus on temporal form is not exclusively found in the aesthetic theories of idealist philosophers, but it also underlies the concept of musical form of music theorists and critics. Because the musical whole was conceived as temporal, Carl Czerny, for example, could define an improvisation as a "magnificent whole." Regarding the improvisatory style that he called "freer improvisation on several themes," he wrote that "there is perhaps no form more capable of placing together and expanding the image of the inner life and the esthetic disposition into a magnificent whole." For here, both the fully whimsical caprice as well as the discipline of a regular composition must be avoided (Czerny 1983 [1836]: 74). The fact that Czerny considers a "magnificent whole" a type of musical creation that defies the "discipline of a regular composition" makes also evident that in his time musical form could be conceived without resorting to the kind of fixed structure on which later formalist approaches were based.[5]

Hans-Georg Nägeli, a music theoretician considered by Edward Lippman to be an early formalist, also defined musical form in terms similar to Czerny's. Nägeli emphasized the temporal experience of listening to music and criticized the application of visual principles to explain music for this "results in overlooking its specific nature" (in Lippman 1992: 297). Music's nature is also for him essentially play, "a play of anticipation, transition, and deception" (ibid.). Lippman notes that Nägeli's approach is not rigorously anti-Romantic. I would take this observation further and affirm that Nägeli's approach is not rigorously "formalist." When form is conceived in such temporal terms, the approach that results is much closer to a phenomenological understanding of music than to the formalist musicological tradition inaugurated by Hanslick.

Samuel Coleridge's 1809 reflections on absolute music are an excellent example of the non-formalist understanding of music prevalent in the Romantic period:

> Certainly there is one excellence in good music, to which, without mysticism, we may find or make an analogy in the records of History. I allude to that sense of *recognition*, which accompanies our sense of novelty in the most original passages of a great Composer. If we listen to a symphony of Cimarosa the present strain still seems not only to recall, but almost to *renew*, some past movement, another and yet the same! Each present movement bringing back as it were, and embodying the Spirit of some melody that had gone before, anticipates and seems trying to overtake something that is to come: and the Musician has reached the summit of his art, when having thus modified the Present by the Past, he at the same time weds the Past *in* the present to some prepared and correspondive future. The Auditor's thoughts and feelings move under the same influence: retrospection blends with anticipation, and Hope and Memory, a female Janus, become one Power with a double Aspect (quoted in Rosen 1995: 73–74, emphasis in original).

In this passage, Coleridge describes the dialectics of memory and expectation essential to modern phenomenological reflection on music. His references to "retrospection" and "anticipation," or "memory" and "hope," as well as Nägeli's "play of anticipation, transition, and deception" are strongly reminiscent, for instance, of twentieth-century phenomenological approaches, such as Gisèle Brelet's (1946) analysis of music in terms of "attention and expectation," and of Paul Ricoeur's (1984) examination of time and narrative in terms of the dialectic of expectation, memory, and attention. Early nineteenth-century approaches to art and music were, in sum, far from formalist and constitute a precedent to twentieth-century phenomenological theories of art.

Originally, therefore, autonomous musical works were understood fundamentally as temporal wholes, as processes, unfolded through time, of self-forming. This understanding was, as I mentioned earlier, substantially different from the idea of autonomy associated with an object-like concept of musical work that developed later in the century. The collapse of these early ideas of aesthetic autonomy is in part responsible for the unproductive dichotomy separating autonomy from the social significance of art. This collapse has also obscured the relationship existing between early Romantic aesthetics and the formation of the Western canon. Marcia Citron (1993: 38) has stated that "the emphasis on music-as-physical-object that arose in the early nineteenth century was instrumental in paving the way for the notion of canon." But, as I have argued, the early nineteenth-century concept of music was far from the idea of physical object. What arose in this period was a concept of autonomous music as temporal self-forming, which became fundamental to the expression of Romantic ideals of freedom and transcendence. It was not this concept of aesthetic autonomy, but the formalist concept of autonomy that, closely linked to the process of canon-formation, resulted in an emphasis on music "as physical object."

Romantic autonomous music was grounded on a fundamentally temporal concept of musical whole. Its meaningfulness relied primarily on the act of temporal shaping itself and on the emotion of witnessing or imagining this act. Later on, these creations were enshrined as canonic and their autonomy was identified with formal beauty. A few decades after the publication of Hegel's *Aesthetics* (1835), his praise of music as "not merely a work of art" had been rendered absurd. Finished, fixed works had become the only object of criticism and music history and, with it, a vibrant period in which musical creations were conceived as autonomous temporal wholes, not as static final products, had been thoroughly forgotten.

Disorder and Emotion: Nineteenth-Century Performance Practice Before the *Werktreue* Ideal

> The performer seems to abandon himself to the impulses of his fancy and feeling, to indulge in a reverie and to pour out unconsciously, as it were, the thoughts and emotions that pass through his mind.
>
> (a London critic on Chopin)

In *Musicking* (1998), Christopher Small describes a concert of Classical music of our times in the mode of an anthropological "thick description." Small highlights the seriousness of the occasion, its minute planning, and its hierarchical organization. Many regular concert-goers already know well the works to be played and innovations to the repertoire are seldom introduced and generally received with reluctance. This is the type of event associated with the "mature" stages of Western music, and with the concept of autonomy—a rigid and solemn occasion where musical works are presented as museum pieces to be contemplated.

Because this way of presenting and listening to music was prevalent in the late nineteenth century, it has been erroneously taken as quintessential to the Western tradition and has been considered the only appropriate setting for performing Western music of any period. The unruly elements of the performance practice of the Baroque and earlier periods—for example, the pervasive use of improvisation—are considered phenomena typical of the immaturity of these stages, tendentiously labeled "early music," which would eventually disappear with the evolution of the tradition. Consider, for instance, Joseph Machlis's (1955: 338) statement in his widely read *Enjoyment of Music*: "the progress of musical art demanded the victory of careful planning over improvisation." (This statement does not appear in subsequent editions of Machlis's book.) The musical practice and aesthetic ideas of the early nineteenth century, however, once again contradict these conventional views. Far from the highly formalized events described by Small, the performing habits of the first decades of the nineteenth century included an array of spontaneous and unceremonious elements. Soloists improvised in private musical parties as well as in public concerts, works were often performed according to highly personal interpretations, virtuoso musicians astonished audiences with sensationalistic musical feats, and concerts given by amateur musicians and with less than solemn audiences were an integral part of the public musical life of the time.

Due to the fact that musicologists have concentrated almost exclusively on the study of works and not on performance practice, these aspects of Romantic music have been mostly ignored or dismissed as unimportant remnants of early, "immature" periods.[6] But these very aspects, I believe, are as essential to Romanticism as the concept of musical autonomy, and are, furthermore, fully compatible with it. These aspects reveal the privileging of emotion and subjectivity characteristic of Romantic aesthetics over order and objectivity. They also suggest that the ideal of fidelity to the work *(Werktreue),* which was supposed to be achieved by means of "objective" interpretations of works, was not necessarily connected to the concept of autonomous music.

To be sure, respect for written works acquired a new relevance in the Romantic period, an era that was strongly influenced by the emergence of modern historical consciousness. For the first time in the Western tradition, musical works of the previous generations were not routinely replaced by the new compositions, but continued to form part of the repertoire (Kerman 1983: 111). There was a historical interest in the music of the masters of the past considered now as predecessors of "modern" composers. The revival of Johann Sebastian Bach by the Romantics is a good instance of this new interest. But the Romantic view of history was more a fascination with the passing of time than a mere fixation with the past. In fact, the interest in novelty and the concern with future generations was just as strong, if not stronger, than the reverence for the past. This sentiment was expressed by Felix Mendelssohn, the composer who contributed the most to the rediscovery of Bach. Despite his great efforts to make Bach's music known and loved, Mendelssohn felt that the repetition of great works of the past could not match the excitement and the emotion of experiencing the new. Concerning the performance of a newly-discovered piece by Bach in 1838 Mendelssohn (1945: 277) wrote: "But even that—to my mind at least—was lacking in the interest one feels in something new and untried; I like it so much when there is that kind of uncertainty which leaves room for me and the public to have an opinion. In Beethoven and Haendel and Bach one knows beforehand what is coming, and always must come, and a great deal more besides."

At the same time, the respect for the masterworks of the past did not translate into a performance practice exclusively ruled by the principle of *Werktreue.*[7] Interpretations that closely followed the score coexisted with highly subjective renderings and with histrionic displays. The following anecdote illustrates these three approaches to interpretation. In 1844 a French enthusiast of Bach's music accused Liszt of being a charlatan and "then asked him to play his famous arrangement for the piano of Bach's Prelude and Fugue in A Minor for organ." Liszt replied,

> "How do you want me to play it?"
>
> "How? But . . . the way it ought to be played."
>
> "Here it is, to start with, as the author must have understood it, played it himself, or intended it to be played."
>
> And Liszt played. And it was admirable, the perfection itself of the classical style exactly in conformity with the original.
>
> "Here it is a second time, as I feel it, with a slightly more picturesque movement, a more modern style and the effects demanded by an improved instrument." And it was, with these nuances, different . . . but not less admirable.
>
> "Finally, a third time, here it is the way I would play it for the public—to astonish, as a charlatan." And, lighting a cigar which passed at moments from between his lips to his fingers, executing with his ten fingers the part written for the organ pedals, and indulging in other tours de force and prestidigitation, he was prodigious, incredible, fabulous, and received gratefully with enthusiasm (quoted in Rosen 1995: 510–511).

Triggered by someone's accusation of charlatanism, Liszt's response could be interpreted as just a defensive exhibition of his ability to play Bach "the way it ought to be played" according to his critic. Liszt, however, did not show a preference for his first performance, but rather offered it as one interpretation among others. Indeed, the second rendering ("as I feel it") is characteristic of Liszt's Romantic sensibilities and embodies the subjective character of an aesthetics of feeling. But the third, the charlatan-like rendering, is not less Romantic: it represents an instance of the sensationalism of virtuoso performances enormously popular in Europe until the mid-nineteenth century. The narrator of the story, witness to the remarkable musical occasion, conveys that charlatanism was not such a bad thing after all: while he refers to the first interpretation as "admirable," and to the second as "not less admirable," the third is described as "prodigious, incredible, fabulous, and received gratefully with enthusiasm."[8]

From the subtle and the intimate to the melodramatic and sensational, music in the Romantic period was meant to arouse emotions at the expense of Classical ideals of beauty and order. To be carried away by emotion, to be spontaneous, to be unpredictable were not imperfections to be overcome, but, rather, expressions of the exuberance and authenticity of the inner life of the artist. Musical pieces were beginning to be considered then as works of art valuable in themselves, that is to say, valuable independently from the particular social function they fulfilled. But this new Romantic sense of autonomy did not translate into a performance practice based on an idea of work as object-like fixed structure. Works were treated with far more flexibility and openness than with the performing standards that became customary a few decades later, and improvisation was often an integral part of musical events (see Wangermee 1950, Ferand 1961, Goertzen 1996). In the later part of the nineteenth century the combination of spontaneity and unpredictability became a main target for the criticisms of musicologists and largely disappeared from public concerts. But only a few decades earlier the public had cherished these aspects of musical performances. The reactions elicited by the element of unpredictability in public concerts ranged from the quasi-mystical raptures reached by listeners of improvisations by Beethoven or Chopin, to the excitement of witnessing the musical risks taken by Paganini or Liszt, to the sheer merriment caused by unexpected events occurring in the midst of public concerts, which were often staged in less-than-formal venues.

The following narration by Louis Spohr of a public concert given by the then-famous violinist Boucher gives an example of the latter. Boucher was a colorful character who used to advertise himself as "le Napoléon des violons," and who would, for example, stop the orchestra in the middle of a performance so as to repeat a passage that he had not played well. In a concert in Lille, France ca. 1820, Boucher was playing a rondo of his own composition that ended with an improvised cadenza. The concert was running late and the musicians had grown tired and impatient, then,

> when the cadence in which Boucher as usual exhibited all his artistic tours de force seemed never likely to end, some of the gentlemen put their instruments into their cases and slipped out. This was so infectious, that in a few minutes the whole orchestra had disappeared. Boucher, who in the enthusiasm of his play had observed nothing of this, lifted

his foot already at the commencement of his concluding shake, in order to draw the attention of the orchestra and the burst of applause it was to bring down from the enraptured audience. His astonishment may therefore be imagined when all that fell upon his ear was the loud stamp of his own foot. Horrified he stared aghast around him, and beheld all the music desks abandoned. But the public, who had already prepared themselves to see this moment arrive, burst out into an uproarious laughter, in which Boucher, with the best stomach he could, was obliged to join (Spohr 1878, vol. 2: 72).

The concert just described was obviously less than ideal for more "serious" musicians like Spohr himself, who by then had begun a sort of crusade in favor of the music of the three masters: Haydn, Mozart, and Beethoven. The performances of Beethoven's string quartets by Spohr and other like-minded musicians, for example, were intended as dignified occasions whose high aesthetic significance demanded an attitude of respect and concentration.[9] This was, after all, the period in which the separation between "serious" and "popular" music was emerging, and voices like that of the critic A. B. Marx were raised against the shallowness of music used as entertainment, such as virtuoso and Italian music (Pederson 1994). The anecdote narrated by Spohr can easily be attributed to the eccentricity of certain individuals and to the amateurism of the orchestra musicians and dismissed as part of an unimportant musical practice at the margins of the true musical standards of the time. Eccentricity and amateurism, however, were pervasive in the musical life of the early nineteenth century. To dismiss these aspects as marginal or irrelevant would amount to an imposition on this era of criteria that were not widespread until decades later. Romantic performance practice, with its combination of seriousness and raucousness, of ecstatic states, and what some critics decried as mere "fleeting sensual pleasures" (quoted in Pederson 1994: 90), should not be understood as the disorderly early stage of a necessarily evolving tradition, but as a music culture in its own right.

The disorderly, imperfect, and overwhelming were in fact basic aspects of the Romantic aesthetics of the sublime that superseded the aesthetics of beauty of the Classical period. The play between order and disorder was central to the Romantic approach to artistic production. Charles Rosen (1995: 96) has discussed the importance of the fragment as a musical form in the Romantic period and affirms that the most successful fragments, "preserve the clearly defined symmetry and the balance of the traditional forms but allow suggestively for the possibility of chaos, for the eruption of the disorder of life." Romantic culture did not shun the chaotic and disorderly, but embraced them as aspects of life. Music, the Romantic art par excellence, was a preferred means to express the tensions between fragment and whole, finite and infinite, seen and unseen. When a tonal piece would never return to the tonic leaving the listener in a suspended state of expectation, when a cadenza could go on forever even risking derision, or when a performer seemed "to abandon himself to the impulses of his fancy" (see quote on p. 11), the Romantics were not expressing a lack of artistic maturity or of seriousness. Rather, they were expressing through music an ideal of freedom and a will to embrace and give meaning to the unpredictable and the contingent.

Autonomous Art: A Light in a Dark Age

What artist has ever troubled himself with the political events of the day anyway? He lived only for his art, and advanced through life serving it alone. But a dark and unhappy age has seized men with its iron fist, and the pain squeezes from them sounds that were formerly alien to them.

E. T. A. Hoffmann

We have seen that the Romantic concept of musical autonomy emerged in the context of a nonformalist aesthetics of music and that the performance practice of the time had little to do with a reified, formalized notion of music. But even if in the early nineteenth century works were not understood in formalist terms, and even if performers did not confine themselves to strict readings of scores, it would still be possible to think of autonomous music as a realm detached from any extra-musical concern. If this was the case, it would perhaps justify the abandonment of the concept of autonomy on behalf of the study of music in culture. But did the idea of autonomy really open an inexorable path to aestheticist positions?

Aestheticism refers to an attitude toward art that was common in the later part of the nineteenth century, according to which artistic creations existed in an isolated, self-justified sphere of the aesthetic. This attitude can be better defined with the aestheticist slogan "art for art's sake." This phrase is found in a Walter Pater passage of 1868 that sums up the aestheticist view: "Of this wisdom, the poetic passion, the desire of beauty, the love of art for art's sake, has most; for art comes to you professing frankly to give nothing but the highest quality to your moments as they pass, and simply for those moments' sake" (quoted in Williams 1983: 171). Pater held as a principle that the end of life is not action but contemplation, and wrote that "in poetry, in art, if you enter into their true spirit at all, you touch this principle, in a measure: these, by their very sterility, are a type of beholding for the mere joy of beholding." The "true moral significance of art and poetry," therefore, is "not to teach lessons, or enforce rules, or even to stimulate us to noble ends; but to withdraw the thoughts for a little while from the mere machinery of life" (ibid.). Oscar Wilde put it more directly, affirming that "all art is immoral . . . for emotion for the sake of emotion is the aim of art, and emotion for the sake of action is the aim of life, and of that practical organization of life that we call society. . . . While in the opinion of society, Contemplation is the gravest sin of which any citizen can be guilty, in the opinion of the highest culture it is the proper occupation of man" (quoted in Williams 1983: 171).

Raymond Williams (1983) maintains that these positions are not essentially different from those held at the beginning of the century by Romantic authors such as Wordsworth or Shelley and argues that the only change is in tone and style. In my view, however, the stylistic changes in prose Williams refers to are not mere superficial and meaningless phenomena, but respond to more profound changes in the views on art and life throughout the nineteenth century.[10] If at the end of the century the concept of autonomous art had taken on the meaning of an isolated realm, in the Romantic period this concept had the connotation of independence more than of the isolation.

Consider for example E. T. A. Hoffmann's statement above quoted (p. 17). Included in Hoffmann's "Extremely Random Thoughts" (Hoffmann 1989: 111), this passage was probably written in 1812, the year Beethoven composed his Seventh and Eighth symphonies.[11] The idea that the music of this time expressed the composer's awareness of a conflictive social and political situation contradicts aestheticist views of this music. Beethoven was the first composer who embodied the Romantic ideal of following only one's own inner voice and who had the financial need to defend his authorship in a post-patronage era (see for example DeNora 1995). But in the early nineteenth century the composer's retreat to find his inner voice did not mean detachment from all other human concerns, but a way to rejoin them at a deeper level. Music no longer needed to fulfill *concrete* social functions, such as accompaniment for an aristocratic ball or a religious service, but this independence from concrete social functions did not necessarily imply that music was considered as isolated from social concerns. It is telling in this regard that Hoffmann, the Romantic critic par excellence, does not attribute the strange sounds of the music of his time to the inner pains, the tortured subjectivities, and personal strivings of composers, but to a "dark and unhappy age" that "has seized men with its iron fist" (Hoffmann 1989: 111).

The idea of the organic autonomy of art was in part an answer the Romantics gave to pressing social and political concerns of their times, marked by the Napoleonic military campaigns throughout Europe and by the increasing mechanization of the means of production. The sacredness of the autonomous work of art, understood as an organism that responds only to internal and natural rules, was a metaphor both for the sacredness of national self-regulation and independence, as opposed to the rule imposed from outside, for example by a foreign invader, and for the sacredness of "natural" as opposed to mechanical means of production.

The "unhappy age" Hoffmann mentioned was that of the Napoleonic wars and of the disenchantment of many who had seen a great revolutionary hero, a champion of new ideas of democracy and freedom, transformed into an imperial invader. Beethoven's well-known withdrawal of the dedication of his Eroica Symphony provides a good example of this disenchantment. Composed in 1803, the *Eroica* was intended as homage to Napoleon. But the following year, upon hearing the news that Napoleon had proclaimed himself emperor of the French, Beethoven "seized the score, tore out the title-page and, cursing the 'new tyrant,' flung it on the floor" (Schindler 1996 [1860]: 116). Later, Beethoven agreed to the publication of the symphony with the subtitle "Per festeggiare il sovvenire d'un grand Uomo" ("to celebrate the memory of a great man"). Schindler, a contemporary of Beethoven who was very close to the composer during the last ten years of his life, reports on the hatred Beethoven felt for Napoleon from the time he became emperor until his death in St. Helena and on Beethoven's final forgiveness. According to Schindler, after Napoleon's death Beethoven had said that

> he had already composed the music appropriate to such a catastrophe, namely the Funeral March in the *Eroica*. He went even further in describing the symbolism of this movement, for the theme of the middle section in C major was supposed to represent a new star of hope in Napoleon's reversed fortunes (his return to the political stage in 1815), and finally the great hero's powerful decision to withstand fate until, at the moment of surrender, he

sinks to the ground and allows himself to be buried like any other mortal (Schindler 1996 [1860]: 116).

Although Schindler warns against any literal interpretations of Beethoven's music, he goes on to affirm that "in this particular instance . . . we must realize his political temperament at the time when he pretended to find in his Funeral March a specific association with the passing of a greatly admired person" (ibid.).

The "dark age" was also the era of industrialization, already pervasive in England at the beginning of the century and steadily spreading over the rest of Europe. From the early years of the century English writers such as Robert Southey (1774–1843) and Robert Owen (1771–1858) had denounced the brutal conditions and devastating effects of the "manufacturing system," criticism that became widespread some years later. Southey contrasted the old "commerce-based" economy with the new means of production which, according to him, reduced human beings to machines and turned everything related to the workmen, such as their living quarters, into things of "unqualified deformity . . . as offensive to the eye as to the mind" (quoted in Williams 1983: 24). For Southey, the physical and moral evil generated by this system affected not only the workers, but also their capitalist employers: "he who, at the beginning of his career, uses his fellow-creatures as bodily machines for producing wealth, ends not infrequently in becoming an intellectual one himself, employed in continually increasing what it is impossible for him to enjoy" (quoted in Williams 1983: 23). Owen, for his part, also contrasted the "happy simplicity of the agricultural peasant" to the evils raised by industrialization. In 1815 he wrote: "The general diffusion of manufactures throughout a country generates a new character in its inhabitants; and as this character is formed upon a principle quite unfavourable to individual or general happiness, it will produce the most lamentable and permanent evils, unless its tendency be counteracted by legislative interference and direction" (quoted in Williams 1983: 26).

Carlyle also complained about the generalization of the mechanical model:

> Not the external and physical alone is now managed by machinery, but the internal and spiritual also. . . . The same habit regulates not our modes of action alone, but our modes of thought and feeling. Men are grown mechanical in head and in heart, as well as in hand. They have lost faith in individual endeavour, and in natural force, of any kind. Not for internal perfection, but for external combinations and arrangements, for institutions, constitutions—for Mechanism of one sort or other, do they hope and struggle. Their whole efforts, attachments, opinions, turn on mechanism, and are of a mechanical character (Carlyle 1869: 234).

Carlyle's complaints about the mechanical age led him to reflect on the lost world of the artisan, not as nostalgic escapism, but as means to criticize the present. As a sphere independent from industrial production and the social ills associated with it, autonomous art or "high art" had, paradoxically, a hidden affinity with the preindustrial world of the artisan. For example, in an essay called *Signs of the Times* published in 1829, Carlyle denounced his epoch as being "not an Heroical, Devotional, Philosophical, or Moral Age, but, above all others, the Mechanical Age. . . . Nothing is now done directly, or by hand; all is by rule and calculated contrivance. . . . On every hand, the living artisan is driven from his workshop, to make room for a speedier, inanimate one. The shuttle drops from the fingers of the weaver, and falls into iron fingers that ply it faster" (ibid.: 233).

Carlyle's and Coleridge's readings of Herder's organicist theories, or of Novalis's distinction between "mechanical" and "dynamic" thinking, had the urgency of finding an intellectual and artistic form of resistance to the fragmentation, and hence dehumanization, imposed by the new division of labor. In the midst of a bleak reality denounced by numerous authors as stripping human beings of their humanity, organic art constituted a realm of freedom and resistance against the new economic order.[12] The autonomy of biological organisms was the preferred metaphor for conceptualizing this independence of artistic creations from mechanical and artificial means, as well as from instrumental considerations.[13] It also provided a means to conceive of art in terms of creations that were free but not arbitrary. According to the organicist paradigm, freedom was equivalent to subjection to organic laws, that is, laws considered to be inherent to one's own nature, and not those imposed from the outside. The emergent concept of aesthetic autonomy modeled after the organic meant, therefore, natural self-regulation and independence from external function.

Organicism had an extraordinary impact on music criticism, providing critics with a powerful theoretical tool to assess the internal coherence of autonomous music (Solie 1980, Montgomery 1992). As Montgomery (1992: 63n) has shown, E. T. A. Hoffmann was one of the first critics to apply organicist thinking to his assessments of Beethoven's music in his ground-breaking essay on his Fifth Symphony. Whereas in the late nineteenth and early twentieth century, organicist-inspired musical analysis such as Schenker's was at the service of formalist views of musical works as self-enclosed wholes, Romantic organicism was not akin to such formalist approaches to music.

First, Schenker interpreted the ideal of organism primarily in terms of structural coherence and the static integration of the elements that make up a whole. He writes for example: "The hands, legs, and ears of the human body do not begin to grow after birth; they are present at the time of birth. Similarly, in a composition, a limb which was not somehow born with the middle and background cannot grow to be a diminution" (Schenker 1979: 6). The Romantics, on the contrary, employed organic models to highlight ideas of spontaneous growth and continuous process to which the concepts of wholeness and structure were dialectically related. Rather than images from animal organisms, Romantic writers preferred vegetal metaphors. Keats for instance wrote: "If Poetry comes not as naturally as the leaves to a tree it had better not come at all" (quoted in Wolfson 1995: 152). Vegetal metaphors, in sum, point to the importance of the ideas of process and growth in Romantic organicism, while animal metaphors, favored by theorists such as Schenker, evoke the ideas of static wholeness that are central to formalist approaches to music.

Second, the organicist thinking that influenced Romantic aesthetics did not suggest the absolute isolation of the work of art, since Romantic organicism was firmly grounded on the belief in a metaphysical unity of the entire universe. If a work of art could be said by analogy to be an organism, it was because the universe was considered a supra-organism that encompassed and connected all its constitutive parts. The autonomy of the work of art was thus a sign of its independence from nonorganic forces and, at the same time, of its vital connection with the Whole. And this organic connection with the Whole was fundamental for art to be regarded as a higher realm that provided a locus of resistance against the threat of widespread mechanization.

The emergence of the concept of aesthetic autonomy in the early Romantic period had, in sum, a social role. Rather than a withdrawal from practical concerns, autonomy at the beginning of the nineteenth century had strong ties to social realities, fulfilling both an ideological and utopian function. In the first case, as Sanna Pederson (1994: 88) has argued drawing from Peter Bürger, autonomous art was, paradoxically, a preferred means for the process of schooling and socialization in bourgeois society: "even while claiming art's ability to withdraw from the demands of instrumental rationality, its proponents were setting up new social purposes and goals for this aesthetic enterprise." In the second case, autonomous art acted as utopian principle providing a way to express and experience alternatives to oppressive social realities. Autonomous art in this context, therefore, was not conceived as a form of escapism, but as a form of resistance. As John Daverio (1993: 2) wrote, "the heady mixture of escapism and ecstasy that is still too often taken as a defining feature of the Romantic endeavor was in fact a surface phenomenon, an artful camouflage for a penetrating and carefully circumscribed societal critique that attempted to come to grips with the disquieting moments in an emerging modern world, thereby wresting from them a measure of value and hopefulness."[14]

If the idea of autonomous art was transformed by the proponents of aestheticism into an isolated—and hence socially irrelevant—sphere of the aesthetic, it was this very idea that had allowed the Romantics to think about art as societal critique and as a source of value and hope. Autonomous art and the idea of the aesthetic itself have, therefore, given rise to radically opposed and mutually exclusive views of art. To a great extent, the difficulties encountered in theorizing art as a productive, and not merely decorative and reproductive, force in culture and society stem from the fact that the same principle that would allow for such an argument—the autonomy of art—is also the source of strong counterarguments to that effect. Furthermore, if the concept of autonomy is what confers on art its critical import, it is this very concept that has made of art a privileged vehicle of ideological distortions. To renounce the idea of autonomy, however, only compounds this complicated state of affairs. Without some sense that art opens up a realm where alternative realities can be explored, art is reduced to a repetition of what already exists and is rendered, therefore, a superfluous and meaningless activity.

If, as Adorno observed, Beethoven's music embodied the struggles and aspirations of the emerging bourgeoisie, the greatness of this music stems from the fact that Beethoven's creative imagination rose above (yet was not detached from) those very circumstances, as Adorno (1989: 209) also understood: "If [Beethoven] is the musical prototype of the revolutionary bourgeoisie, he is at the same time the prototype of a music that has escaped from its social tutelage and is esthetically fully autonomous, a servant no longer." Or, to give a more concrete example, if Beethoven had in fact been inspired by a question about paying a bill ("Muss es sein?"), and the answer that it must be paid ("Es muss sein!") when he composed the motives of the String Quartet, op. 135, these motives and their development have allowed us experience a great deal more than a recount of somebody's financial difficulties and Beethoven's sense of humor, despite the fact that finances and humor are not foreign to great art either.

Conclusion

In his lucid defense of the "literary" character of literature and, in general, of the aesthetic character of art (as opposed to a reduction of literature and art to political positioning), George Levine (1994: 3) has written: "I am trying to imagine the aesthetic as a mode engaged richly and complexly with moral and political issues, but a mode that operates differently from others and contributes in distinctive ways to the possibilities of human fulfillment and connection." In the same spirit, my aim has been to contribute to an idea of Western classical music as a tradition deeply engaged with the social and cultural world from within which it emerged, but also as participating of the autonomous realm of the aesthetic. In order to be able to hold these two aspects together it would be necessary, I have argued, to disentangle the notion of the autonomy of art from its late nineteenth-century association with formalism and aestheticism.

Neither a reified concept of musical work nor a highly formalized performance practice are inherent in the Western classical tradition. What is generally understood as the world of Western classical music constitutes a set of beliefs and practices that took hold in this tradition as late as the second half of the nineteenth century. Before this time, musical works were understood in a fluid, open, and dynamic manner, akin to contemporary phenomenological understandings of art. At the same time—and this is the fundamental point I have aimed to make in this essay—this phenomenological, flexible, and socially-anchored understanding of music was compatible with the new ideas of autonomy that emerged around the turn of the nineteenth century.

A reflection on the original meaning of autonomous music can help us to retain both a sense of autonomy without renouncing music's links with its social context and the social roots of music without renouncing its independence. The musical life of the early nineteenth century also offers an inspiring image of classical music, where seriousness is not confused with pomposity, where the public acts of making and of listening to music involve the excitement of the new, and where there is room for the unexpected.

NOTES

1. By "Romantic period" and "Romanticism" I refer exclusively to the artistic movements that originated in the 1790s and declined in the 1840s, that is, the period that has been often defined as "early" Romantic in order to differentiate it from a later period also considered to be Romantic.

2. Elsewhere I have argued this thesis at length, proposing 1848 as the year that symbolically marks the turn from a Romantic, phenominological approach to music to post-Romantic and formalist approaches (Sancho-Velázquez 2001).

3. Hanslick's idea of form is nonetheless still influenced by the idealist conception. But his emphasis on the permanent and fixed character of musical structure marks the turn towards the formalist approaches that developed later in the nineteenth century and reached a peak during the twentieth.

4. Two years after the publication of *The Beautiful in Music* (1854), he was appointed to a position at Vienna University, the first university music professorship ever created.

5. Carl Czerny's views on music were hardly atypical of his time. A pupil of Beethoven and Liszt's teacher, Czerny (1791–1859) had been called by Chopin "the oracle of Vienna" for his influence on musical matters. His treatise on improvisation was published in 1836.

6. Carl Dahlhaus, for example, maintains that work "is the central category of music, and hence of music historiography as well" (Treitler 1989: 170). But as Leo Treitler (1989: 170–171) has observed, "the 'work' concept has a history that is at least a thread in one of the central plot-lines of Western music history; it cannot be taken as a premise for that history."

7. Lydia Goehr (1992: 242) has argued that the *Werktreue* ideal "pervaded every aspect of practice in and after 1800 with full regulative force." Though I agree with her analyses of the links between *Werktreue*, formalist aesthetics, and the canonization of Western music, I have argued elsewhere that these developments did not impact Western music until the collapse of Romanticism around the middle of the century, and that the ideal of *Werktreue* was not pervasive until then (Sancho-Velázquez 2001).

8. Liszt himself was ambivalent about his career as a virtuoso and after 1848 abandoned his tours as a soloist and concentrated on conducting and composing. In my view, Liszt's turn participated of a generalized move away from Romanticism.

9. When Spohr (1784–1859) wrote his memories at the end of his career the musical world was undergoing dramatic changes, and it is highly probable that—consciously or unconsciously—he was reading his own life and his role in the history of music under the new high-art ideal. It could be argued that in his autobiography Spohr was much more interested in evoking "serious" occasions—such as the performances of Beethoven's and his own works—than less solemn musical events.

10. Ironically, Williams's downplaying of the significance of stylistic differences in prose seems to agree with the aestheticist tenet that art exists in a vacuum unaffected by extra-artistic concerns.

11. "Extremely Random Thoughts" was first published in *Zeitung für die elegante Welt* in 1814, and later published as part of Hoffmann's first book, *Kreisleriana*. David Charlton mentions circumstantial evidence that Hoffmann was working on it in 1812 (Hoffmann 1989: 53).

12. In Germany, as well as in other European countries and the United States, industrialization not only began later than in England, but it developed at a much slower pace. Around 1840 continental countries were still slowly adopting and adapting to the revolution in the modes of production launched by England (see for example Lerner, Meacham, Burns 1993: 709f). Whereas the Romantic movement first flourished in Germany and then influenced England and other countries, English Romanticism and its reinterpretation of this movement in the light of a reaction against industrialization had in turn an impact on the German Romantics, who were increasingly aware of the changes gradually imposed in society by the new forms of production. The first studies of Karl Marx were written in the 1840s.

13. The term "instrumental" is used here in the sense of Adorno's critique of "instrumental reason," a notion that refers to a form of thought that operates in analogous manner to the capitalist form of production, that is to say, a form of thought exclusively guided by self-interest that translates into domination of nature and of other human beings. By using Adorno's terminology in this context I am purposefully drawing attention towards the connection of Adorno and other Frankfurt School thinkers to the critique of the rise of industrialization mounted by the early Romantics.

14. By "Romantic" Daverio also refers to the period usually defined as "early Romanticism." More concretely, he adapts the dates 1772–1829 proposed by Friedrich Schlegel (Daverio 1993: 3).

REFERENCES

Adorno, Theodor W.
    1997   *Aesthetic Theory.* Translated by Robert Hullot-Kentor. Minneapolis: Univer-
                  sity of Minnesota Press.
    1989 [1962]   *Introduction to the Sociology of Music.* Translated by E. B. Ashton. New York:
                  Continuum.

Brelet, Gisèle
    1961 [1946]   "Music and Silence." In Susanne K. Langer, ed., *Reflections on Art: A Source
                  Book of Writings by Artists, Critics, & Philosophers.* New York: Oxford Univer-
                  sity Press, pp. 113–121.

Carlyle, Thomas
    1869   *Critical and Miscellaneous Essays, Vol. 2.* Chicago: The American Bookmart.

Citron, Marcia J.
    1993   *Gender and the Musical Canon.* Cambridge: Cambridge University Press.

Czerny, Carl
    1983 [1836]   *A Systematic Introduction to Improvisation on the Pianoforte. Opus 200.*
                  Translated and edited by Alice L. Mitchell. New York: Longman.

Daverio, John
    1993   *Nineteenth-Century Music and the German Romantic Ideology.* New York:
                  Schirmer Books.

DeNora, Tia
    1995   *Beethoven and the Construction of Genius: Musical Politics in Vienna,
                  1792–1803.* Berkeley: University of California Press.

Ferand, Ernst
    1961   *Improvisation in Nine Centuries of Western Music.* Cologne: A. Volk Verlag.

Goehr, Lydia
    1992   *The Imaginary Museum of Musical Works.* Oxford: Clarendon Press.

Goertzen, Valerie Woodring
    1996   "By Way of Introduction: Preluding by 18th- and Early 19th-Century
                  Pianists." *The Journal of Musicology* 14(3):299–337.

Hegel, Georg W. F.
    1991 [1835]   *Aesthetics: Lectures on Fine Art,* 2 vols. Translated by T. M. Knox. Oxford:
                  Clarendon Press.

Hoffmann, E.T.A.
    1989   *E. T. A. Hoffmann's Musical Writings: Kreisleriana, The Poet and the Com-
                  poser, Music Criticism.* Edited by David Charlton. Translated by Martyn
                  Clarke. Cambridge: Cambridge University Press.

Kerman, Joseph
    1983   "A Few Canonic Variations." *Critical Inquiry* 10:107–26.

Lerner, Robert E., Standish Meacham, and Edward McNall Burns
    1993   *Western Civilizations, Their History and Their Culture.* New York: W. W.
                  Norton.

Levine, George
    1994   "Introduction: Reclaiming the Aesthetic." In George Levine, ed., *Aesthetic &
                  Ideology.* New Brunswick: Rutgers University Press.

Lippman, Edward A., ed.
    1988   *Musical Aesthetics: A Historical Reader, vol. 2: The Nineteenth Century.* Stuyvesant: Pendragon Press.
    1992   *A History of Western Musical Aesthetics.* Lincoln: University of Nebraska Press.

McClary, Susan
    1991   *Feminine Endings: Music, Gender, and Sexuality.* Minneapolis University of Minnesota Press.

Mendelssohn, Felix
    1945   *Letters.* Edited by G. Selden-Goth. New York: Pantheon Books.

Montgomery, David
    1992   "The Myth of Organicism: From Bad Science to Great Art." *The Musical Quarterly* 76(1): 17–66.

Pederson, Sanna
    1994   "A. B. Marx, Berlin Concert Life, and German National Identity." *19th-Century Music* 18(2): 87–107.

Rajan, Tilottama
    1995   "Phenomenology and Romantic Theory: Hegel and the Subversion of Aesthetics." In John Beer, ed., *Questioning Romanticism.* Baltimore: John Hopkins University Press, pp. 155–78.

Ricoeur, Paul
    1984   *Time and narrative,* vol 1. Translated by Kathleen McLaughlin and David Pellauer. Chicago: University of Chicago Press.
    1985   *Time and Narrative,* vol. 2. Translated by Kathleen McLaughlin and David Pellauer. Chicago: University of Chicago Press.
    1988   *Time and Narrative,* vol. 3. Translated by Kathleen Blamey and David Pellauer. Chicago: University of Chicago Press.

Rosen, Charles
    1995   *The Romantic Generation.* Cambridge: Harvard University Press.

Sancho-Velázquez, Angeles
    2001   "The Legacy of Genius: Improvisation, Romantic Imagination and the Western Musical Canon." Ph.D. Dissertation, University of California Los Angeles.

Schenker, Heinrich
    1979   *Free Composition.* Translated by Ernst Oster. Longman: New York.

Schindler, Anton Felix
    1996 [1860]   *Beethoven As I Knew Him.* Edited by Donald W. MacArdle. Translated by Constance S. Jolly. Mineola, NY: Dover Publications.

Small, Christopher
    1998   *Musicking: The Meanings of Performing and Listening.* Hanover: Wesleyan University Press.

Solie, Ruth A.
    1980   "The Living Work: Organicism and Musical Analysis." *19th Century Music,* 4(2): 147–156.

Spohr, Louis
    1878   *Autobiography,* 2 vols. Translated by the publishers. London: Reeves & Turner.

Treitler, Leo
    1989   *Music and the Historical Imagination.* Cambridge: Harvard University Press.

Wangermee, Robert
    1950   "L'improvisation pianistique au debut du XIXe siècle." In *Miscellanea Musicologica Floris Van der Mueren.* Gent: Drukkerij L. Van Melle, pp. 227–53.

Williams, Raymond
    1983   *Culture and Society 1780–1950.* New York: Columbia University Press.

Wolfson, Susan J.
    1995   "Romanticism and the Question of Poetic Form." In John Beer, ed., *Questioning Romanticism.* Baltimore: John Hopkins University Press, pp. 133–54.

Cuma agus Craiceann/Shape and Skin: Metaphor and Musical Aesthetics in Tory Island

LILLIS Ó LAOIRE

University of Limerick and Loyola Marymount University

In Memoriam Séamus Ó Dúgáin 1928–2000

"Aesthetics" is of central concern to the study of ethnomusicology. Although the term itself may not be found explicitly among many groups (Merriam 1964, Jones 1971, Becker 1983), this should not prevent us from seeking to identify the metaphorical categories through which music is considered to be pleasing by such groups. The discussion may be complicated by the fact that the Western aesthetic has been regarded as a transcendental and universal standard across cultures, and, moreover, that it has often been appropriated and promoted as part of a colonial discourse. This paper concerns itself with the aesthetics of Gaelic music and song as part of the cultural life of Tory Island, where Gaelic, or Irish, is the dominant language of the community and where Gaelic songs form a significant part of local culture. In attempting to highlight the metaphors that underpin the poetics of music, dance, and song in Tory, I will concentrate upon the contextualized uses of certain words in the Irish language that I consider to be highly significant. By providing an interpretation of the complex of relations that exists among such words, the world disclosed by them will be more readily apprehended. In such an interpretation, I adopt a hermeneutical approach, following the theories of art and mimesis advanced by Hans-Georg Gadamer and Paul Ricoeur, whose phenomenological and ontological stance I have found particularly useful for such an exploration.

Before embarking on an interpretation of the poetics of music, dancing, songs and singing and their attendant aesthetic, however, it may be useful to consider the words of the celebrated Scottish writer, Iain Crichton Smith (1928–1998), himself a native of a Gaelic community on the island of Lewis in Scotland, similar to Tory in many respects. In an essay entitled "Real People in a Real Place," he describes the singing traditions of the Western Isles (Crichton Smith 1986: 45):

> Such a society is not interested in the aesthetic in any real sense. It has been said, for instance that the standard of singers in the Highlands is not high but this, however, is to judge the singing in a wrong way. Angus Macleod, a Gaelic singer, sang with great fervour,

in a voice from which the notes emerged like solid boulders. In my opinion he sang certain songs most lovingly. No purist would ever be able to convince me that Macleod's singing was not beautiful and powerful: the passion of the singing, the solidity of the notes, appealed to a profound resonance in my own nature, and was thus for me the highest pitch to which singing could attain.

The islander, as I have said, is not concerned with the aesthetic and is not interested much in modern poetry . . .

When taking into account the title of his essay, Smith, in my view, contradicts himself here in his use of the phrase "in a real sense," as if his own vivid description of an excellent performer's ability to move the listener were not "real." He seems to be answering allegations that Gaelic singing is not of a high aesthetic standard, considering this to be a wrong judgment. Apparently, his difficulty lies in his perception of the reality of his modern readership as different to the reality of island life, and that island reality lies outside the terms of reference of the modern. The modern is the desirable standard to which everything else must be compared. Because of the normative, hegemonic power of the aesthetic standard of modernity, anything that does not attain it is considered inferior. It is patently obvious that Smith does not believe island life to be lesser, but nevertheless, he remains locked in a polar opposition of perceived differences between Hebridean cultural backwardness and "modern" reality. Angeles Sancho-Velázquez (1994) has critiqued modern aesthetics as a socially constructed phenomenon in which she convincingly argues against epistemologically defined, universalist definitions of the aesthetic. Adopting a hermeneutical stance in relation to aesthetics, she opposes Merriam's purely scientific definitions, cast in what might be termed the traditional European mode derived from Kant. Rather, she advocates the inclusion of culturally situated meaning within aesthetics, reasoning that the questions need to be changed, if aesthetics is to become a cross-cultural project. In the context of Los Angeles, she asks among other questions, what the reasons for music making are, and what the musics of the city are saying (1994: 48). These questions coincide to a large extent with my own inquiry into the practice of music, dance and song on Tory. I offer interpretations here in an attempt to reveal partially the world which is disclosed by entertainment on the island.

Place

Tory is located in Donegal, in the northwest of the Republic of Ireland, nine miles from the nearest point on the mainland. It is three miles long and one and a half miles wide at the widest point. The population stands at about 160 year round, although it was formerly much larger, comprising some 400 individuals in 1851 (Fox 1995 [1978], Hunter 1996). An attempt to move the islanders to the mainland in the late seventies and early eighties was resisted, although ten families did leave the island permanently in 1981 to live in local authority housing on the mainland, at Falcarragh. Since then, services and communications on the island have been steadily improving, although problems of unemployment and emigration continue to remain formidable.

The people of Tory have always been renowned in the northwestern region of Ireland for their prowess as singers, dancers, and musicians. Indeed, one song fragment, possibly composed in the early twentieth century, applies the name *Baile an Phléisiúir*, the "Village of Pleasure," to the island. My work on the song tradition of Tory has taken the form of observing the dances and other musical events during short visits to the island. I also formed close relationships with some of the older singers who were born around the end of the 1920s and the beginning of the 1930s, especially Éamonn Mac Ruairí (1928–) Teresa McClafferty (1931–), and the late Séamus Ó Dúgáin (1928–2000). I have recorded songs from all three and conducted interviews with them during 1995 and again in 1997. I also consulted John Ó Duibheannaigh (1920–) of Rannafast in mainland Donegal, a noted authority on the Irish language and folklore of the region. What is presented here is largely based upon those interviews.[1]

Questions and Approach

The questions I will ask concerning the aesthetics of Gaelic song in this paper owe much to the poststructural hermeneutics of Paul Ricoeur and Hans-Georg Gadamer.[2] My examination will concentrate on the configuration and representation of music in Tory and on linguistic concepts and metaphors that are integral to them. Such an approach proceeds from Gadamer's (1989: 103) claim that language "has performed in advance the abstraction that is, as such, the task of conceptual analysis." By this Gadamer suggests that the examination of a language itself may reveal the beliefs that underpin the worldviews of its speakers. It is a view with which I concur and which forms the basis of my subsequent interpretation in this paper. The interpretation of meaningful action concerned with the proper realization of the musical situation is also crucial for its revelation.

An ontological approach, that is, broadly, one founded upon the temporal condition of being-in-a-world, is particularly useful for an interpretation of the poetics of Tory entertainment, since the body in motion is central to its activities. The idea of play as the mode of being of art, which is a central idea in Gadamer's work, is important in my examination. Such a claim holds that play is devoid of a purposive practical element beyond the game itself, in which the players must lose themselves if they are to achieve its end. When aesthetic enjoyment is viewed in this light, it provides an opportunity to overcome the divide constructed between object and subject, characteristically invoked in the treatment of aesthetics in mainstream European art. An ontological view identifies a dialectical relation between appropriation and distanciation, where the primary encounter with a tradition also brings about a distanciúion of prior assumptions and prejudices. Moreover, as Huizinga has argued (1955 [1938]: 10): "play creates order, *is* order. . . . Play seems to lie in the field of aesthetics. . . . Play has a tendency to be beautiful." Such a notion establishes clear links between the Irish idea and Gadamer's concept.

"In the to-and-fro movement of play, everyday reality becomes metamorphosed, into an intensified and 'truer' reality" (Gadamer 1989: 101–129; Ricoeur 1991: 91). In this context, it is noteworthy that the usual word for "art" in the Irish language is *ealaín*.

This term, however, is not exactly equivalent to English "art" in that it also may carry meanings of "science" or "skill," particularly poetic or musical skill. It may also include the idea of "craftsmanship" or "performance" as well as "trickery" and "prank playing." In fact, in everyday spoken language it is often the latter meanings of wiliness that are foregrounded. *Caitheamh aimsire* is another important term, signifying "pastime" or "entertainment," in other parts of Ireland, which Glassie (1982) claims to include everything from food and drink to singing and music. Glassie (1975: 107) also accurately compares entertainment in Fermanagh to an "exacting test of verbal, musical and dancing abilities," which has clear resonances with the high critical standards applied in Tory Island.

A thick description (Geertz 1973) of the poetics of entertainment in Tory island in terms of play has much to reveal about the aesthetic preconditions upon which it is founded. Any such account must, in the first place, focus upon dance. Dancing has always been a central entertainment for ordinary Irish people (Breathnach 1977), with Tory being no exception. Today, dancing continues to be important to both young and old. Formerly, most dances were usually held in the winter, but with the decline in inshore fishing and small farming practices, they now take place more often in summer, a pattern that has been called "seasonal reversal" (Brody 1973: 18–40). I have described elsewhere how dances were organized during festive times of the year (Ó Laoire 1996, 1999a, 2002). Until the mid-1950s, these dances were held in the island school house on festive nights associated with the major annual religious festivals, the greatest event of the year being St. Patrick's Day, when all islanders, if it was within their power, made a concerted effort to be there for the celebration of the holiday, many returning especially from seasonal labor migration in Scotland. The dances were painstakingly organized and rigorously supervised by young island men in their late teens and early twenties, particularly those from the island's western village, the location of the island school. Everything was perfectly arranged so as to ensure that the events proceeded in a proper manner, transforming the event into an *oíche mhór*, "a big night," so that its performances and memorable incidents become woven into the fabric of everyday life through the retelling of them, a part of island *seanchas*, oral history, conversation, or talk. Furthermore, in the days and nights that followed, performances were fully critiqued, so that if someone had confused the order of a song's text in some way or made a similar mistake in a dance, this would be minutely discussed, indicating the proper or correct manner in which it should have been executed. The verb used to express this practice is *loisc le*, which usually means "scorch," perhaps referring to the embarrassment that might follow from such a rebuke. The term for this correctness is *ceart*, sometimes *i gceart*, an adjective signifying "right" or "correct." Its opposite term *ciotach* "wrong," is used to describe mistakes. Significantly, *ciotach* may also mean left handed, a point which I will return to later. Good performances are said to have *cuma*, "a (proper) shape, appearance," sometimes *cuma* and *craiceann*, "appearance" and "skin" or "finish." Allen Feldman (1999: 1) refers to the extent of the term *craiceann* as he observed its use in South Donegal, where he previously researched the fiddling tradition:

> The local performance culture, in its oral, musical and choreographic forms, was the anchoring symbolization of economic infrastructure, kin and kith reciprocities, and the

labor practices of an increasingly unstable agrarian society. In southwest Donegal music-making, field cultivation, stone walls and thatched roofs were meant to exhibit *craiceann*, an aesthetically pleasing 'skin' or finish that was the seal of craft, pride, emotional invest-ment and memory.

The word "finish" above, as used by Feldman, is a further nuancing of what is meant by the terms *cuma* and *craiceann*. His extension of the term to cover not only performance but also labor indicates, correctly I believe, that the aesthetic extends to both and, in this respect, does not differentiate rigidly between "art" and "work" or "craft." This is consonant with the semantics of the word "*ealaín*" discussed above. A related English word used by Éamonn Mac Ruairí, when speaking with quiet pride of his daughter's house keeping abilities, will further clarify the semantic range of the terms: "*Tá* taste *iontach ag Helena*" (Helena has wonderful *taste*). He was commenting not only upon the product of her labor, but also the discerning and proper manner in which she carried out her tasks. Her work and her approach to it could also be said to exhibit *cuma* and *craiceann*.

Art and labor, then, may be discussed using the same terms and within related semantic fields disclosing that art is not segregated from other aspects of culture but is considered to fall within the same remit. Nevertheless, a dialectical tension also exists between the two domains where those overconcerned with entertainment were some-times ironically characterized as not being *i gceart*, that is, not right (in the head), or *fallsa* "lazy." Despite this tension, verbal wit and eloquence, storytelling ability, music, dance, and song continue to be highly regarded, such that entertainment and perfor-mance are viewed as a kind of work. As a *poeisis* or making, music, dance, and song recreate reality by raising reality above itself in the space set apart for them. Ricoeur (1991: 137–155) sees the mimetic process of this recreation as having three moments. Drawing upon the practical field of experience (prefigured reality), narratives unfold their worlds in front of themselves. The receiver or reader encounters this narrative, appropriating it, thereby enlarging his own horizon of understanding. In so doing, the text reshapes the world of the reader, presenting him with a new horizon. In this way the reception of new texts leads to a new and intensified understanding of reality on the receiver's part.

The workings of entertainment in Tory and particularly of the dance and its con-stituent parts can be regarded as such a case. The "text" here is the action undertaken by the islanders, their meaningful and purposive efforts through preparation for and execution of skilled performances in order to augment their own reality in a meaning-ful way (Ricoeur 1981: 197–221). Play and ritual, according to Gadamer (1989: 116), only attain proper realization in performance, and the "chance conditions" pertaining to performance also form an integral part of the whole. Significant here, I believe, also is the etymological connection highlighted by Gadamer between the German word *Spiel* and its original meaning, "to dance."

Preparation for the Dance

The way in which the dance space was prepared can be interpreted as a clear demarcation of the special precincts for the event, thus creating the conditions for "the emergence of new dimensions of experience and reality" (Ricoeur 1991: 134). The schoolhouse was the only building on the island large enough to accommodate the numbers attending. There has been a school in Tory since 1839, with the present building dating from 1849. Dancing in the school was certainly not regarded as unusual in an anonymous (1899) late-nineteenth-century account, and until 1956, when another building became available, the school house was the usual location for such events (Ó Colm 1995 [1971]). Occasionally, during the day, however, the pier itself might also be used. Initially, the islanders would have to get permission from the priest to hold a dance, since the priest was the manager of the school building and often the sole figure of external authority on the island.

Some priests did not approve of dancing and often were inclined to refuse. Others gave consent grudgingly, and a small number did not object to dancing at all. Having got the key, the room itself had to be prepared, the desks set aside, and the long, low stools known as "forms," pronounced "furems," set around by the wall to provide seating, especially for the elders.

Lighting was also very important. The aim was to have the place as brightly lit as possible and sometimes the organizers would have as many as eleven lamps. These lamps had to be requested from their owners and some had only one part of a lamp, so that where different owners contributed different parts to make a whole, it was imperative, to avoid squabbles, that the proper part be returned to its rightful owner. Hugh Dixon (1890–1957) was the first islander to own a "tilley" lamp and Éamonn Mac Ruairí asked him for the loan of it, shortly after he had acquired it. [3] He remembers the long convoluted conversation in which he had to engage, before eventually summoning up the courage to ask for the lamp. The owner consented, but brought it to the schoolhouse himself. William Rodgers (1905–1995) also had a lamp that was particularly bright. When the organizers were successful in borrowing it, it would be given pride of place in the center of the ceiling. Often, when oil was in short supply, candles had to suffice. These left black sooty marks on the wall, which had to be cleaned the following day, for fear of incurring the wrath of the priest or of the teacher.

Other details had also to be meticulously attended to. Protruding nails in the floorboards were driven more deeply into the wood with shore stones, to avoid snagging the dancers, and the floor was also sprinkled with water to prevent the dust from rising. All of these preparations testify to the care of the young men in providing the best location possible for the enjoyment of their fellow islanders. People attending the dance would go to considerable lengths to dress their best in an effort to achieve a "personal aesthetic triumph" (Pitt Rivers 1971: 70). The young women, in particular, sent away for dress patterns and had them made up by other island women who had some training in dressmaking. Bright floral patterns were favored. Likewise, there was a tailor to suit the men. In this way a special space for the occasion was prepared. These preparations can be regarded as involving the aesthetic concepts of *cuma* and *craiceann*, the proper "shape" and "skin" or "finish" without which no greatness could be anticipated. Subsequently, characteristics of island culture were displayed in the representations that the islanders produced *of* themselves and *for* themselves and others. Dances were strictly supervised and proper behavior was demanded of, and imposed upon, all present. Despite the fact that the priest might not always be in favor of dancing, his presence was regarded as another element contributing to the night's success, probably because order was more easily achieved because of it. To the present day, dances begin late around 11:00 p.m. or so and continue for several hours afterwards. Children were also subject to the same conditions and school goers were obliged to leave at midnight, usually accompanied by their mothers—a restriction imposed by the priest.

In this way, the enclosed space prepared for the dance, like the closed world of play that Gadamer (1989: 112) argues lets down one of its walls, also opened onto the islanders' world, thereby mediating their experiences of island life, and enabling them to identify positively with it.

The Dance

Dancing is, according to Huizinga (1955 [1938]: 165), "a particular and particularly perfect form of playing," a view that has been borne out by many subsequent studies. Dance, a multi-sensory activity which creates a particular atmosphere and changes the dancer's bodily state, in turn facilitates the emergence of certain emotions (Fuller Snyder 1972: 256). Through dance, the stimulation of the body provides and communicates a kind of excitement (Hanna 1979: 68) capable of facilitating a kind of ecstacy. It is, furthermore, an enactment of social and gender relations (Quigley 1985, Cowan 1990). Although dance and song are not explicitly linked, dance often functions as the precursor of song performance (Zumthor 1990: 158–9). Young people were particularly fond of dancing and, as long as their health allowed, older people continued to take the floor. I remember clearly, on one of my first visits to Tory in the early seventies, how, after playing a football match on the island, the islanders gathered to provide entertainment for us. The older women were the first out dancing. A fondness or desire for anything, and in this case for dancing, is called *dúil* in Irish. This "desire" is a central element in the success of the dance, the anticipation and the excitement generated by the run up to it, culminating in the event itself. Although smaller events occurred in people's houses, dances in the school house occurred relatively rarely and can be regarded as the "formal mechanism for gathering the community together" (Glassie 1982: 74), also found in Newfoundland (Quigley 1985: 59). They were highly prestigious occasions, which increased the *dúil*, the "desire" or "expectation," with which people looked forward to them, *mar bheadh cat ag fanacht le luchóg*, as Éamonn memorably expressed it, "like a cat waiting for a mouse." The intensity of this *dúil* or desire for the event to go well contributed in large part to the success of the night. It also raised the stakes, however, putting pressure on all performers to strive to execute their performances well, recalling Glassie's idea of an exacting test. This included not only the "stars" who were renowned for their skilled execution of the Hornpipe (Figure 1) or the Maggie Pickie (solo step dances), or the singers, but the group dancers as well. The elders surveyed the proceedings with great watchfulness, noting any departure from the norms of good performance for future criticism.

Such vigilance contributed greatly to the festive atmosphere of the dance of course. The small size of the school house (about 18 by 35 feet) meant that on nights such as these, the crowd present would be rather large, making the night "warm" or

The Liverpool Hornpipe

Figure 1. The Liverpool: Tory Dancers' favorite tune for the solo Hornpipe.

"hot," in Irish *te*. I consider that such a value is linked to the *dúil* or "desire" which I have been discussing, in that the anticipation or desire for the event contributed strongly to its emotional warmth when it finally took place. The desire of anticipation then became transformed into the desire to achieve a big night. This can be viewed metaphorically in terms of warmth. The maintenance of the high pitch of excitement in the night was metaphorically known as keeping the night "up," *suas*. Allowing the night to become "cold," *fuar* or to go "down," *síos*, was avoided at all costs.

These metaphors are part of a complex of concepts central to an understanding of the aesthetics of entertainment in Tory and must first be understood as referring to bodily experience. The heat referred to is, I consider, first and foremost a physical heat, which is also interpreted metaphorically. On a visit by me to Tory in August 1987 during the island's summer festival, the presence of large crowds at the dance, coupled with the vigorous activity on the floor, certainly contributed to the heat of the night, although at the time, its connection with the night's success was not apparent to me. The heat is, moreover, contingent upon having a large crowd. It would be very difficult for a small crowd to achieve the correct conditions for this physical and metaphorical heat. A set dance at such an event, where the hall was only half-full, might be called a "cold set," *cúrsa fuar* (Ó Laoire 2000, 2002).

It is relevant here that this heat is also linked to kinship. People who are closely related and who assume responsibility for each other's well being are considered to be "warm to one another," *te dá chéile*, (Ó Laoire 2000, 2002). This is much more than simple friendliness and encompasses the frequency of positive interaction deemed proper for close kin. It is sometimes called "clannish" in English. The heat at the dance, then, can be regarded partly as the representation of the ideal community, where the desirability of mutual responsibility and interdependence was symbolically manifested.

The wish to achieve this feeling of heat is further confirmed by the fact that in the fifties, when Éamonn Mac Ruairí, Séamus Ó Dúgáin and others were organizing the dance, they were faced with a problem regarding its configuration. When they assumed responsibility for the event, it was clearly divided into two constituent parts, marked by the departure of the elders when the last songs had been sung. At that time, the songs were sung during one period after a prolonged bout of dancing. The young men considered this unsatisfactory, believing that the departure of the elders left the schoolhouse looking "cold," *fuar*. To remedy the situation, they deliberately changed the configuration of the dance, interspersing songs between every few dances so that all the songs would not be performed together. The elders, because of their great desire for hearing songs, were induced to stay for a longer period and, correspondingly, the pitch of the night would not descend, thus leaving it feeling "cold." This is striking in view of what I have been saying regarding the elders' strictness concerning proper performance. Their departure might have been regarded as a positive turn, allowing a more relaxed atmosphere to prevail. On the contrary, however, the presence of such a vigilant and critical group was crucial to the realization of the desired goals of "heat," *teas* and of keeping the night "up," away from descent into the mediocre, lackluster, and the "cold." Such metaphors may be regarded as forming a coherent composite of the theory of a life cycle and through that a world view which associates life with light and warmth and death with cold and darkness (Lakoff and Turner 1989: 87). The orientational metaphors "up" and "down" are also consonant with such an interpretation (Lakoff and Johnson 1980). It is significant in this case that most of the schoolhouse dances were held during the darkness of winter, between Halloween and St. Patrick's Day and Easter. Significantly, what was considered the biggest event of the year, St. Patrick's Day, was held in the middle of Lent, which was, before Vatican II, a time of severe restrictions of fasting and abstinence. Again, the dance can be read as warding off the cold and darkness of the winter with the metaphorically constituted warmth of the celebration of island life. In this respect it can be said to resemble the carnivalesque, representing to some degree a resistance to such Lenten constraints (Bakhtin 1984). The world of dance and song unfolded in the specially configured precincts of the dance in Tory island, then, invokes the extended present, a mediation of the interplay of memory, expectations for the future, and the exigencies of the present (Ricoeur 1991: 49).

Individual Performances

When sufficient dances had been performed, soloists would begin to be called out for either step dances or songs. Many were regarded as being more than ordinarily proficient in these areas, and a certain rivalry existed between some individuals. Two of those still regarded as great singers of the past are a sister and brother Kit (1880–1953) and John Tom Ó Mianáin (1889–1967).[4] They lived in the East End of the island with another sister Sarah (1891–1980). John Tom, in particular, was highly regarded as a singer on the island and when present at the dance would always be called upon to sing. He usually sang two songs, the request for the second distinguishing him as a better than average performer. John Tom's singing was particularly admired because his clear enunciation of the words. "*Phronouncálfadh sé na focla go maith*" (he would pronounce the words well) I was told by a younger contemporary who remembered his singing vividly. Her use of an English loan word, *phronouncálfadh*, reflects her wish to pinpoint exactly what she considered best about John's singing. His *glór cinn*, his "head" or "individual voice" is often compared to the pipes, one of the reasons he was so sought after. From good quality archive recordings made by RTÉ, the Irish national broadcasting service, in the late forties and mid-fifties, it is possible to get some idea of the qualities which made him so much admired (Ó Laoire 2002). The voice is deep, clear, and resonant with a strong nasality in articulation. This quality lends a sharpness or hardness of tone to the voice, which was, I believe, in part a declamatory tactic calculated to transmit the voice distinctly throughout the school house. Similarities between John Tom's voice and the tone of the bagpipes can, for me, be heard, in the same way that they can be identified in the voices of other more renowned Irish traditional singers, for example, Joe Heaney, Darach Ó Catháin, and Nioclás Tóibín. Characteristics can, then, be recognized in John Tom's voice that allow us to at least glimpse what a traditional aesthetic entailed and to understand better what the term *binn* "sweet, melodious" signified in such an aesthetic. It might indeed be labeled the "grain" of the voice, which Barthes describes as "the materiality of the body speaking its mother tongue" (Barthes 1996: 46). I believe that these are the qualities that were associated with the individual voice that Éamonn calls the *guth cinn*, "the head voice." Ciarán Carson (1986: 10) has also discussed this term in relation to traditional singing but I believe that his use of the term reflects a usage more influenced by familiarity with mainstream musical terminology.

Eamonn Mac Ruairí has remarked of John's singing that: "*Nuair a cheolfadh John Tom 'Scairteach Áranna' agus 'Amhrán na Scadán' bheadh oíche mhór i dtigh na scoile!*" (When John Tom would sing '*Scairteach Áranna*' ("The Shouting of Aran") and '*Amhrán na Scadán*' ("The Song of the Herring"), there would be a big night in the schoolhouse!) (See figure 2.)[5]

This statement seems relatively simple and uncomplicated, but in light of the metaphorical meanings we have been discussing it can be seen that it assumes a thorough practical knowledge of the context in which he sang. The two songs mentioned here are also important. One is a lament for a tragic drowning that occurred of the coast of Aranmore Island on the West Donegal coast, probably in the nineteenth century (Figure 2).

The other also concerns the sea, but is a composition of Éamonn Dooley Mac Ruairí (1856–1931), an islander who made a number of songs at the turn of the twentieth century. It is a lighthearted backward look at the poet's life as a herring fisherman now that he is old and is probably the island's most popular song today, being regarded as something of a local anthem (Ó Laoire 1996, 2002). John Tom was a sterling performer because he had a remarkable voice, famous for its clarity and for the ease with

Figure 2. *Scairteach Áranna* "The Shouting of Aran."
Song sung by John Tom Ó Mianáin, at the Tory dances.
From the singing of Éamonn Mac Ruairí and Séamus Ó Dúgáin.

Scairteach Áranna

1
Tá scairteach mhór mhór á dhéanamh in Árainn
Ag iarraidh orainne na cladaí fhágáil
Ach imigí shibhse ós sibh tá sáraí
'S cha philleann muidinne go raibh lucht den leathach linn.

2
Shíl muid féin go raibh muid láidir
'S go ndéanfas muid bulaíocht mhór an lá sin
Ach tháinig an plúchadh is cha léir dúinn Árainn
'S cha raibh fios ár dtuairisc in aon chuan in Éirinn

3
Chuir bean chupaí in iúl do Mháire
Go mbeadh siad aici ar thús na mbádaí
Chrom sí a ceann agus rinne sí foighde
'S ar dheireadh na scéalta bhí an báthadh déanta

4
A Mháire Bhán bhocht a bhéal na céille
A chailín stuama thar a raibh mhná in Éirinn
Tá tú sa bhaile inniu 's nach dubh clár d'éadain
'S go bhfuil fhios ag an tsaol gurb í do chlann a chráigh thú

5
'Mhuire is a Rí nach seo an truaighe
Mise agus Máire Bhán bhocht a bheith scartha ó chéile
A raibh mo chroí inti go barr na méar
S go raibh sí liomsa ar an nádúr chéanna.

6
Cuirimse scrios agus léan ar Árainn
Sí bhain díomsa mo thriúr fear breátha
Ba deise nádúr is a bhí múinte
Is a bhí ar aghaidh ins na leabharthaí Gaeilg.

Translation
"The Shouting of Aran"

1
There is a great shouting being done in Aran
Asking us to abandon the shores
But all of you should depart since you have been overcome
And we won't return until we bring back a load of sea-wrack.

2
We thought ourselves that we were strong
And that we would achieve great feats that day
But the blizzard came and we couldn't see Aran
And no one in any of the harbors of Ireland knew our whereabouts.

3
A woman reading cups said to Mary
That they would return to her aboard the first boats
She bowed her head and remained patient
But at the end of the stories the drowning was done.

4
My poor fair-haired Mary, my speaker of reason
Wise beyond all the young women of Ireland
You are at home today and how dark is your brow
And the world knows that your children have tormented you.

5
Mary and King, isn't this the pity
My poor fair-haired Mary and I to be apart
Whom my heart loved to her very fingertips
And she acted towards me in the same way.

6
My curse on Aran with sorrow and destruction
It has taken from me my three fine men
Who were so good-natured and courteous
And who were well advanced in Gaelic learning

which the lyrics might be followed. John also sang the songs in the proper configuration, never becoming confused or forgetting the words as others might do. His efficacy
as a performer helped make the night *maith* "good" and thus effect the transformation
of the night into an *oíche mhór* "a big night." His success was also, however, due to his
desire for singing, since he is remembered as constantly practicing his songs even
during the performance of household chores. His success links the *dúil*, the desire of
anticipation to the desire to perform according to *ceart* "right" in order to achieve
cuma and *craiceann*, the proper "shape" and "skin" or "finish." That is to say that both his
intense interest in song and in acquiring the correct way of a song were conveyed in the
conviction of his performance, which contributed greatly to the listeners' enjoyment of
his singing, since it confirmed their expectations of music, text, and presentation. Discussing this exact point with me, Teresa McClafferty remarked concerning her own
view of good performance:

> *Tá daoine a bhfuil dúil acu in amhrán thar amhrán eile—tá daoine ag gabháil cheoil atá*
> *ábalta ar amhrán a cheol agus nach mbíonn ábalta ceann eile a cheol chomh maith, nó*
> *caithfidh tú dúil a bheith agat san amhrán le bheith ábalta brí agus misneach a chur ann.*
> *Caithfidh tú dúil a bheith agat ann.*

> (There are people who prefer one song to another—there are people who sing who can
> sing one song and who cannot sing another equally as well, for you must have *dúil* [desire]
> for the song to be able to put *brí* [life/meaning] and *misneach* [courage] into it. You must
> have a desire for it.)

Séamus Ó Dúgáin (Jimmy Duggan) (1928–2000), who acted as one of my con-
sultants for this study, deserves mention in this regard. A visiting journalist wrote of
him during the island's crisis in 1983 (Tóibín 1990: 116): "Among the dancers one man
had been remarkable. He knew the steps inside out and he performed them with
incredible skill and some small flourishes. He danced with extraordinary seriousness
and intensity."

The accuracy of this observation is borne out by his contemporary, Éamonn
Mac Ruairí's assessment of Jimmy's contribution to dances, stating that when Jimmy
was called out to perform, he was always sure to do something that would keep the
night "up." The extraordinary individual was an important figure in the achievement of
a dance's climax, then, someone who possessed the *brí* "life," or "energy," and the
misneach "courage" to make the night a lively and exciting one. This ability alone was
not what others appreciated, but the willingness of the individual to share his or her
talent freely in order to include all participants in its glow (Spencer 1985: 16).

The connection between individual agency and the complex of metaphors associated with entertainment is remarkable. In Irish, the words *glór* or *guth* designate
voice, the second, significantly, also being synonymous with a song air or tune. *Cuirtear*
guth leis an amhrán "a voice is put with the song," literally is one way of saying a song is
sung. Another term for a song air or melody, *fonn*, is important in relation to Teresa's
foregrounding of *dúil* "desire" and its importance for delivering a convincing performance having *brí* and *misneach*. Ó Dónaill's Irish-English dictionary gives three
further meanings for the word *fonn*: (1) a base or foundation, and arising from it
(2), territory or land, with (3), signifying the desire or mood which takes someone to

accomplish something. *Dúil* "desire" has been demonstrated as being central to the successful realization of a "big night" and of its component parts, particularly as regards the performance of song. In connecting the term *guth* with *fonn* in all its meanings, I imply an identification between *fonn*, "desire," "song air," *dúil*, "desire," and *guth*, "voice, song air," relating song directly to the fervor necessary to bring the night to the highest pitch. I further suggest that these metaphorically rich valuations situate song at the highest level of entertainment as practiced in dance in Tory (Glassie 1982: 37). Such a claim does not at all negate the centrality of preparation, of instrumental music, of group and solo dancing, and all the other action which contributed to the transformation of the night into an event which went beyond its merely ostensive reference to disclose a world in its own right (Ricoeur 1981: 220). On the contrary, as I have been arguing, these were absolutely necessary to ensure the successful performances of songs, since without them, song could not achieve its most profound efficacy. Moreover, the tacit understanding embodied by the semantic relations I have identified between aesthetic evaluations of the singing and the most intense moments of performance seem to support such a claim. This serves to remind us, furthermore, that the complexity of the physical act of singing, so often taken for granted, is surpassed in performance where, as Walter Ong (1990: ix) has stated, "the culmination of voice is not merely any use of language, but song."

I have discussed elsewhere in detail how members of one island family constructed a matrix of meaning around a particular song, *A Phaidí a Ghrá* (Paddy, my love), which they linked specifically with the early and tragic demise of their brother (Ó Laoire 1999b, 2002). A coincidental correspondence between his first name and that of a character in the song enabled the creation of a new metaphorical association with the narrative alluded to therein. I argue that an explicitly erotic love song came to be interpreted in terms of the tensions between marital and sibling relationships in Tory. Furthermore, the link between love and death in folk song, well known throughout northern Europe (Toelken 1995), and emigration were also interpreted in a fashion emblematic of many aspects of island life. Ricoeur's idea that "metaphors produce new configurations of meaning by extending the polysemy characteristic of natural languages" (1981: 39) in a redescribed and iconically augmented reality (1991: 117, 149) illumines how this new association transforms the erotic song's referential meaning by creating a new metaphorical constellation of meaning, capable of expressing the dilemmas of maturity, emigration, death, family loyalty, desire for marriage, and even the survival of the island community. The performance of this song carried on for a prolonged period of perhaps fifty years at the dance in Tory and may be read as a subtle and shifting commentary upon many aspects of island life, identifying the dance with Turner's liminal space "where the central values and axioms of the culture are potentially scrutinized" (1967: 167).

This is consonant with the letting down of one of the walls in Gadamer's closed circle of meaning, so that the participants may encounter themselves. The absolute silence and stillness demanded for the performance of songs contrasted starkly with the charged, patterned body movement and excitement of the dancing. Moreover, the freer, less constrained rubato rhythm of the slower songs also signified a change of mood. Songs such as *A Phaidí a Ghrá* or *Scairteach Áranna* were empowered by the conditions in which they were performed to attain the maximum potential of their immanent meaning, eliciting feelings of longing, grief, pining, or nostalgia, known as *cumha* pronounced [ku:i]. This is an important concept not to be confused with the orthographically similar term for "shape" and "appearance," *cuma*. When the night was being kept *suas* "up," when it was *te* "warm, hot," when performances exhibited "proper shape and finish" or *cuma* and *craiceann*, an intense longing feeling, *cumha*, could be efficaciously evoked The expressive power of songs were further enhanced by their juxtaposition with lively dance music in jig, reel, hornpipe, polka, and highland tempos and the singing of humorous songs, also in quicker tempo, which elicited laughter and merriment. Songs such as *Amhrán na Scadán* (The Song of the Herring), or *An Seanduine Dóite* (The Burnt-Out Old Man), describing a young woman's dissatisfaction with her aged and impotent husband, examined in a lighter mode issues broached in the tragic songs, so that each both leavened and complemented the other and spurred the participants on to the *ekstasis* of a successful event. Gadamer (1989: 131) reads such a change as the creation of a circle of meaning complete within itself, a "transformation into structure," giving rise, in the case of the sad songs, to what he calls a "tragic pensiveness." He identifies such a feeling as the deepening of a spectator's continuity with himself or herself through the "self-knowledge" and "relief" gained by participation (1989: 131/133). In this respect, Gadamer's idea may be considered very closely akin to the Gaelic idea of "pining grief or longing," disclosed by the term *cumha*. This is considered an extremely intense emotion by Irish speakers, and it also considered necessary to express this or other strong emotions by letting out its *racht*, its burden or pent-up energy, in a strategy resembling catharsis. Indeed, it is worth noting here that the term *cumha*, in the older Gaelic language, was the explicit term for the instrumental lament composed by professional harpers, suggesting a connection between such feelings and musical expression (Ó Madagáin 1981). *Cumha*, in this case, importantly contrasts with the related but distinct term for "lonesomeness" and the "feeling of a lack of company," known as *uaigneas*. "Pining grief," or *cumha*, is linked to "right," *ceart*, "proper shape," *cuma*, "heat," *teas*, keeping the mood "up," *suas* so that the dance is transformed into "a big night," *oíche mhór*. In the same way loneliness, isolation, lack of company, or fear of the supernatural, or *uaigneas*, may be associated with the "coldness" or *fuacht* of a night which was going downwards "*síos*." Although similar, in the sense that they both refer to emotional states which are covered by the related terms "loneliness" or "lonesomeness," the terms *cumha* and *uaigneas* refer, through the interconnected matrix of associated semantic fields I have been discussing, to very different states. I suggest that *uaigneas* has more negative associations of isolation associated with the metaphors of downward motion and coldness, where *cumha* seems to me to have more positive associations of affectionate memories associated with the heat, and upward orientation, associated with a good night. *Cumha* is a different kind of emotion, which, although sorrowful, is considered to be affirming in that it reinforces the values of kinship and community reciprocity which the dance exemplifies. This may also be extended to cover a life-and-death polarity.

Conclusion

The dynamics of this matrix can be considered also to refer to a cosmological pattern, in that an "upwards" orientation, *suas*, may refer to a southwards direction (*deas, deisceart*) and "down" or "downwards," *síos*, to a northwards direction (*tuaidh, tuaisceart*). The south is seen as the source of light where a northerly direction is considered dark, unwelcoming, and cold. Importantly these are also linked to the right (also *deas*) and the left sides of the body, recalling *ciotach* "left" or "wrong," previously mentioned (Ó Laoire 2000, 2002). This reveals a coherently constructed, metaphorically mediated world, a perspective which broadly suffuses all discourse and action. It also communicates in some way how Gaelic speakers' reality is constituted, and how they convey to themselves "those truths about themselves and the world that they consider more than ordinarily permanent" (*an fhírinne úd fúthu féin agus faoin saol a mheasann siad a bheith buan thar an ngnáth*," translation mine) (Ó Crualaoich 1989: 15). In adopting a hermeneutical approach founded on an ontology where "ways of being" are mediated by cultural signs and works, it is possible, as Sancho-Velázquez (1994) has advocated, to interpret the cognitive categories of musical performance in a way not predicated upon whether people possess the category of "aesthetics in any objective reverifiable sense" (Feld 1990: 233); rather, the project becomes a cross-cultural one, asking "how to describe the quality of experience they feel and my relation to it" (ibid).

My investigation of metaphors referring to the poetics of entertainment in Tory has, to some extent, disclosed a world with rich and subtle shades of meaning. In regarding the mode of being of the component events of the dance in this world as play, following Gadamer, it becomes possible to reveal that such matters are taken extremely seriously, despite the lack of an overtly practical purpose. And yet, perhaps, the imagining through music, dance, and song of a utopian representation was a sufficient purpose. F.H.A. Aalen and Hugh Brody (1969: xviii), in their introduction to a socioeconomic study of the decline of the community in Gola, another Donegal island, now uninhabited, once mention the importance of morale for the psychological well being of the community but do not touch upon it afterwards. As Glassie noted in Fermanagh (1975: 25), "For people whose days pass in rough work, an occasional break for enjoyment is not a trivial matter. Entertainment makes a hard life durable."

A study of Tory islanders' sense of place in 1989 found that the foremost attractions of island life were "aesthetic," mainly concerned with quality of life (Bryce 1989). Islanders' music making, dancing, and singing contribute strongly to their understanding of the validity of their reality in their own place. Crichton Smith's opposition of island life with "aesthetics," "modernity," and "reality," may suggest that this is the "real" debate that continues to motivate the community. Mediated poetically through music, dance, and song, the world of the Tory islanders, as I have discussed in this paper, sustains a living island community, determined to find ways of dealing with the challenges presented by the realities of the twenty-first century.

NOTES

1. For an explanation of the development of these relationships, see Ó Laoire 2003.

2. I was introduced to the theories of Gadamer, Ricoeur and others by Professor Roger W. H. Savage, as a visiting scholar at the Department of Ethnomusicology and Systematic Musicology at UCLA, during the academic year 1996–1997, on a Fulbright Scholarship. I am indebted to Professor Tim Rice for acting as my host and for facilitating my visit in every way on that occasion. I am also grateful to Niall Keegan, The Irish World Music Center, University of Limerick, for the transcription of "The Liverpool Hornpipe," and to Sandra Joyce, also of IWMC, for transcribing "The Shouting of Aran." Thanks also to Jeff Janeczko for help with formatting.

3. A "tilley" lamp was a paraffin lamp, operated by a pumping action, widely used before the advent of electricity in Ireland. The name comes from the manufacturer. The last major phase of rural electrification began in Ireland in 1956.

4. The "Tom" here is a patronymic, a naming system common in Tory and among other Gaelic speaking communities. This system may also use the mother's name. Sometimes, one member of a family may be known by the father's name, while another uses the mother's (see Fox 1995 [1978]).

5. The text and translation of *Amhrán na Scadán*, "The Song of the Herring" may be found in Ó Laoire 1996. A recording may be heard on the CD accompanying Ó Laoire 2002 (Track 1).

REFERENCES

Aalen, F. H. A. and Hugh Brody
    1969   *Gola: The Life and Last Days of an Island Community*. Cork: Mercier Press.

Anonymous
    1899   "Feis Ceoil on Tory Island." In *Fáinne an Lae* (Gaelic League Paper), 87.

Bakhtin, Mikhail
    1984   *Rabelais and his World*. Translated by Hélène Iswolsky. Bloomington: Indiana University Press.

Barthes, Roland
    1996   "The Grain of the Voice." In M. Huxley and N. Witts, eds., *The Twentieth Century Performance Reader*. London: Routledge, pp. 44–52.

Becker, Judith
    1983   " 'Aesthetics' in Late Twentieth Century Scholarship." *World of Music* 25 (31): 65–80.

Breathnach, Breandán
    1977   *Folk Music and Dances of Ireland*. Cork: Mercier Press.

Brody, Hugh
    1973   *Inishkillane: Change and Decline in the West of Ireland*. London: Jill Norman & Hobhouse.

Bryce, Nuala
    1989   "An Irish Island's Sense of Place." MA thesis, Department of Geography, University of Edinburgh.

Carson, Ciarán
    1986   *Pocket Guide to Irish Traditional Music*. Belfast: Appletree.

Cowan, Jane K.
   1990   *Dance and the Body Politic in Northern Greece.* Princeton: Princeton University Press.

Crichton Smith, Iain
   1986   "Real People in a Real Place." In *Towards the Human: Selected Essays by Iain Crichton Smith.* Edinburgh: MacDonald Publishers, pp. 13–73.

Feld, Steven
   1990   *Sound and Sentiment: Birds, Weeping Poetics and Song in Kaluli Expression.* Pennsylvania: University of Pennsylvania Press.

Feldman, Allen
   1985   *The Northern Fiddler.* Belfast: Blackstaff.
   1999   *The Northern Fiddler—Irish Traditional Fiddle Playing in Donegal and Tyrone 1977–79.* (Exhibition catalogue). Dublin: Irish Traditional Music Archive.

Fox, Robin
   1995 [1978]   *The Tory Islanders: A People of the Celtic Fringe.* Cambridge: Cambridge University Press.

Fuller Snyder, Allegra
   1972   "The Dance Symbol." *New Dimensions in Dance Research: Anthropology and Dance—The American Indian, CORD Research Annual*: 247–260.

Gadamer, Hans-Georg
   1989   *Truth and Method.* Translated by Joel Weinsheimer and Donald G. Marshall. New York: Continuum.

Geertz, Clifford
   1973   *The Interpretation of Cultures.* New York: Basic Books.

Glassie, Henry
   1975   *All Silver No Brass: An Irish Christmas Mumming.* Bloomington: Indiana University Press.
   1982   *Passing the Time: Folklore and History in an Ulster Community.* Dublin: O' Brien Press.

Hanna, Judith Lynne
   1979   *To Dance is Human: A Theory of Non-Verbal Communication.* Austin: University of Texas Press.

Hunter, Jim
   1996   "Tory Island—Habitat, Economy and Society." *Ulster Folklife* 42: 38–75.

Huizinga, Johan
   1955 [1938]   *Homo Ludens: A Study of the Play Element in Culture.* Boston: The Beacon Press.

Jones, Michael Owen
   1971   "The Concept of the Aesthetic in the Traditional Arts." *Western Folklore* 30 (April): 77–104.

Lakoff, George and Mark Johnson
   1980   *Metaphors We Live By.* Chicago: University of Chicago Press.

Lakoff, George and Mark Turner
   1989   *More than Cool Reason: A Field Guide to Poetic Metaphor.* Chicago: University of Chicago Press.

Merriam, Alan
   1964   *The Anthropology of Music*. Chicago: Northwestern University Press.

Ó Colm, Eoghan
   1995 [1971]   *Toraigh na dTonn*. Indreabhán: Cló Iar-Chonnachta.

Ó Crualaoich, Gearóid
   1989   "Litríocht na Gaeltachta: Seoladh isteach ar Pheirspeictíocht ó Thaobh na
                 Litríochta Béil." In P. Ó Fiannachta, ed., *Litríocht na Gaeltachta, Léachtaí
                 Cholm Cille XIX*. Maigh Nuad: An Sagart, pp.8–25.

Ó Laoire, Lillis
   1996   "Ar Chreig i Lár na Farraige: Traditions of Song from Tory Island." *Ulster
                 Folklife* 42: 79–97.
   1999a   "Big Days, Big Nights: Entertainment and Representation in a Donegal Com-
                 munity." *Irish Journal of Anthropology* 4: 73–83.
   1999b   "Údair Úra: New Authorities: Cultural Process and Meaning in a Gaelic
                 Folksong." *Iris Nua Éireannach/New Hibernia Review* 3(3): 131–144.
   2000   "Metaphors We Live By: Some Examples from Donegal Irish." *Western Folk-
                 lore* 59 (Winter): 33–48.
   2002   *Ar Chreag i Lár na Farraige: Amhráin agus Amhránaithe i dToraigh*. (On a
                 Rock in the Middle of the Ocean: Songs and Singers in Tory.) Indreabhán:
                 Cló Iar-Chonnachta.
   2003   "Fieldwork in Common Places: An Ethnographer's Experiences in Tory
                 Island." *British Journal of Ethnomusicology* 12(1): 113–136.

Ó Madagáin, Breandán
   1981   "Irish Vocal Music of Lament and Syllabic Verse." In R. O'Driscoll, ed., *The
                 Celtic Consciousness*. Toronto: McClelland and Stewart, pp. 311–332.

Ong, Walter J.
   1990   "Foreword." In Paul Zumthor, *Oral Poetry: An Introduction*. Translated by
                 Kathryn Judy Murphy. Minneapolis: University of Minnesota Press, pp. ix–xii.

Pitt Rivers, Julian A.
   1971 [1954]   *The People of the Sierra*. Chicago: University of Chicago Press.

Quigley, Colin
   1985   *Close to the Floor: Folk Dance in Newfoundland*. St. Johns, Newfoundland:
                 Memorial University.

Ricoeur, Ricoeur
   1981   *Hermeneutics and the Human Sciences*. Translated by John B. Thompson.
                 Cambridge: Cambridge University Press.
   1991   *A Ricoeur Reader*. Mario J. Valdés, ed. Toronto: University of Toronto Press.

Sancho-Velázquez, Angeles
   1994   "Interpreting Metaphors: Cross-Cultural Hermeneutics as Hermeneutic
                 Project." *Selected Reports in Ethnomusicology* 10: 37–50.

Spencer, Paul
   1985   *Society and the Dance: The Social Anthropology of Process and Performance*.
                 Cambridge: Cambridge University Press.

Toelken, Barre
   1995   *Morning Dew and Roses: Nuance, Metaphor and Meaning in Folksongs*.
                 Urbana: University of Illinois Press.

Tóibín, Colm
    1990   "The Island that wouldn't go to sleep." In *The Trial of the Generals: Selected Journalism 1980–1990*. Dublin: Raven Arts' Press, pp. 112–120.

Turner, Victor
    1969   *The Forest of Symbols: Aspects of Ndembu Ritual*. Ithaca: Cornell University Press.

Zumthor, Paul
    1990   *Oral Poetry: An Introduction*. Translated by Kathryn Judy Murphy. Minneapolis: University of Minnesota Press.

The "Supermen" and the "Normal People": Music, Politics, and Tradition in 1990s Serbia

BRANA MIJATOVIC

University of California, Los Angeles

During the devastating political, economic, and cultural circumstances of 1990s Serbia, voices of political and cultural opposition to the regime of Slobodan Milosevic took many forms. Musical genres as diverse as rock, rap, reggae, Byzantine ethno-jazz, New Balkan music, and recreated Serbian village singing resonated with these oppositional voices. One singer-songwriter, Djordje Balasevic, even created his own genre of protest songs that could loosely be described as pop music. One music genre, however—newly composed folk music, or turbo-folk—supported the political agendas of the regime and served as a catalyst for extreme nationalistic passions.[1] These two genres—the pop music of Djordje Balasevic and newly-composed folk music—represented opposite political ideals. The political significance of each rested on a different understanding of Serbian history and tradition, thereby shaping political and social life by expressing specific cultural meanings that created and reinforced different senses of moral responsibility and solidarity.

Music's mobilization for different political purposes in Serbia illuminates how music can operate in both productive and destructive ways by shaping ideas of solidarity and community. One of the German philosopher Hans-Georg Gadamer's (1900–2002) great contributions to hermeneutical philosophy was his elucidation the role history and tradition play in the process of understanding. Understanding, for Gadamer (1989: 294), unfolds "on the basis of expectations of meaning drawn from our own prior relation to the subject matter." Since we are always situated within traditions, historical realities of the society into which we are born affect our experiences. Our prejudices—our judgment of a situation before any other elements of that situation have been examined—condition our understanding. "However, understanding in its fullest potential (sense) is only possible when the interpreter examines the legitimacy of his prejudices, their origin and validity" (ibid: 267). Through becoming aware of our prejudices, we are able to acquire a better understanding of what significance tradition has for a present time, that is, what kinds of ideas the tradition is based on and what influence those ideas have on shaping political orientation.

The conflicting understandings Serbian history and tradition set the stage for accepting as "true" specific rhetorical and symbolic elements that were used in different music genres for different purposes and ends. As one of the most powerful means for affirming communal "truths," music genres that evinced both pro- and anti-war orientations created solidarity through a sense of moral allegiance to particular visions of the Serbian community, its tradition, and its history.

History and Politics

At the beginning of the 1990s, the political situation in Serbia was by no means transparent. On the contrary, several social analysts referred to the "opacity of the social world experienced by ordinary citizens of Serbia in the 1990s," and the "experiential messiness" of living in Serbia under Slobodan Milosevic's regime (1989–2000) (Zivkovic 2001, Gordy 1999, Djurkovic 2002). A series of dramatic and traumatic events characterized life in Serbia in the last decade of the twentieth century. These events led to the extreme deterioration of the quality of everyday life and the relentless and rapid compounding of layers of "twisted moral universes" propagated by the media, to which people in Serbia were subjected over a long period of time (Zivkovic 2001).

The strain of the civil wars in Croatia and Bosnia and the coercive regime of Slobodan Milosevic brought poverty, the criminalization of society, and destruction to Serbia. All this was intensified by the years of international economic sanctions and the three-month long bombing of Serbia by forces of the North Atlantic Treaty Organization in 1999.

The economic sanctions affected the most elementary activities of everyday life. By limiting the economy's ability to function legitimately, these sanctions created opportunities for the "gray economy" and illegal activities, which escalated into organized crime that the government covertly supported in order to maintain some semblance of stability. The unprecedented rise in criminal activities was not only tolerated but in many cases openly supported by the state (See E.B. 2003, N.N. 2003, Obradovic 2000, Adzic 2002, Teodorovic 2003). The cumulative effect of the sanctions contributed to the powerlessness felt by ordinary citizens (Gordy 1999). A restricted flow of information from outside of Serbia compounded the psychological and emotional toll on individuals in Serbia, who experienced a constant decline in their living conditions and who were affected in a variety of ways by the horrors of the civil wars. The web of conspiracy theories propagated by the state media, the dissemination of facts on Serbia's victimization and endangerment, the speech of hatred,[2] including death threats and actual killings of those who dared to challenge or disagree with the official politics, and the initial lack of any serious Western political or cultural support of the oppositional forces within Serbia served to further strengthen Milosevic regime and intensify the effects of his politics (for detailed analysis see Brankovic 1995, Curguz Kazimir 2001, Dimitrijevic 1995, Dinkic 1995, Djurkovic 2002, Gordy 1999). The complete collapse of political, economic, and cultural life on the institutional level, the increasingly negative status of Serbia and Serbs in the world media, and their exclusion from the larger political and cultural sphere of Europe was an unprecedented experience for Serbian citizens. While the communist rule of Josip Broz Tito (from 1945 till his death in 1980) curtailed some freedoms, primarily freedom of speech and religious expression, Serbia and Yugoslavia were politically and economically stable and their international reputation was high. During the period from the 1950s to the 1980s, Yugoslavia was regarded as an important factor of stability, not only in the Balkans but in Europe as well (Pribicevic 1995). Yugoslavia's international standing changed in the years following Tito's death in 1980, when the complicated system involving a rotating federal presidency of six members made "decision-making without a final arbiter ultimately . . . impossible" (Judah 1997:156). Each republic and province increasingly demanded that their local and ethnic national interests be put above those of the state. Dennison Rusinow (1995:14) states that it was "the calculations and/or ineptitude" of the politicians from different Yugoslav republics, together with "a decade of mounting economic, political and social crisis . . . [that] transformed endemic tensions and conflicts among its diverse nationalities into collective existential fears for their communal survival that progressively infected them all."[3] This gradual, decade-long accumulation and transformation of conflicting interests into fear for survival, spurred on to a great extent by the electronic and print media in each republic, ultimately led to the break-up of Yugoslavia.

Even if the break-up of Yugoslavia after the death of Tito was inevitable, the wars were not. They were a result of the "creation of new national states in which the leadership of the individual republics brought them into conflict over the distribution of Yugoslav territory, borders and ethnic boundaries" (Pesic 1996:9).[4] In this process of creating new national states, culture, and particularly music, assumed a crucial role in providing a means through which people identified with particular ideas of nationhood, solidarity, and belonging.

Newly-composed Folk Music

In her study of newly-composed folk music (*novokomponovana narodna muzika*) in the former Yugoslavia, Ljerka Vidic Rasmussen (1999) discussed this music's empowering effect for rural migrants to the cities in the period from 1960 to 1992. She examined the ways in which newly-composed folk music (NCFM) served to establish the migrants' social presence within the contested space of normative and alternative cultures of the city. During the 1990s in Serbia this genre become aligned with the politics of the Slobodan Milosevic regime. Newly-composed folk music and its variants supported the political agendas of the regime through its lyrics and video presentation and through its appearance in specific social contexts.

The genre of newly-composed folk music developed in the 1960s in the former Yugoslavia as a modernized version of arrangements of traditional folk music. The term indicated that this music was composed in the vein of the older folk tradition. Rasmussen (1991:128) stated that newly-composed folk music was "a commercial embodiment of a variety of musical traditions found in Yugoslavia," functioning as a genre, a style, and a musical system. It included regional patterns (Serbian, Bosnian, and Macedonian music) as well as features of other musical cultures from Turkish and Greek to Western European pop.

In 1989 a talented Yugoslav/Montenegrin rock musician living in Belgrade, whose stage name was Rambo Amadeus, produced the album "*O Tugo Jesenja*" ("Oh,

Autumn's Sorrow") entirely based on the parody of newly-composed folk music and
called it "turbo-folk." The newly coined term "turbo-folk" implied a mix of intrinsically
foreign elements, such as the combination of "folk" lyrics and melodies with a sound
increasingly modernized through the use of electric instruments such as synthesizers,
electric bass and electric guitar, and the use of music phrases characteristic of the rock
genre (see Kronja 2001 and Djurkovic 2002 for a more detailed explanation of this
term). Since the early 1990s the term turbo-folk was often used synonymously with
the term newly-composed folk music, since in many cases there were no clear cut stylistic differences between songs marketed as turbo-folk and those marketed as NCFM.

However, the term turbo-folk increasingly came to refer to songs whose lyrics
glamorized violence, national extremism, masochism, and excessive hedonism. While
in the 1970s and 1980s expressions of love and nostalgia for an idyllic village life characterized the repertoire of NCFM, in the early 1990s the NCFM repertoire dealt primarily with patriotic themes that glorified Serbian history, along with themes that
showed a fascination with power obtained by force.

The history of the relationship between Serbian folk music and politics illuminates why this particular genre facilitated the cultural promulgation of violence that
supported Slobodan Milosevic during the 1990s. The use of folk music for political
purposes extends back to the nineteenth century, when the weakening of the Ottoman
Empire and the Habsburg Empire prompted political programs for the creation of
nation-states in the Balkans. The idea of a national identity promoted the formation of
the nation-state. Cultural production of the common people, or folk, offered one of the
most powerful ways to mobilize political sentiments by referring to the nation's
tradition.

Since the nineteenth-century nationalist movements, national tradition in Serbia
has been connected to the Serbian Orthodox Church, the national myth of the Battle
of Kosovo, and the history of the medieval Serbian Kingdom. The national tradition
was expressed in music through the Serbian folk liturgy, through epic songs sung with
the accompaniment of *gusle* (a bowed lute instrument with one or two strings and very
limited melodic capabilities) as one of the main propagators of the myth of the Battle
of Kosovo, and through folk songs arranged and harmonized according to European
musical romanticism of the nineteenth century. Both the musical styles and other
artistic expressions of national tradition were associated with the idealized village life
and the idealized peasant. The romantic idealization of the *Volkgeist*, or the spirit of the
folk, as the source of national culture and customs constituted one reason for this connection. Another reason was the role peasants played in Serbian history:

> Peasantry constituted the main force in all the processes that made Serbia a modern
> nation-state. It played the dominant role in uprisings and wars that liberated Serbia (in the
> 19th century and the Balkan wars of 1912–13 and WWI and WWII), enlarged it and made
> it respected. Finally, peasantry was arguably the main pillar of Serbia's economic develop-
> ment. . . . Therefore, in Serbia it is possible to use the symbolism of peasantry to . . .
> glorify the greatness of the nation (Naumovic, cited in Zivkovic 2001:224).

Naumovic's comment, however, failed to indicate that even today Serbia retained a predominantly rural character in social and cultural terms (Ramet 1996:70–88). Thus, the

majority of the population could identify with "the symbolism of peasantry to glorify the greatness of the nation" in the late 1980s.

It was primarily the rural population in Serbia that supported both the nationalist movement and the ascendance of Milosevic to power in the late 1980s. Through playing upon the countryside's patriarchal values, and in particular the notion that the collective has primacy over the individual, nationalistic rhetoric of the late 1980s found a fertile ground in the population of the countryside. By arguing that the needs of the individual must to be subjugated to the needs of the collective in order to fulfill the goals of Serbian nationalism and by looking to the romanticized past as the ideal for future moral conduct, the regime was able to steer public opinion in its favor by emphasizing the elements of tradition that it found suitable for its goals.

The Milosevic regime's political misrepresentation of Serbian identity distorted Serbian tradition in two ways: as made up of uniquely Serbian cultural traits and achievements and as set in opposition to the rest of the world. This understanding of the tradition was summed up perfectly in the lyrics from an NCFM song: "We Serbs are Supermen, alone against the world." This lyric represents an example of the uncritical acceptance of nationalistic ideology on the part of the majority of NCFM creators, performers, and audiences. In a self-aggrandizing manner, the whole nation is endowed with limitless, superhuman powers on the one hand, and characterized by xenophobia towards the world at large, on the other.

Two Serbian historians, reflecting on the situation during the 1990s, offered insightful comments on the reasons for such a misappropriation of tradition:

> We are not sufficiently familiar with our tradition. We do not approach it critically and analytically, to see what it is made of and how, but in an uncritical and idolizing way. A tradition of a people is not fixed (*fiksirana*) once and for all. It consists of a number of often contradictory ideas which make up [something like] a quilt. All traditions are synthetic. We are talking about ours as being pure, specific, unique, but people in less inhibited (*inhibiranim*) places are aware that their tradition is [like] a quilt, made out of [many] different parts" (Dimitrijevic 1999).

> The survival of a people, even with all pragmatic and real-politik adjustments to the trends of the world politics, cannot be assured without an unambiguous point of reference. And that [point of reference] would be the rereading of tradition, which would constantly be critically examined. During the last fifty years our past has been continually misinterpreted in its important segments, and the depiction of history was extremely simplified and distorted in a way that created a false historical consciousness and a false image of ourselves. . . . Our tradition and world trends should not be opposites [as they were regarded by the Milosevic regime]" (Batakovic 2000).

Reasons for the popularity of nationalistic ideology in Serbia in the 1990s were numerous and have been explored in a number of studies (for example, Brankovic 1995, Colovic 1994, Bozic-Roberson 2001, Zivkovic 2001).

One of the most significant modes of its actualization was the arousal of passions through the abuse of particular elements of Serbian tradition. The means through which this awakening of nationalistic fervor was most passionately communicated was music. Perhaps the most telling examples of the role music played in connecting the sense of self, nation, and tradition were the mass rallies in support of Slobodan Milosevic in the late 1980s and early 1990s.

At these gatherings Slobodan Milosevic's speeches publicly glorified the greatness of the Serbian nation, thus lifting the ban on the expression of Serbian national feeling. Such public glorification of the Serbian nation represented a new development in Yugoslav political rhetoric. However, the most striking aspect of Milosevic's speeches was not their content, but the reaction of his audiences to them:

> It is hard to imagine the intensity of the excitement of the masses, at last permitted to broach the strictly-guarded taboo of national feeling, *to roar out the old forbidden songs at the top of their voices* [italics mine]. It might bear comparison with audience excitement at the first pornographic films: an ecstatic explosion, an orgiastic rush towards the forbidden fruit. For months, hundreds of thousands of people did little else but attend mass meetings, always pushing the limits of the permissible a little further in their expression of national feeling (Brankovic, cited in Zivkovic 2001: 243, fn 7).

Nationalistic feelings were most passionately expressed through "roaring out the old forbidden songs at the top of their voices." The old songs that provoked the "ecstatic explosion" and the "orgiastic rush" referred to particular moments in Serbian history: the Balkan Wars (1912–1914), the First World War, and the Chetnik movement (the Serbian royalist-oriented resistance and a political opposition to the Communists) in the Second World War. All of these songs were forbidden after the Second World War, some for their expressions of Serbian national identity, and some for their ethnocentric territorial claims from the times when Serbia was first emerging as a political entity in the nineteenth–century. The singing of forbidden songs in the political context of mass rallies generated emotions that fueled nationalist fervor. Through the "experience of simultaneity" in unison singing (Anderson, as cited in Turino 2000:173) and a heightened emotional charge, this collective participation in performance of a previously forbidden practice "allowed people to begin not only to imagine the nation, but to have the experience of being part of it" (Turino 2000:174). That these songs were all in various ways related to the historic experiences of wars that defined Serbian geopolitical status within Europe was not lost on the aspiring nationalist politicians, as subsequent historical development attested. For those who participated in the performance of such songs in this historic moment, being part of a nation meant remembering the historic battles and wars as events that created, sustained, and defined Serbian nation.

This sudden public appearance of "old forbidden songs," which were sung openly and without repercussions, sparked the production of songs promoting nationalistic feelings that justified the wars through the association of its lyrics and music with the misappropriated elements of Serbian tradition. These new songs used aspects of historical, religious, and musical tradition to promote intolerance towards other nations and support the actions of the regime. Some authors see these types of songs as belonging to the "patriotic-warrior" version of the turbo-folk genre (Tarlac 2001, Kronja 2001).

One of the most popular singers/songwriters in this (sub-)genre was Baja Mali Knindza, who was also known as Mirko Pajcin. Knindza gained popularity at the outset of the wars in the early 1990s with his catchy stage name, which combined the image of the undefeatable cartoon characters of Teenage Mutant Ninja Turtles and the town of Knin in Krajina, Croatia, where the fighting began in 1991. The lyrics of his songs ranged from asserting Serbian identity through stating the goals for the war to a direct call to arms to "brothers Serbs." He recorded over twenty albums and sold several million records, not counting pirated albums.

Knindza sought to inspire the Serbian people to join the wars in Croatia and Bosnia through invoking historical figures from the Serbian kingdom of the thirteenth century as well as figures from the famous national myth of Kosovo battle heroes of the late fourteenth century in his lyrics. His musical style relied heavily on the "*sumadijski*" style of the newly-composed folk music tradition for its impact. The paradigm of Serbian "*sumadijski*" style included references to Serbian *kolo,* a circle dance in a fast tempo with continuous sixteenth-note movement in a 2/4 time signature locally known as *dvojka* (two). It was preeminently characteristic of the central Serbian Sumadija region but, along with the characteristic sound of the accordion on which it is often played, it has come to be understood as signifying Serbian identity.

For Serbian people living in Serbian enclaves in Bosnia and Croatia, Knindza's references to this historical and mythic heritage had a heightened importance because it reflected their political reality. Many felt that, in order to protect their homes, it was necessary to go to war. However, this music was not only promoted in the Serbian enclaves in Bosnia and Croatia, but in Serbia as well, in order to mobilize even those whose lives and properties were not threatened. Knindza's songs exploited the fear and anxiety of Serbs from Bosnia and Croatia and gave them a feeling of empowerment that the government did not provide in their everyday life. By evoking the elements of tradition that spoke of glorious battles, territorial expansion of kingdoms past, and brave heroes, his songs promulgated feelings of a "just cause" that prompted many Serbs from Serbia to go to war in Bosnia and Croatia. By alluding to common historical roots in the medieval Serbian kingdom, NCFM songs fueled the dominant political rhetoric that, as a spiritual aspect of shared cultural traits, "Serbianness" (*srpstvo*), ought to be important to every Serb and that "we are all in this together."

Following the political speeches that glorified the Serbian people as great and invincible, dancing *kolo* to NCFM songs at mass rallies in support of Slobodan Milosevic further solidified these views and served to reassure those present that nothing wrong was actually going on, at a time when thousands of people (including Serbs living in Croatia and Bosnia) were being killed, chased from their homes, and reduced to living in despair and suffering, and when refugees were coming to Belgrade *en masse* from different parts of the former Yugoslavia. Celebratory characteristics in this music's lyrics and tunes, together with its accompanying visual aspects and dances in public performances, presented a striking musical corroboration of Milosevic's claim that Serbia was not at war, and everything was as it should be, as his campaign slogan, *Tako Treba* ("[And] that's how it should be"), suggested.

The image of perfect order and happiness that was portrayed through the performance of NCFM made the audience feel good about themselves. To a great extent, the genre's projection of this illusory sense of well-being accounted for its popularity. By promoting a belief in the justness of the extreme nationalist goals and actions, and the upcoming glory as a fulfillment of their common destiny, this music united people behind the regime's political cause. Yet, this constructed representation was in striking contrast to the reality of life in Serbia. The dystopia of everlasting celebration and happiness became all the more alluring as destruction, poverty, and death overwhelmed everyday life. People were offered a dissembling picture of utopia and, as long as they believed in it, they did not have to reflect on the reality of their lives and work on changing their circumstances.

Pop Music of Djordje Balasevic

A community of resistance, which the famous pop singer-songwriter Djordje Balasevic designated as the community of "normal people," saw through the lies and deception propagated by the numerous political and cultural figures within the Milosevic regime. Balasevic critiqued the regime's rhetoric regarding war, nationalism, oppression, and destruction of the country through a combination of simple but powerful musical expression and lyrics that exposed the inconsistencies between the behavior, the rhetoric, and the ideas used to justify the regime's actions.

Throughout its history, pop music in Serbia spoke to those who shared an openness towards and interaction with the ideas and cultures beyond the local, and whose outlook on the world was in the widest sense cosmopolitan. According to Vojislav Simic (1999:86), a renowned jazz composer of the older generation, the first examples of pop music in Yugoslavia dated to the period of the 1930s. Songs such as romances, chansons, waltzes, tangos, and fox-trots, which were composed under the influence of Italian, Spanish, and French music and American jazz, created a large repertoire of domestic jazz and light (*laka*) music in the years after World War Two. The foundation of the Radio Belgrade Light Music Orchestra in 1948 provided a strong impetus for Yugoslav composers to create new songs, as the opportunities for performing them and the interest of the public began rapidly increasing. Inspired by European popular song festivals, music producers began launching festivals all over Yugoslavia, thereby increasing the demand for pop songs and creating a flourishing pop scene (Simic 1999:87). This flourishing scene clashed with the ascendance and propagation of newly-composed folk music, which reached its peak during the nationalist fervor of the early 1990s. The ban on broadcasting Croatian and Bosnian bands, which accounted for a majority of pop-music production in the former Yugoslavia, virtually eliminated the pop sound from Serbian airwaves. The political and social situation in Belgrade narrowed the cultural spaces for rock and pop music performance and production by curtailing the creation of light pop lyrics and sounds.

Djordje Balasevic was the only pop singer/songwriter who in the 1990s continued not only to produce albums and tour, but to criticize constantly the Milosevic regime. His song "*Sloboda-ne*" (1992) was the first in Serbia to directly attack Milosevic by pointing to specific instances of rhetorical manipulation by the state-run media. His 1993 song *"Krivi smo mi"* ("It's Our Fault"), critiqued the actions of the ordinary people who "stepped aside," effectively letting those in power assume their positions. In contrast to the prevailing attitude of the media in blaming everyone else, from foreign powers to "historical destiny," for the current situation in Serbia and former Yugoslavia, the song *"Krivi smo mi"* encouraged ordinary people of all nationalities to rethink *their* personal engagement with political activism. It suggested that ordinary people did have political power and that speaking up and taking a stand is an expression of that power. Balasevic's *"Covek sa mesecom u ocima"* ("A Man With a Moon in His Eyes") (1993) was one of the most powerful anti-war songs of the 1990s. In contrast to the NCFM songs that used tradition to glamorize the "national cause" and the wars, this song used tradition to illustrate the human, material, and spiritual losses that the wars had brought. Instead of evoking the past kingdoms and mythical heroes, Balasevic sang of one man's memories of his life before the war and of the village tradition whose defining elements were the large weddings, the communal work, and the solidarity among neighbors. In contrasting those memories with the memories of war (the muddy trenches, the sounds of grenades, and the sights of destruction), this song left listeners to come up with their own conclusions, to examine and reevaluate their prejudices about what war actually entails, and whether one's tradition in that process is affirmed or destroyed.

In the song "The Legend of Geda the Stupid" (1998) Balasevic critiques Slobodan Milosevic using allegory and humor. The song describes a series of anecdotes about a gambler called Geda recounted by different members of a land-owning family who complain about their relative. At the very beginning of the song it becomes obvious that this is actually an allegorical tale about Slobodan Milosevic. Illustrating his character, mindset, and rhetoric using double-entendre in a series of vignettes, Balasevic succeeds in making the song both opaque (for the uninitiated) and a safe place for conspiratorial moments of recognition among those who identify with this song's message.

Performed for the first time in Belgrade's concert hall *Sava Centar* during one of Balasevic's traditional New Year's concerts in January of 1998, "The Legend of Geda the Stupid" had an enormous impact. During the following spring and summer it became a sign of recognition among people who blasted it from their cars in the city streets, daring the policemen to intervene. People honked their horns to show approval, sang the refrain together, and developed this as a street game. Recognizing that one was not alone in one's anti-regime stance and that one could actually enjoy this stance openly with other people in the streets while the uninitiated looked on was empowering. By replacing feelings of personal isolation and fear with those of solidarity and collective understanding, this song presaged a shift in power and facilitated the conditions for political action among ordinary people. In the following years this song was performed at anti-regime demonstrations all over Serbia, and it always evoked euphoric responses from the audience.

During 1993, Balasevic began greeting his audience at the opening of his concerts with "Good evening, normal people, I know that you are here." This greeting confirmed a community of people who identified themselves as "*Normalni*" ("normal people") amidst the wars and chaos of the former Yugoslavia. The term "normal" was also a colloquially stated aspiration for many citizens of the former Yugoslavia during the previous decade: to remain normal in abnormal times (See also Timofejev 2001).

While this greeting referred to the many different instances of everyday life that increasingly had begun to look like Alice's Wonderland, Balasevic particularly critiqued the madness of extreme nationalism and intolerance, and emphasized the loss of people and homeland. As one of the painful results of the general "abnormality" of life under extreme nationalism, he frequently talked about people in other republics who emigrated abroad or who remained in Serbia, enduring forcefully imposed separations due to the wars and the new regimes in Croatia, Bosnia, and Serbia.

The wars inflicted on peoples from the republics of Croatia and Bosnia all but extinguished social contacts among the people of Croatia, Bosnia, and Serbia. Traveling between these areas during the first part of the 1990s was not possible except for the military (after 1995 special visas were required) and telephone connections with these former republics were disabled. The official media in all three republics broadcast only political news from the other republics that corresponded with their respective national interests. For a number of years no Croatian or Bosnian music, theater troupes, or writers were mentioned in the Serbian media, and vice versa. This lack of cultural contact with the other parts of the former Yugoslavia, in the first part of the 1990s, before Internet connections became widely available, was experienced as a deep cultural loss. But more than that, it was contact with the people that was missed the most.

During the 1990s, Balasevic began giving concerts abroad, something that had previously been reserved for the NCFM singers. Before the 1990s most of the Serbian community outside Yugoslavia were so-called "guest-workers," who were interested exclusively in NCFM. Due to the large emigration during the 1990s of different social strata whose music interests were rather varied, Balasevic began getting calls to perform in Sydney and Melbourne (Australia), Chicago and New York (U.S.A.), Toronto and Vancouver (Canada), and throughout Europe.

All his audiences—in Serbia, Slovenia, Croatia, and Bosnia, as well as in America, Canada, Australia—shared the pain of having lost a homeland and with it, their people. In the former Yugoslavia most Yugoslav citizens regarded people in all the republics as their countrymen. After the break-up of Yugoslavia some people still considered the people from the other republics their compatriots due to cultural and emotional ties. Others with nationalistic sentiments made a distinction between people of their ethnicity and all others. By identifying themselves as "normal," Balasevic and his audience refused to associate themselves with the new nationalistic divisions and rejected them as meaningless. In one of his interviews Balasevic stated, "I have my own, parallel people, that is neither geographically nor politically divided" (Karanovic 2001). At a concert held in Belgrade in 2001, fans attended from Zagreb and Split in Croatia, Sarajevo in Bosnia, Skopje in Macedonia, and Podgorica in Montenegro. The enormous difficulties involved in obtaining visas and traveling through the former Yugoslavia made this an extraordinary event. Balasevic's fan club, the "Optimists" from Split, Croatia have managed to follow Balasevic in the past decade from Maribor in

Slovenia, to Vienna in Austria, to Prague in the Czech Republic, to Budapest in Hungary, and to Belgrade in Serbia.

This community of "normal people" at Balasevic's concerts regards the whole planet as its homeland. This sense of community refers not only to the fact that its members were physically spread all over the globe, but it also expresses a profound aversion to the extreme nationalistic sentiments that they abhorred.

Balasevic's continuing efforts to connect, inspire, and spread the word about this community of "normal people" through his songs and in his concerts inspired the creation of a fan website *(ne)normalni Balasevicevci* in January 1999. Self-described as "those whose Internet search always begins with the keyword Balasevic, a keyword which began to serve as a recognition of Normals" (http://www.Balasevic.org/ under (Ne)normalni), the creators of this site illustrate this geographical and national/ethnic diversity. The founder and moderator of the site works in Bajina Basta, West Serbia; the graphic design work is done in Sweden; the complete site design is realized in Belgrade; some parts are done in Zagreb, Croatia; and the music editor works in Stara Pazova, north of Belgrade. The founder and moderator of this site, Dejan Savic (2002), describes the goal of the website: "Djole's songs and books, and his struggle, was a code through which we recognized each other and Internet was a way to cross the barricades and borders." Detailed statistics reveal that the site has about seven hundred visitors daily who come from, among other places, Saudi Arabia, United Arab Emirates, Australia, Zimbabwe, Samoa, Mexico, Chile, United States, and Canada. The website contains the extensive archive of newspaper and e-magazine articles devoted to Balasevic, news about Balasevic's concerts, fan chat room, a photo gallery from the concerts, lyrics from all the songs, short video clips from some of Balasevic's concerts, and audio clips from all of his albums.

Although the website was created primarily out of the need to spread the word of resistance to the extreme nationalist madness through the virtual world, it also promoted a number of successful actions in the real world. One notable action involved breaking through the regime-media blockade and spreading the news about the police violence on Belgrade streets in 2000. During protests against the closing of several independent media, a boy was brutally battered by the police. Upon hearing this news, Balasevic decided to cancel his appearance at the sold-out concert in the Serbian town of Nis. He asked the members of his fan site for help in sending his letter in which he explained his cancellation to the independent media. His intent was to have "a cancelled concert ring further and louder then the held one could" (Vasovic-Mekina 2000). Due to the involvement of the site visitors, who found the contact information for all the independent media in Serbia, by noon that day everyone cited Balasevic's statement. The very next day the message crossed the border of Serbia and a translation of his letter appeared in the Slovenian and Macedonian press.

In February 2002, the founder of the site was asked by an interviewer if there is still a need for the resistance in Serbia now that the regime has been brought down from power. He answered:

Just in case, as a subtitle to our site, there are words [from Balasevic's song "To Live in Freedom"] "this heart beats the eternal rhythm of resistance." As long as the fact that I have an Albanian, Bosnian or a Croatian friend is not viewed as normal but abnormal, it would be necessary to defy the primitivism and intolerance (Savic 2002).

Conclusion

Both NCFM and Djordje Balasevic's pop songs appealed to a sense of moral responsibility and solidarity among people. While the newly-composed folk music genre related to tradition as a script to be reenacted, with battles to be won and heroes to lead the whole nation to the imagined glory of the past and right perceived historical wrongs, Balasevic viewed tradition as a living part of the present, as something to be protected from destruction. Furthermore, while NCFM singers and songwriters expounded on the exclusiveness of the Serbian tradition, Balasevic viewed it as a quilt, which the diversity of people and ideas only made more beautiful.

Both music genres inspired people to take action: one towards and the other away from war. Among some of the decisive factors for such opposite stands, paradoxically united by the underlying belief that each represents the highest moral good of the community, was on the one hand the acceptance of inherited values, painful memories of past events, and prejudices, *as they were*, and on the other hand the willingness to examine them against the light of the present. In that process music played a powerful role both in bringing the outdated ideals from the past to the present, as in NCFM and emphasizing the interconnectedness of people and the beauty of life in the present, as in Balasevic's songs. There always exists a possibility for social and political change and a hope that people will reevaluate their prejudices, their knowledge of history and tradition, and, through cultural production, create a better future.

NOTES

1. In Serbian intellectual discourse the distinction can be made between *nationalism in a positive sense* and *extreme nationalism*. *Nationalism in a positive sense* refers to asserting the self-identity of the people, while *extreme nationalism* is expressed through aggressive attitudes towards other nationalities. Patriotic feelings in these two forms of nationalism have very different means of expression and consequences. Some even understand extreme nationalism, with its intolerance of other ethnicities and a fanatic favoritism toward ones' own, as a degenerate form of patriotic feeling (Ninkov n.d.).

2. Developed from extreme nationalism, "the speech of hatred" (*govor mrznje*), cited in Bugarski 1997, Cvetkovic 1999, Skiljan 2002, and Toncic n.d., became a tool for powerful political manipulation in all the former Yugoslav republics involved in wars. Through political speeches and written media, it continually expressed xenophobic, misogynist, racist, and militant attitudes towards all aspects of life.

3. Within Serbia, this was manifested through politicians' abuse of nationalist sentiments in order to promote the view of the inevitability of wars with Croatia and Bosnia (Pesic 1996). In Croatia, the resurgence of Croatian nationalism followed the electoral victory of ardent Croat nationalist Franjo Tudjman, whose slogan "Croatia is for the Croats" (rather than for citizens of Croatia) and the new constitution, which proclaimed that Croatia is homeland to the Croatian nation alone, brought fear to the Serbian population living in Croatia (Sack and Suster 2000). In Bosnia, the resurgence of Islamic fundamentalism, along with influences from Serbia

and Croatia, similarly induced instability and mistrust in its multi-national population (Serbs, Croats, and Muslims).

4. Pesic states that it was this insistence to create "congruence between nation and state by the configuration of the population" (Pesic 1996:10) that led to war. This could have been avoided if the governments of Croatia, Bosnia, and Serbia had considered other political options such as the "legalistic approach to the 'national question,' or a struggle for an adequate position of the minority, including non-discrimination, personal (cultural) and political-territorial autonomy, along with free cultural links with the homeland, and so on" (Pesic 1996:11). Since the positions of the Serbian minority and their representatives in Croatia were far from homogeneous (ranging from co-operation with Croatian government to co-existence with Croats to secession from Croatia), it is clear that war was not the only political option available. The war was ultimately the result of the politicians' personal interests in gaining or reinforcing their power.

REFERENCES

Adzic, A.
2002   "Vise od 100 kriminalaca nosilo legitimacije DB" ("More Then One Hundred Crime Figures Held the State Internal Security ID's"). *Blic News* (November). http://www.blic.co.yu/arhiva/2002-11-13/strane/hronika.htm (Last accessed September 2004).

Batakovic, Dusan
2000   "Graditi od temelja jednu bolju Srbiju" ("Building a Better Serbia From the Ground Up"). *Kisobran* (May): 6. Also at http://www.kisobran.com/kisobran/jun00/str6.html (Last Accessed May 2002).

Bozic-Roberson, Agneza
2001   "The Politicization of Ethnicity as a Prelude to Ethnopolitical Conflict: Croatia and Serbia in Former Yugoslavia." Doctoral Dissertation, Western Michigan University. Kalamazoo, Michigan.

Brankovic, Srbobran
1995   *Serbia at War with Itself: Political Choice in Serbia 1990–1994*. Translated by Mary Thompson-Popovic and Mira Poznanovic. Beograd: Sociological Society of Serbia.

Bugarski, Ranko
1997   *Jezik od mira do rata*. Beograd: Cigoja Stampa XX vek.

Colovic, Ivan
1985   *Divlja knjizevnost: Etnolingvisticko proucavanje paraliterature*. Beograd: Nolit.
1994   *Bordel ratnika: folklor, politika i rat*. Beograd: Biblioteka XX vek.

Curguz Kazimir, Velimir, ed.
2001   *The Last Decade: Citizens in the Struggle for Democracy and An Open Society 1991–2001*. Group of Authors. Belgrade: Media Center.

Cvetkovic, Margita
1999   "Jezik Nasilja: Intervju sa Rankom Bugarskim" ("The Language of Violence: Interview with Ranko Bugarski") *Nezavisna Svetlost*. http://www.svetlost.co.yu/arhiva/99/215/215-4.htm (Last accessed December 2002).

Dimitrijevic, Branislav
    1999   "U visku se lepo uziva." *Blic News* (January). http://blic.gates96.com/blicnews/no26/1aktuel/aktuel7.htm (Last Accessed May 2001).

Dimitrijevic, Vojin
    1995   "The International Community and the Yugoslav Crisis." In Nebojsa Popov ed., *The Road to War in Serbia: Trauma and Catharsis*. Budapest: Central European University Press, pp. 633–659.

Dinkic, Mladjan
    1995   *Ekonomija destrukcije: velika pljacka naroda* Beograd: VIN.

Djurkovic, Milos
    2002   *Diktatura, nacija, globalizacija*. Beograd: Institut za evropske studije.

E.B.
    2003   "Mafija od 1993 sa ispravama DB" ("Organized Crime Figures with the State Internal Security ID's Since 1993"). *Blic News* (April) http://www.blic.co.yu/arhiva/2003-04-15/strane/tema.htm#2 (Last accessed May 2003).

Gadamer, Hans-Georg
    1989   "Elevation of the Historicity of Understanding to the Status of a Hermeneutical Principle." In *Truth and Method*. Second edition, revised by J. Weinsheimer and D.D. Marshal. London: Sheed and Ward, pp. 265–306.

Gordy, Eric
    1999   *The Culture of Power in Serbia: Nationalism and the Destruction of Alternatives*. University Park, PA: Pennsylvania State University.

Judah, Tim
    1997   *The Serbs*. New Haven, CT: Yale University Press.

Karanovic, Zorica
    2001   "Novogodisnji koncerti Djordja Balasevica; Muzicka radionica duse." ("Dordje Balasevic's New Year Concerts: Music Workshop for the Soul") *Politika* (December) http://www.balasevic.org/arhiva/stampa/31122001_politika/ (Last Accessed March 2003).

Kronja, Ivana
    2001   *Smrtonosni sjaj: msovna psihologija i estetika turbo-folka*. (*The Fatal Glow: Mass Psychology and Aesthetics of Turbo-Folk Subculture*) Beograd: Tehnokratia.

N.N.
    2003   "Obicni i neobicni kriminalci" ("Regular and Irregular Crime Figures"). *Danas* (March) http://www.danas.co.yu/20030331/dijalog.htm (Last accessed August 2004).

Ninkov, Zvonko
    n.d.   "Sta je nacija i postoji li ona stvarno?" ("What is a Nation and Does it Really Exist?") http://novabarselona.webhouse.co.yu/arhiva/Broj8/nacija.html (Last accessed May 2002).

Obradovic, Ljubisa
    2000   "Organizovani kriminal: Mafija odlazi s rezimom?" ("Organized Crime: Mafia Leaves with the Regime?"). *Nezavisna Svetlost* http://www.svetlost.co.yu/arhiva/2000/274/274-4.htm (Last Accessed September 2004).

Pesic, Vesna
1996   "The War for Ethnic States." In Nebojsa Popov, ed., *The Road to War in Serbia: Trauma and Catharsis*. Budapest: Central European University Press, pp. 9–49.

Pribicevic, Branko
1995   "Relations with the Superpowers." In Sabrina Petra Ramet and Ljubisa S. Adamovich, eds., *Beyond Yugoslavia: Politics, Economics, and Culture in a Shattered Community*. Colorado: Westview Press, pp. 435–460.

Ramet, Sabrina Petra
1996   "Nationalism and the 'idiocy' of the countryside: the case of Serbia." *Ethnic and Racial Studies* 19 (1):70–88.

Rasmussen, Ljerka Vidic
1991   "Gypsy Music in Yugoslavia: Inside the Popular Culture Tradition." *Journal of the Gypsy Lore Society* 1 (2): 127–139.
1999   "The Newly-Composed Folk Music of Yugoslavia (1945–1992)." Doctoral Dissertation. Middletown, Connecticut, Wesleyan University. UMI Microform 9936237.

Rusinow, Dennison
1995   "The Avoidable Catastrophe." In Sabrina Petra Ramet and Ljubisa S. Adamovich, eds., *Beyond Yugoslavia: Politics, Economics, and Culture in a Shattered Community*. Boulder, Colorado: Westview Press, pp. 9–21.

Sack, A. L. and Zeljan Suster
2000   "Soccer and Croatian Nationalism: A Prelude to War." *Journal of Sport and Social Issues* 24(3): 305–320.

Savic, Dejan
2002   "Priča o srcu koje bubnja večni tam-tam otpora" ("The Story of a Heart That Beats the Everlasting Tam-Tam of Resistance") (May) http://www.balasevic. org/arhiva/stampa/05022002_com/ (Last Accessed October 2002).

Skiljan, Dubravko
2002   "Jezik i identitet" ("Language and Identity") http://www.pobjeda.co.yu/ arhiva/novembar2002/2711/rubrike/kultura/kultura_8.htm (Last accessed December 2002).

Simic, Vojislav
1999   "Development of Jazz and Light Music in Our Country." *New Sound: International Magazine for Music* (Belgrade) 13: 86–92.

Tarlac, Goran
2001   "Ratni turbo-neo folk: novi heroji, novi pevaci" ("Warmongering Turbo-Neo Folk: New Heroes, New Singers"). In Goran Tarlac and Vladimir Djuric Djura, eds. *Antologija Turbo Folka: Pesme iz Stomaka Naroda*. Belgrade: SKC, pp. 61–96.

Teodorovic, Milos
2003   "Veza organizovanog kriminala s policijom: Razmrsiti Miloseviceve cvorove." ("The Connections Between Organized Crime and Police: Untying Milosevic's Knots"). *Danas* (February) http://www.danas.org/programi/ aktuelno/2003/02/20030220203310.asp (Last accessed September 2004).

Timofejev, Aleksandar
    2001   "Da budemo normalni" ("To Be Normal"). *Nin*. Beograd. http://www.nin.co.yu/2001-11/28/20823.html (Last accessed April 30, 2003).

Toncic, Bojan
    N.D   "Govor mrznje pol diktatu politicara: Intervju sa Aljosom Mimicom" ("Speech of Hatred as Dictated by Politicians: An Interview with Aljosa Mimica") http://www.nuns.org.yu/srpski/dosije/12/8s.asp (Last Accessed January 2003).

Turino, Thomas
    2000   *Nationalists, Cosmopolitans, and Popular Music in Zimbabwe*. Chicago: University of Chicago Press.

Vasovic-Mekina, Svetlana
    2000   "Necu da pevam dok tuku klince." ("I Don't Want to Sing While They Beat the Kids") *Vreme* (January) http://www.balasevic.org/arhiva/stampa/010700/index.htm (Last Accessed May 2003).

Zivkovic, Marko
    2001   "Serbian Stories of Identity and Destiny in the 1980s and 1990s." Doctoral dissertation, The University of Chicago. Chicago, Illinois, UMI Microfilm 9997195, Bell and Howell Information and Learning Company.

Hieroglyph, Gesture, Sign, Meaning:
Bussotti's *pièces de chair II*

PAUL ATTINELLO
University of Newcastle upon Tyne

Between 1958 and 1960, Sylvano Bussotti, Italian composer of the avant-garde, composed various works that are published as the song cycle *pièces de chair II* for piano, baritone, female voice, and instruments (Bussotti 1960).[1] These "pieces of flesh," suggesting chunks of musical material ripped apart but still warm with expressive power, consist of some twenty-seven separate pieces (depending on how they are counted). Most of these are one- or two-page works for baritone and piano on texts in Italian, French, or German (Bussotti's first and second languages and his then lover Heinz-Klaus Metzger's first), along with fragments of ancient Greek, Hebrew, Latin, English, Armenian, and Hungarian. Notable exceptions to this basic model are the interspersed (and also separately published) *five piano pieces for david tudor* (Bussotti 1959), a famous series of works presented at Darmstadt at a course on music and graphics in 1959, and also part VII, the extended "Voix de femme" for female voice and various scattered instruments, which was written for Cathy Berberian.

The *pièces de chair* can be considered as an anthology of Bussotti's early experiments with notation and graphics (but not by any means a complete anthology, as the scores of the *sette fogli* (Bussotti 1963) present yet other approaches). These are not engraved, but handwritten in the composer's distinctive calligraphy. Some are in specific and fairly traditional notational systems; others include patches of suggestive graphics; some are dense, difficult to read "portraits" of notation; but none are really what is normally called "pure graphics," as all are based to some extent on musical symbols in a way typical of Bussotti's work. Other important aspects of the song cycle are the multilingual tangle of erotic (especially, and flagrantly, homoerotic) texts and the nonlinear network of interrelations and identities among the songs. However, the most striking aspect of the score remains the element of visual expression and its concomitant visual allure; along with Bussotti's more important works from the period of 1958 to 1969, their rhizomatic fusion of the linear and the holistic, the rational and the surreal, presents a distinctive problem in analysis and interpretation. An additional problem with studying the *pièces de chair* is the lack of available recordings; the composer tends to dislike recordings in any case (a fact that has undoubtedly limited his public visibility over four decades). His resistance to maintaining or distributing tapes, even those made under his direction, makes the interpretation of the score as a performance text even more difficult than it might be.

The received wisdom we usually employ to read the more canonic works of the Darmstadt "school" is inadequate to the aesthetic and cultural implications of these pages. That received wisdom is, of course, rooted in our cultural understanding of music and of notation, which is still remarkably normative in its insistence on notation as a transparent instrument of objective communication. My attempts to find an alternative means of understanding—to find another place to stand, so to speak—pull ideas of the Frankfurt school and poststructuralist thinkers into the discussion. Our usual readings of those philosophies focus on their ability to dismantle value systems, on the subtle political attack, the deconstruction of discourse, the psychoanalysis of projections, and irrational logic. While these all have great power, such force can be frustratingly limited after a while, since techniques of dismantling ideology can only be used so many times to erase the same discursive space before a critically terminal boredom sets in.

Fortunately, Ulmer's 1985 monograph on *Applied Grammatology* generates conceptual possibilities that move in a more productive direction. Ulmer points out that Derrida has actually been engaged with several projects, of which deconstruction is only one. But, as the title suggests, another, completely separate, project is that of grammatology, or the science of writing; and therein lies a tale.

Looking at the Graphic Score

It is useful in this context to examine the preconceptions and implications of some technical discussions of graphic scores, particularly those that refer to Bussotti. Reginald Smith Brindle's 1987 textbook on what was then "new music," which tends to focus on the European avant-garde, discusses the meaning and viability of graphic scores in a way that is subtly problematic. He clearly regards such work as having some value, as he discusses it extensively; but he repeatedly implies that calligraphic and theatrical gestures are not quite real music, and that they are not to be taken too seriously. For instance, in speaking of the very last page of *pièces de chair II*—part XIV, the "piano piece for David Tudor 4" (Bussotti 1960: 55)—Smith Brindle (1987: 87) says:

> [R]adical means of stimulating improvisation without the stumbling block of notation have been used. . . . Some graphic scores may indicate distinct musical parameters. . . . Other graphic scores may deliberately omit any notational sign or indication of a musical shape. The composer's one aim is to stimulate the performer's musical creativity through a graphic design. Some composers are extremely able draughtsman, and obviously find it irresistible to turn a musical score into a work of art. Sylvano Bussotti, for example, is quite outstanding both as an artist and as a musician, so that in some cases one wonders whether the final page of a score is the consequence of a primarily visual conception, or whether the music came first. The . . . ['piano piece for David Tudor 4'] was derived from a drawing made in 1949 and reset as a music score in 1959.

In his generalized discussion of graphic scores, Smith Brindle imbeds certain concepts that have interesting implications. The composer's desire to stimulate creativity is called "one aim," thereby suggesting that it is a limited and teleological aesthetic plan, not to mention one that excludes other usually important processes. The desire to create graphics for pleasure is, on the other hand, "irresistible"—suggesting a temptation to be fought by any respectable musician. A distinct causality is also implied: the musical score is "turn[ed] . . . into" a work of art, implying that the score has some kind of previous existence; thus, composition consists of sound conceived, which is then translated into the communicative code of notation, from which it can be retranslated into performed and experienced sound. Turning a score into a work of (visual) art thus becomes an inventive addition to the normal procedure. Such a directed plan is, of course, an acceptable traditional semiotic path; but what if a drawing is created *as* a drawing, not as a graphic score? Smith Brindle wonders whether the visuals or the "music" came first, before he gives his example—an example of something that happens intermittently in Bussotti's scores—of a case where the visuals come first, indeed a decade earlier. What, then, is the music? Clearly, the conceived sound is the justifiable artistic gesture, with the performed sound as its empirical validation. What if the visual *is* the musical, however—either by some kind of more indirect reference, or by the understanding that no conceived sound prefigures the performed sound? Smith Brindle's attempt to explain Bussotti's work via his understanding of its intent and function—that is, the assumption that the primary purpose of the score is to present accurate, practical notation for performance—continues in his analysis of a later work for the stage by the composer.

> Some of Bussotti's scores, through their pictorial presentation, became very enigmatic as music, and the only way to interpret some of his notation would seem to be through well-prepared improvisation. The example . . . from *la passion selon Sade* [p. 8 of the published score] . . . shows all kinds of elements—stage directions, lighting indications, fragments of music, words to be sung (or spoken?), instrumentation, gestures, etc., but the exact performance of this page . . . will need considerable preparation if a consistently good presentation is to be guaranteed (Smith Brindle 1987: 89).

The concept of a "consistently good presentation" is of great interest here. As the discussion revolves around concepts of notation, the implication is that a good score is one where the notation can be read in some reproducible manner—if not such that each performance is similar, then such that each performance is "consistently good." This reflects essentially positivistic and scientist attitudes towards reproducible results, and of course views the performers as a pure conduit of the composer's conceived sound work. This is not to say that notation as the source of a reproducible performance is necessarily problematic in all cases. It is merely to raise the question: what definition of notation and of music could include Bussotti's work in a productive way?

It would be interesting to consider some of the other definitional writing that affects the way we view graphic scores, notably those with characteristics similar to Bussotti's. Such works as Karkoschka's (1966) typology of avant-garde notation, Griffith's (1981) history of avant-garde composers, Goodman's (1976) analysis of artistic gesture, and Ingarden's (1986) study of the identity of the work of music can all be analyzed in terms of their presuppositions. Such presuppositions are, of course, attempts to create an axiomatic basis from which to overcome the difficulties attendant on the aesthetic analysis of normative Western musical works, difficulties that can be maddening in the interpretive, semiotic, and even ontological spheres. Admittedly, many of the major arguments of musical aesthetics and analysis were never intended to deal with graphic scores or other avant-garde experiments. But there may be a rather neat way through these difficulties in the context of sociology.

Nattiez (1990: 41) engages with the problem of defining music from a semiological position by first examining various principles similar to those implied but not explicitly examined by Smith Brindle. The definitions of music from the contexts of acoustics, poetics, and aesthetics (as the latter was formerly defined, that is, as the study of "the beautiful" rather than the study of art) all get into trouble at the outer margins of musical poetics. How does a notation- or sound-oriented definition of music accommodate Schnebel's (1969) "music to read," Cage's *4'33"*, or, of course, this Bussotti score? Nattiez employs anthropologist Jacques Molino's transformation into symbolic terms of Mauss's "total social fact" to redefine the boundaries of music. Originally constructed to deal with problems of studying non-Western cultures, this seems to be one of the many ethnomusicological concepts that we need to turn back onto our own society. A music redefined via the idea of a "total musical fact" suggests that all of the activities, signs, and concepts that have been attached to music—including the above examples—must be considered as part of the musical universe, whatever distinctions or values are later applied. This suggests that attempts to define the musical versus the extramusical, whether considering movement, behavior, ritual, symbolism, narrative, or any possible kind of notation whether functional or not, is pointless—all of it *is*, indeed, music, and all of it *must* be seen as music if one is to make sense of varied cultural contexts.

Nattiez also reflects on Ruwet's rearticulation of unusual cultural products as peripheral. As Ruwet says, "We must remind ourselves that . . . we live in an age in which it has become possible (without undue risk) for anyone to baptize anything as 'music,' 'poetry,' or 'painting'," (quoted in Nattiez 1990: 42). Nattiez (1990: 42–3) agrees:

> In the West, the general context of the musical fact assures that . . . special cases . . . are quickly marginalized. Moreover, their creators now perceive them (even if they do not say so publicly) as a way of 'speaking' in music about music, in the second degree as it were, to expose or denounce the institutional aspect of music's functioning.

Although this may seem rather condescending in establishing the intentions of avant-garde activity, it applies very well to Cage, and I think also to Schnebel's beautiful book of para-notation. These are works that can easily be seen as essentially schematic, suggesting an axis of musical time perpendicular to one of musical space (that is, pitch); like Earle Brown's elegant score for *December 1952*, they are designs whose characteristics can be described, for the most part, geometrically. As long as such graphics retain a certain figural aspect, they can be subsumed into the world of notation via an only slightly expanded acceptance of what a signifying figure is allowed to be.

It is my argument that Bussotti's work cannot be subsumed in this way—and this in spite of the fact that most of his graphic scores, even such bizarre mutations as *sette fogli* or the "piano piece for David Tudor 4," have a close relation to the signs and significations of traditional notation. The example in Figure 1 is based on evocative recreations of musical figures, drawing musical notation into the realm of visual art,

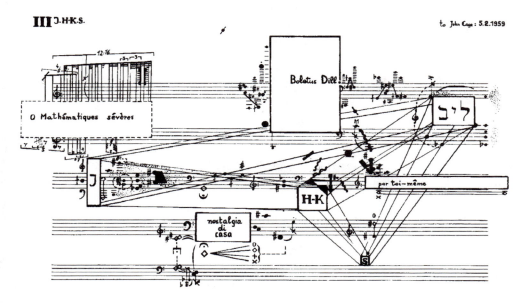

Figure 1. Bussotti, *pièces de chair II*, p. 6.
© Casa Ricordi—BMG Ricordi S.p.A.—Used by permission
A thoroughly graphic score. Note references to the first names of Bussotti, Cage, and
Metzger ("S/J/H-K") and the name of a Cageian mushroom dish ("Boletus Dill").

where the density and grace of lines and forms cannot be accounted for in terms of a symbol set.

It is interesting that this work alone of the cycle is then transcribed, as may be seen in the next example (Figure 2), into a more "notative" notation, implying that the composer does not expect the original graphic of part III to be a performable piece on its own. Perhaps this is simply not a song, or a score, but the *hieroglyph* for a score: and that brings us to grammatological concerns.

Pieces of Grammatology

What is the point of a quarter note? Well, of course, that question has a very dense answer, depending on the quarter note. But let's just speak of the notated quarter note here, the usual spot with a line attached, formed in accord with Western traditions. It represents a sound, probably a pitched one, that lasts for a particular length of time, depending on the context established by the metric grid in which it occurs. It is thus a visual object that represents an aural object. That is why it exists, that is its point.

What is the point of the letter "s"? Same kind of answer: it exists because it represents a sound, a phoneme that varies somewhat among speakers and across dialects and languages, but that is fairly recognizable. After all, sibilants are a very particular class of phoneme, and an "s" is the easiest sibilant to produce.

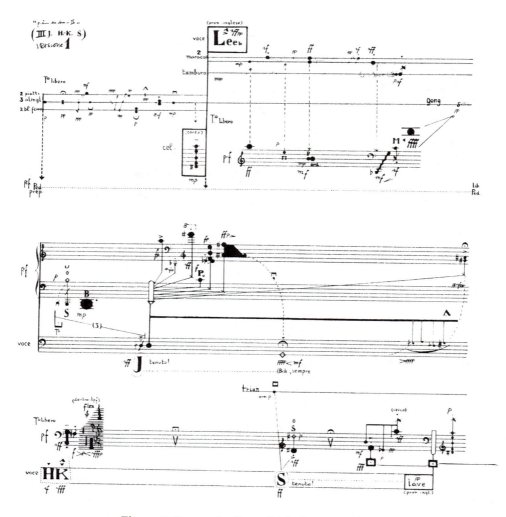

Figure 2. Bussotti, *pièces de chair II*, p. 7, detail.
© Casa Ricordi—BMG Ricordi S.p.a.—Used by permission
The beginning of the first "version'" (transcription) of part III.

What is the point of ∫, the sign that resembles an elongated 's', that represents the integral function? When I write ∫ f(x), what is the value of those symbols? The first symbol has no phonetic value of any kind, and the "f," the "x," and the parentheses represent complex nonverbal operations that can only be spoken of in terms of description or process.

Where does the phonetic end and the hieroglyphic begin? Derrida, and Ulmer after him, claims that the relation between the two is not historically fixed, but has changed in recent history.

> The nonphonetic moment in writing threatens and subverts the metaphysics of the proper ('self-possession, property, propriety, cleanliness') first of all by decomposing the substantive: 'Nonphonetic writing breaks the noun apart. It describes relations and not appellations. The noun and the word, those unities of breath and concept, are effaced within pure writing. . . . It is to speech,' Derrida notes of nonphonetic writing, 'what China is to Europe' . . .—the outer margin of logocentrism. Theoretical grammatology adopts hieroglyphic writing as a model, translating it into discourse, producing thus in philosophy distortions similar to those achieved in those movements, labeled 'cubist' and 'primitivist,' which drew on the visual arts of non-Western cultures in order to deconstruct the look of logocentrism. (Ulmer 1985: 18)

And, perhaps, in those modernist techniques that created parallel distortions in the symbolic codes of music. Crucial in the definition of grammatology is the difference between the letter and the hieroglyph, a difference that was understood clearly in the West only after the Rosetta Stone was deciphered.

> Far from being rejected owing to ethnocentric scorn of things non-Western, the hieroglyph was excessively admired as a form of sublime, mystical writing. Derrida credits . . . Freret and Warburton . . . with creating an 'epistemological break' that overcame these obstacles. . . . Then a systematic reflection upon the correspondence between writing and speech could be born. The greatest difficulty was already to conceive, in a manner at once historical and systematic, the organized cohabitation, within the same graphic code, of figurative, symbolic, abstract, and phonetic elements. (Ulmer 1985: 6)

Derrida's understanding of our culture—the one that has so much video and television in it, the one where mathematical and cybernetic syntaxes have replaced so much discourse that was once verbal—is rooted in the realization that the hieroglyph, the ideogram, has returned to central importance. This is a reflection on the ideas expressed by McLuhan, but Derrida has shown how McLuhan's ideas are really simple surface formulations of a change, an "epistemological break" that goes much deeper and changes our perceptions—or more accurately that already changed our perceptions, long before we ever noticed. Hieroglyphs, and even more Chinese ideograms, are frequently presented in encyclopedia articles as cumbersome, primitive, and peripheral to the central work of language and writing; but the forces that created ideograms are strongly at work in our culture, remaking our codes to become more visual and to develop characteristics separate from and beyond their need to convey aural information.

Graphic scores are generally presented in music histories and theories as peripheral. But what if they are not peripheral at all: what if they move us into spaces that we could not have realized in a "pure" notation, in a transparent symbol set? We still use letters; we still read and write books. And we still use quarter notes, clean and without calligraphic ornament. But perhaps we should not insist that all of our quarter notes stay clean; perhaps the ornaments will grow of their own accord, whether we like it or not. Those ornaments may be like the vines that overcome the stage at the end of Henze's opera *The Bassarids*; they express the ability of nature, the feminine, and the physical to overcome the hierarchy of control established by thinking men. The final lines of Auden's stage description run:

The flames sink. . . . Of the palace, only a jagged blackened wall is left. . . . Vines descend and sprout everywhere, wreathing the columns, covering the blackened wall (Auden and Kallman 1991).

This efflorescence is symbolic in this work, and its parallel musical expression—the sensual overloading of contrapuntal textures typical of much of Henze's writing, as it was of Richard Strauss—is still largely contained within traditionally determinate relationships between notation, sound, performer, and listener. Bussotti exposes the spectral quality of such relationships, showing their limitations in the dazzling illumination of the possibilities that can be made to exist out beyond them. In a brief essay, Barthes (1976: n.p.) exults in Bussotti's work:

> When Bussotti lays out his page and, in a stroke that is full, black, calligraphic, covers it with staves, with notes, with signs, with words and even with drawings, he does not content himself with transmitting to the executants of his work the operations that effect it, as was done by the old musical manuscript—where the Jansenist [that is, predestined] form, if one can say that, was quite well represented by the figured bass; it constructed a homological space, wherein the surface—since the page is condemned to be only a surface—wanted to be, with rage, with precision, a volume, a scene, striated with lights, traversed by waves, broken by silhouettes; and again, all at the same time (and these are the stakes): on the one hand a *grimoire* of multiple signs, refined, coded with infinite minutiae, and on the other hand a vast analogical composition in which the lines, the sites, the evasions, the stripes have the power to suggest, if not to imitate, *that which really happens* on the scene of hearing. . . . A manuscript by Sylvano Bussotti is *already* a complete work: the theater (the concert) begins at the graphic apparatus which must transmit the program.

The theatrical, combined with the graphic—and, of course, the erotic, the intensely physical—are all elements that are usually considered "extramusical" or of secondary importance, if not actually antagonistic to "real" musical concerns. Yet these are all elements that Bussotti constantly foregrounds in his scores. For a paradigm to compare with these, consider a crucial statement of Ulmer's (1985: xii):

> [Grammatology] could be described as non-Euclidean—the humanities equivalent of non-Euclidean geometry—in that it builds, in defiance of the axioms of dialectics, a coherent, productive procedure out of the elements of writing considered traditionally to be mere ornament, not suitable for fostering true knowledge. The ultimate deconstruction of the logocentric suppression of writing is not to analyze the inconsistency of the offending theories, but to construct a fully operational mode of thought on the basis of excluded elements (in the way that the non-Euclideans built consistent geometries that defied and contradicted the accepted axioms).

To me, that sounds like the scores of Sylvano Bussotti. In his work, our musical signs are not bypassed or surpassed, but instead expanded, their hieroglyphic facets added back into a code that had become all too much a tool, a thing to be used and minimized, since the subtler notation of the fourteenth century. These musical pages invent, they caress, explode, and reach out to us, seductively recreating our first childish impressions of scores before we could read the signs—asking us to fall in love with them, all over again.

NOTES

1. Versions of this article were read at the University of California, San Diego, in May 1993 and the University of Tasmania, Hobart, Australia in December 2001, as well as appearing in my dissertation (Attinello 1997) and in Italian translation (Attinello 1995).

REFERENCES

Attinello, Paul
    1995   "Geroglifico, gesto, segno, significato: analisi di *Pièces de chair II* de Sylvano Bussotti." Translated by Roberto Favaro. *Musica/Realtà* 46 (March): 111–121.
    1997   "The interpretation of chaos: a critical analysis of meaning in European avant-garde vocal music, 1958–68." Ph.D. dissertation, Los Angeles: University of California.

Auden, W. H. and Chester Kallman
    1991   *The Bassarids/Die Bassariden*. Libretto in recording booklet. Vienna: Koch Schwann.

Barthes, Roland
    1976   "The score as theater." Preface to Francesco Degrada, *Sylvano Bussotti e il suo teatro*. Milano: Ricordi, one unnumbered page. Author's translation.

Bussotti, Sylvano
    1959   *five piano pieces for david tudor*. London: Universal.
    1960   *pièces de chair II pour piano, baryton, une voix de femme, instruments (1958–59–60)*. Milan: Ricordi. First published in 1970.
    1963   *sette fogli, una collezione occulta*. London: Universal Edition.

Goodman, Nelson
    1976   *Languages of Art: An Approach to a Theory of Symbols*. Indianapolis: Hackett.

Griffiths, Paul
    1981   *Modern Music: The Avant garde since 1945*. New York: George Braziller.

Ingarden, Roman
    1986   *The Work of Music and the Problem of its Identity*. Translated by Adam Czerniawski. Berkeley: University of California Press.

Karkoschka, Erhard
    1966   *Das Schriftbild der neuen Musik*. Celle: Hermann Moeck Verlag.

Nattiez, Jean-Jacques
    1990   *Music and Discourse: Toward a Semiology of Music*. Translated by Carolyn Abbate. Princeton: Princeton University Press.

Schnebel, Dieter
    1969   *MO-NO: Musik zum Lesen/Music to Read*. Köln: M. DuMont Schauberg.

Smith Brindle, Reginald
    1987   *The New Music: The Avant-garde since 1945,* second edition. Oxford: Oxford University Press.

Ulmer, Gregory
    1985   *Applied Grammatology: Post(e)-Pedagogy from Jacques Derrida to Joseph Beuys*. Baltimore: Johns Hopkins University.

Hermeneutics, Adorno, and the New Musicology

ROGER W. H. SAVAGE
University of California, Los Angeles

Since Joseph Kerman challenged musicology to overcome the limitations of formal analysis and criticism, the idea that music belongs to a world isolated from everyday social realities has been under attack.[1] Postmodern musicology's legitimacy derives from its claim that aesthetic formalism abstracts the work from its social, cultural, and historical context. Yet, postmodernist critiques of formalist aesthetics fail to confront Theodor W. Adorno's troubling assertion that music's autonomy is the condition of its social truth. Kerman calls for a new musicology that would challenge traditional musicology's critical myopia by situating music's meaning in the broader context of its socially conditioned production and its historically situated reception. Postmodern musicology responds to this call by denouncing traditional disciplinary ideals that privilege the concept of the musical work as a self-sufficient aesthetic entity. According to Lawrence Kramer (1992), musicology has been slow to hear the *Gotterdämmerung* already in progress in other scholarly disciplines. For musicologists schooled in poststructuralist literary theory, cultural studies, and feminist criticism, the idea that music transcends material exigencies dissembles music's socially constructed character. Consequently, critical musicology exercises its authority by deconstructing absolute music, thereby advancing the discipline beyond traditional doctrine through opposing formalist aesthetics with socially informed critique.

This opposition links postmodern musicology with Theodor W. Adorno's music criticism. Adorno's aesthetic theory represents a critical alternative to the formalist concept of the self-contained musical work. For Adorno, music's distance from society is its first social characteristic. His theory of the art work therefore contests the formalist convention that music's aesthetic autonomy isolates it from its social context. By identifying the work's social truth with the critically distanced position it takes on society, Adorno aligns aesthetic criticism with social critique. Music therefore entails more than the illusion of transcendence that postmodern musicology deconstructs. From Adorno's vantage point, the work's autonomy evinces the critical opposition to reality that is the condition of the work's social truth.

Although Adorno's perspective on music's relation to social reality prefigures new musicology's rejection of formalist aesthetics, postmodernist deconstructions surpass Adorno's critical standpoint in denouncing absolute music's claim to autonomy. Yet, despite critical musicology's appeals to hermeneutics, deconstructive strategies decode socially constructed meanings and unmask concealed political agendas at the expense of the mediation Adorno struggles to preserve between music's autonomy and its social facticity. By acceding to the schema inaugurated by Kant's subjectivization of aesthetics, socially oriented deconstructions of absolute music repeat Adorno's failure to confront the impasse arising from his two-fold concept of art.

Kant's justification of a subjective principle of taste inaugurated art's separation from reality by divorcing aesthetic judgments from their surrounding cultural ethos. Adorno's concept of a work's autonomy draws upon this schema as instituting the difference between an authentic art work and empirical reality. For him, a work's autonomy is essential to its critical social function. As aesthetic illusions, works are socially true through opposing the instrumental character of social life. Their autonomy, which is the mark of their distance from empirical reality, is the repository of their truth. This truth is a function of the work's semblance character. Hence, the enigmatic figure that conjoins the work's autonomy with its semblance of truth harbors a content that is more than an illusory effect of the work's artifactual character.

This impasse, where art's enigmatic semblance of truth presupposes art's separation from reality as the condition of its critical content, calls for a hermeneutics of musical works. Postmodern critiques' occultation of the subjectivization of aesthetics and its historical effects eliminates this enigma. Yet the power works exercise by contesting and subverting reality evinces their capacity to distance themselves from that reality. New musicology's appropriation of Adorno's socially informed music criticism overlooks the productive function of this distance. By deepening the paradox of a work's distance from reality, the impasse within Adorno's aesthetic theory compels music criticism to reevaluate postmodern musicology's deconstructive strategies through a hermeneutical consideration of the power of thought and imagination at work.

Absolute Music, Musical Formalism, and Musical Hermeneutics

The idea that absolute music—instrumental music invested with the metaphysical dignity of the Absolute—transcends the material conditions of its production unites the new musicology through its opposition to this metaphysical pretense. Through the influences of cultural studies, ethnomusicology, and post-structuralist and critical theories, contemporary music criticism rejects the conceit of absolute music's aesthetic autonomy. In renouncing musical formalism, contemporary music criticism cultivates interpretive strategies that aim at decoding music's social and political meanings. These strategies' interpretive characters align music criticism with musical hermeneutics; a common hostility toward formalist aesthetics unites them. Yet through this alignment, contemporary criticism conceals from itself the distance that separates its interpretive practices from philosophically hermeneutical reflections on the musical work.

Hermann Kretzschmar's (1990 [1902]) struggle against Eduard Hanslick's aesthetics anticipates the destruction of the idea that a musical work's form represents a self-sufficient meaning. Kretzschmar's musical hermeneutics offers a humanistic alternative to Hanslick's aesthetic program. Hanslick's renunciation of a Romantic metaphysics of feeling advances the cause of positive science by identifying the beautiful in music with the play of tonal forms. Kretzschmar counters by raising musical hermeneutics to the highest rank of music theory. Turning to the aesthetic doctrine of affects, Kretzschmar identifies music's motives and themes with specific feelings and affects in order to make accessible the full understanding of the works of the great masters.

Kretzschmar's humanistic reply to Hanslick's formalism rejoins Richard Wagner's concept of absolute music. Inspired by Feuerbach's "philosophy of the future," Wagner regarded absolute music's emancipation from myth, poetry, and dance as a necessary step leading to the total work of art. The *Gesamtkunstwerk* overcomes absolute music's deficiency with regard to the demand for clearly defined, individual emotions by investing musical expression with a positive content. Kretzschmar's musical hermeneutics echoes the function of Wagner's leitmotif technique by identifying music's tonal drama with definite feelings and moods. Illuminating the soul of the works of the great masters by penetrating music's form constitutes a positive interpretive method that consummates the "desire only to relive the life of others" (Kretzschmar 1990 [1902]: 6) as objectified in the spirit of musical works. Kretzschmar's aesthetics of themes, which constitutes the cornerstone of his musical hermeneutics, lays out instrumental music's drama of affects and feelings (Kretzschmar 1990 [1905]). Despite the differences between Wagner's music drama and Kretzschmar's aesthetics of themes, the programmatic intent of his musical hermeneutics aligns this hermeneutics with Wagner's positive thrust.

As a language beyond language, absolute music's sublime ineffability gives wing to thoughts, feelings, and emotions beyond the external sensual world. This idea invests instrumental music with an indeterminate quality that Wagner's music drama, Hanslick's formalist aesthetics, and Kretzschmar's musical hermeneutics intend to overcome. Hanslick rejects Wagner's aesthetic-historical program when, by giving the concept of absolute music a positive designation, he identifies music's ideal content with the tone-structures themselves. This ideal content rests solely with music's "tonally moving forms," whose construction conforms to natural laws governing both the "human organism and the external manifestations of sound" (Hanslick 1986 [1891]: 29, 30). Kretzschmar's renunciation of this scientific ideal preserves the positive intent of Wagner's aesthetic program. Hence, in turning against the "poetic conceit of unspeakability," which Carl Dahlhaus (1989: 63) identifies with the metaphysical authority invested in musical works by romantic aesthetics, this musical hermeneutics weaves together Wagner's programmatic and Hanslick's formalist agendas. Kretzschmar's aversion to Hanslick's program did not prevent him from deriving music's expressive content from a work's formal features. Through his opposition to Hanslick, his musical hermeneutics establishes a method where descriptions of successive moods and feelings invest music's formal structure with a narrative content.

Deconstructing Absolute Music

Contemporary responses to romantic and formalist conceits align deconstructions of music's aesthetic autonomy with Kretzschmar's hermeneutics. By surpassing positivist and formalist methods of music scholarship through critiques of the musical work's self-sufficiency, contemporary music criticism replaces Hanslick's aesthetics of form with analyses of music's worldly content. Influenced by developments in literary criticism, social theory, and contemporary philosophy, critical musicology promulgates the suspicion that absolute music harbors political, social, and ideological meanings. This suspicion turns against the formalist doctrine of music's autonomy, a doctrine that ratifies the role that aesthetic consciousness plays in distinguishing between art and reality and that, for a critical musicology, consecrates the illusion of transcendence invested in the idea of absolute music. This illusion marks the distance between absolute music and social reality that critical musicology intends to overcome. Critical musicology deconstructs this distance as a function of formalist and romantic conceits, despite the hold exercised over this deconstruction by the subjectivization of aesthetics. By replacing formalist aesthetics with a materially grounded aesthetics of content, critical musicology reprises Kretzschmar's program by shifting his hermeneutical agenda onto the social plane.

Denouncements of formalist and positivist conceits foreground the difference between formalist and sociological conceptions of a work. From the vantage points of these competing perspectives, the distance separating a musical work from social reality appears either as absolute or as an ideological phantasm. From the standpoint of the work's aesthetic autonomy, the distance between the work and the world is absolute. From the conflicting standpoint, this distance dissimulates political, cultural, and ideological interests by concealing the work's socially constructed character. The opposition is intractable. Transcendence and autonomy, and music's proximity with the social world, represent two poles of a metaphysical divide. On one side, the work's self-sustaining ideality holds sway. On the other, the discourse of music's socially contingent nature dominates strategic disclosures of its cultural and political significance.

This opposition ratifies the conceptual frame imposed by the history of art's opposition to reality by inverting it. Lawrence Kramer argues that musical autonomy, and even the relative autonomy Carl Dahlhaus espouses, is a chimera, and that "neither music nor anything else can be other than worldly through and through" (Kramer 1992: 9). For him, the illusion of immediacy sanctioned by the idea of a purely musical experience within the cultural preserve of high-art music dissembles how musical experiences are concretely situated in the worlds of composers, performers, and listeners. Mediating structures, "usually positioned outside music under the rubric of context" (Kramer 1992: 10), are inscribed within music's immediacy effects. Yet by setting music's worldliness against the illusion of transcendence, he conforms to the conceptual frame he intends to overturn by reversing music's distance from social reality.

Susan McClary's deconstructions of absolute music consecrate this reversal. By identifying absolute music's master narrative with a hegemonic political agenda, she intends to decode socially hegemonic meanings. For her, the interlocking schemata of tonality and the traditional sonata form constitute the ideological backbone of this master narrative. Absolute music, she argues, only appears "to make itself up without reference to the outside world . . . [because] it adheres so thoroughly to the most common plot outline and the most fundamental ideological tensions available within

Western culture" (McClary 1993: 333). Tonality "operates according to a standard sequence of dynamic events, giving the music it organizes a distinctly narrative cast" (McClary 1993: 330). Sonata form throws this standardized tonal procedure into relief. The first theme represents the masculine protagonist. A second theme follows, which is semiotically marked as the feminine Other. The return of these two themes in the tonic key at the movement's close resolves the conflict between them at the expense of the identity of the Other. According to McClary, this tonal adventure depicts the implied protagonist's assertion of his identity as a natural imperative, thereby concealing the absolutist political narrative it enacts.

This interpretive strategy identifies socially constructed representations of gender identities and sexual promiscuity with the ideological containment and marginalization of differences, thereby contesting the formalist claim that absolute music operates according to purely musical principles. On this reading, the double gesture that confines differences by means of the subjugating strategy of absolute music's master narrative also puts the feminine Other on display. From the outset, tonal resolution demands that tonality's rational frame contains "whatever is semiotically or structurally marked as 'feminine' " (McClary 1991: 15). For McClary, this double gesture is in essence social. Framed as an object of surveillance and fascination, tonality's discursive force marks out and marginalizes the contagion of the Other as a cultural exercise of social violence.

McClary's critique echoes Kretzschmar's programmatic methods by identifying the formal procedures of tonality and sonata form with a narrative content. Although she relies on narrative studies and semiotics, her deconstructions of absolute music extend beyond hermeneutics to social critique. In her study of Brahms' *Third Symphony*, she claims to trace contradictions of bourgeois subjectivity by penetrating the formal procedures that seem impervious to such analyses (McClary 1993). While she acknowledges her debt to Adorno's music criticism, she argues that her concerns with gender and race were not among Adorno's priorities. Through her critique, she intends to reveal the links between music and society that Adorno attributes to music's social mediation. Yet, by correlating formal procedures with a politically motivated narrative agenda, she subordinates the critical difference between music and society, which Adorno attempts to capture dialectically, to a social semiotics of gender.

This difference foregrounds the dilemma confronting postmodern musicology. The destruction of formalist conceits, together with absolute music's ideological demystification, abolishes the distance separating music from reality. Yet this distance, which the bourgeois cult of art-religion sanctifies for aestheticism's sake, is critical to a work's capacity to contest and subvert reality. Critics who deny this capacity defend the condition they struggle against. By shifting the topos of art's imitation of nature onto the social plane, deconstructive strategies that supplant absolute music's metaphysical dignity excise the possibility that music's aesthetic figuration is more than a weapon in the struggle for position and power. To the extent that postmodern musicology's authority derives from formalism's failures, its legitimation confirms music's worldliness against the principle of music's aesthetic differentiation. The possibility of music's critical difference notwithstanding, absolute music's social deconstruction occludes the dilemma raised by the question of a critical or productive relation that transgresses the conceptual frame imposed by the subjectivization of aesthetics.

Aesthetic Criticism and Social Critique

Adorno's self-consciously modernist music criticism embodies the dilemma engendered by absolute music's postmodern demystification. By dialectically capturing music's relation to social reality, Adorno's critical theory maintains a determinate difference between empirical existence and a critical surplus, which in music and art is the emblem of their truth. This surplus, which distinguishes the work's truth content from its aesthetic semblance, exceeds the meaning the work has as an autonomous entity. Conversely, music's autonomy, which is its first social characteristic, is the condition for this truth content's appearance. Adorno's formulation of music's relation to reality coincides with this paradox. Negatively dialectical, it evinces the dilemma of a critique at pains to distance itself from musicology's formalist and positivist proclivities and from reductive sociological analyses.

The idea that a critique of music's social significance should take its bearing from music's aesthetic constitution sets Adorno's critical project apart. For him, neither formalist analyses nor vulgar sociological ones do justice to the demand to decipher music's critical content. The cheap sovereignty of sociological analyses dismisses works' "immanence of form as a vain and naïve self-delusion" (Adorno 1997: 238). By ignoring their aesthetic constitution, such analyses subordinate art works to abstract social correlations. Formal analysis is equally suspect. By making itself absolute, it capitulates to the ideological reification that Adorno argues it struggles against when devoting itself "to the artworks internally rather than deducing their world-views" from outside (Adorno 1997: 180). Positioned equidistantly from formalist and vulgar sociological standpoints, critical sociology offers insights into music's essential relation to society through music's dialectical deciphering (Adorno 1976: 194). Hence for Adorno, aesthetic criticism and social critique coincide.

The paradox of music's critical surplus springs from Adorno's claim that autonomous music's distance from society is its first social characteristic. This claim circumscribes the tension between illusion and truth. Unlike Nietzsche (1967 [1886]: 18), for whom art's dissembling illusion is the "subtle last resort" against truth, music's and art's semblance character is the condition of a social truth that surpasses a work's artifactual nature. Consequently, the task of aesthetic criticism and social critique is not to feign false proximity, as though musical works directly and realistically reproduced real social conditions. Rather, critique recovers the truth manifest through music's semblance character by deducing the difference between art and empirical existence while recognizing the limit that critical social theory imposes on sociological analyses of music's aesthetic constitution.

The autonomy Adorno requires of music and art deepens the paradox instituted by a necessary difference between aesthetic phenomena and social reality. Autonomous art is social only through its determinate opposition to instrumental modes of social domination. Autonomous art's refractory objectification of socially unresolved antagonisms shatters the illusion of harmoniously reconciled interests and practices.

Its semblance character is therefore the repository of a social truth that militates against the violence inflicted upon individuals within a rationally administered world.

Adorno's two-fold characterization of music and art captures the enigma of a work's semblance and truth. As autonomous, each work forms a singular aesthetic monad. As a social fact, each work takes a position on society by anticipating a reconciliation within society that would bring to an end the violence of position and power. Art's and music's double character embodies the essence of this negative dialectical premise. Musical works and works of art—the "social antithesis of society"—objectify a social truth that, while it is not empirically deducible, illumines social reality's antagonistic unity (Adorno 1997: 8).

The paradox that singular works achieve this truth through the artifice of their production dominates Adorno's critical aesthetic theory. In light of this paradox, the task of deciphering a works' truth involves more than denouncing its aesthetic character. For Adorno, aesthetic semblance is critical to autonomous art's utopian function. Consequently, a work's truth content, which takes shape as the semblance of the true, conjoins music's and art's innermost paradox (that is, aesthetic semblance is the condition of a work's truth) with their enigmatic utopian impulse. That truth is something that cannot be made deepens the paradox of music's artifice. Since "what is true in art is something nonexistent," only the semblance of the true testifies to what in reality does not yet exist (Adorno 1997: 131). Yet for Adorno (1997: 135), "because for art, utopia—the yet-to-exist—is draped in black," in all its mediations art evinces its enigmatic impulse by registering only the possibility of possibilities. Confined to "the imaginary reparation of the catastrophe of world history," utopia is the refuge for a "freedom, which under the spell of necessity did not—and may not ever—come to pass" (Adorno 1997: 135, 133). Authentic works recall a condition of freedom suppressed by society's bent toward rational administration. Yet, in concretizing utopia without betraying it to merely empirical existence, the remembrance—the anamnesis—of this condition binds art's semblance of truth to the paradox that authentic works, which determinately negate social reality by taking a position on it, are incapable of prefiguring practical alternatives.

A Critical Impasse

The idea that autonomous works oppose society and, as society's determinate *other*, recall a condition of freedom that has not yet come to pass, separates Adorno's social critique of music from postmodernist deconstructions. Where deconstructions of absolute music denounce a work's autonomy by identifying socially encoded meanings with hegemonic social and political agendas, Adorno's enigmatic formulation of music's social truth preserves the distance between music and social reality on which a work's critical function depends. Deconstructing the idea of absolute music surpasses Adorno's critical strategy by occluding the condition of a work's possibility for contesting, subverting, or refiguring reality. The occultation of music's first social characteristic—that is, its distance from empirical reality—distinguishes critical musicology's demystification of absolute music from Adorno's dialectical investment in its autonomy. However, Adorno's paradoxical formulation of art's social truth does not escape the contradiction of music's negative dialectical relation to society. Caught up in the attack on modern reason's conversion into the instrument of social violence, the paradox of art's semblance of truth reproduces the performative contradiction of his critique's relentless negativity.

The strategy of *ad hoc* negation Adorno pursues leads to a critical impasse. Jürgen Habermas (1987: 119) argues that when the "suspicion of ideology becomes *total*, but without any change of direction," the performative contradiction that this totalizing critique engenders paralyzes the critical ambition of transforming reality. Trapped in the vicious paradox of incessant negativity, Adorno's negative dialectical strategy holds out "scarcely any prospect for an escape from the myth of purposive rationality that has turned into objective violence" (Habermas 1987: 114). Authentic art's aesthetic semblance reprises this performative contradiction through its enigmatic figuration of truth. Without being able to say what the right reality is, authentically autonomous works remonstrate against existing reality as if, through their opposition, they testify to an oppressive reality's utopian *other*.

This performative contradiction, where autonomous works reproach social existence without offering any practical alternatives, condemns music and art to mute protest. Unable to say what the right reality is without betraying the promise of utopian fulfillment, art works preserve the consistent sense of nonidentity that distinguishes Adorno's negative dialectical strategy from postmodernist deconstructions. As society's other, authentic works oppose the imposition of domination through their mediate relation to social forces and circumstances of production. Yet, through their determinate opposition to society's continuing lack of freedom, they hold out scarcely any hope for surpassing the reality they assail.

Genius and the Subjectivization of Aesthetics

The impasse in Adorno's music criticism places postmodernist deconstructions of absolute music in a different light. Critical musicology's destruction of formalist conceits intersects with Adorno's rejection of the idea that music's aesthetic worth can be distinguished from its social truth. Yet, Adorno's renunciation of vulgar sociological analyses, which regard works only as aesthetic extensions of socially constructed positions and identities, presupposes a difference between art and reality. This difference, which is constitutive of art as such, distinguishes Adorno's critical enterprise from critical musicology's reversal of musical transcendence. This reversal collapses the opposition that Adorno's paradoxical formulation of music's aesthetic truth struggles to maintain. The opposition between music and reality that for Adorno is the condition of music's social truth, and its postmodern reversal, spring from Kant's subjectivization of aesthetics. Adorno's negative dialectical formulation also labors under the schema inaugurated by Kant. Yet the claim of art's constitutive difference, which anchors the paradox of art's distance from social reality in his critical strategy's performative contradiction, indicates the path of a reflection that conjoins this difference with the power of imagination.

This path traverses the effective history of the subjectivization of aesthetics. Nineteenth-century philosophy of art consecrates Kant's subjectivization of aesthetics by investing art's symbolic quality with its own positivity and by justifying music's and art's aesthetic autonomy as the greatest achievement of subjectivity. Influenced by Goethe, the idea that the symbol emerges organically in the unity of the work's sensible appearance and the expression of the life and mind behind it expands into a universal aesthetic principle. As the "poetic formation of experience (Erlebnis)," music and art embody the essence of this experience in aesthetic form (Gadamer 1991: 80). Hence, the "pure" work of art, and the experience (Erlebnis) of it, represents the highest standard of value. In the nineteenth century according to Hans-Georg Gadamer (1991: 59), "the concept of genius rose to the status of a universal concept of value and—together with the concept of the creative—achieved a true apotheosis." By seizing upon Kant's statement that "fine art is the art of genius" (cited by Gadamer 1991: 58), German idealism erected a philosophy of art based on this transcendental principle. Even the return to Kant proved incapable of dislodging the phenomenon of art and the concept of genius from the center of aesthetics. Consequently, the metaphysical question of truth in music and art continued to dominate aesthetics, even when its original cultural and philosophical context had been left behind.

The concept of genius provides the point of contact with Kant's aesthetics that facilitates marking out the art work as the object of aesthetic experience. Gadamer (1991: 82) argues that when Schiller transformed Kant's concept of taste into a moral demand, "Schiller took the radical subjectivization through which Kant had justified transcendentally the judgment of taste and its claim to validity, and changed it from a methodological presupposition to one of content." By reinterpreting Kant's anthropology, Schiller isolates art and the experience of it from mundane reality. Aesthetic consciousness and its correlates, aesthetic education and the creation of a cultured society, provide a bulwark against reality by giving flight to the freedom of the human spirit in its purely aesthetic state.

By contrasting art with reality, and by differentiating between the pure work of art and the mundane world of everyday experiences, romantic consciousness cultivates the idea, adopted by socially informed critique, that music and art belong to an entirely separate domain. The subjectivization of aesthetics, which begins with Kant's transcendental grounding of the judgment of taste, culminates in the idea that the aesthetic life's conscious cultivation demands that the art work, and the experience of it, be dissociated from worldly contexts. The methodological abstraction that aesthetic consciousness performs by disregarding the work's rootedness in a life context enables the work to become visible as a "pure" work of art. Once defined as appearance in contrast to reality, art attains a standpoint of its own, thereby establishing "its own autonomous claim to supremacy" in contrast to the life contexts from which aesthetic consciousness tears it (Gadamer 1991: 82).

Sociological deconstructions that take art's opposition to reality as their starting point occlude the hold that the subjectivization of aesthetics exercises over music criticism, musicology, and even ethnomusicology. Reactions against the concept of the work and its institution in the culture of the nineteenth century seek to reverse the effects of Kant's subjectivization of aesthetics by locating music's meaning in its social, cultural, and historical context. However, descriptions and analyses of music's social and cultural significance, and critiques of music's symbolic value as a form of capital used to exercise social violence by other means (Bourdieu 1977: 183 ff.), accede to the schema that relegates a work's truth to an otherworldly realm. When, in order to deconstruct the idea of absolute music and to decipher its social content, social critique allies aesthetics with ideology, it only shifts the metaphysical topos of music's spiritual essence onto the social plane. Adorno's negative dialectical strategy also fails to break free of this schema. Consequently, his two-fold concepts of art and its truth remain locked within a performative contradiction that is the inheritance of Kant's critique of taste.

Towards a Hermeneutics of Music Criticism

The failures of Adorno's and postmodern musicology's criticism to confront the subjectivization of aesthetics calls for a different response to music's abstraction from its life contexts. McClary and Kramer deconstruct the separation between music and social reality that Adorno claims is the condition of autonomous music's critical vehemence. Yet, the performative contradiction in Adorno's critical theory attests to the impossibility of deriving music's capacity to contest and subvert reality from the aesthetic schema inaugurated by Kant. Strategic interpretations that identify absolute music with socio-political agendas attain their positive significance by mapping an ideological content onto music's formal features. By investing traditional musical hermeneutics with a critical program, they ratify this schema's historical hold.

These failures compel critique to confront its philosophical presuppositions and to renew itself by reflecting upon the traditions that nurture it. By starting from the impossibility of deriving the power works exercise from the schema inaugurated by Kant, a hermeneutics of music criticism begins with the mode of being that belongs to singular works. Where thought and imagination are at work, singular works augment our understanding of ourselves and our world by transcending reality from within existing socio-historical horizons. This ontology of the work, in which a work achieves its self-presentation in the mode of play (Gadamer 1991: 101 ff.), explodes the idea of aesthetic transcendence. A work is neither the object of formal analysis nor is it the cultural artifact of sociological inquiry.

Like all cultural works, music belongs to the life contexts that support its creation, transmission, and reception. However, works enrich these contexts through the power of thought and imagination at work in them. By suspending everyday reality and its purposive relations, works unfold worlds that enlarge our own. The *epoché* of reality that works effect is only the negative condition for social reality's refiguration. Paul Ricoeur argues that the paradox of productive reference shatters the traditional prejudice that works refer to reality by reproducing it in aesthetic form. The paradox that only "the image which does not already have its referent in reality is able to display a world" breaks with the idea of imitation as a copy or reflection of reality (Ricoeur 1991: 129). By mobilizing the concept of mimetic representation, this paradox extricates this concept from critiques of the representative illusion and returns it to its field of play. Henceforth, imitations effected by works can no longer be seen to reduplicate reality, but are instead creative renderings of it.

The fecundity of imagination—the wellspring of the work's power to contest, subvert, and transfigure reality—attests to the power of thought in prefiguring new possibilities. Imagination, when it is productive, evinces this power of thought at work. Imagination and thought consequently join with judgment in establishing the ground for a work's communicability. Correspondingly, we understand ourselves only through the detour that cultural works provide. In "contrast to the tradition of the *cogito* and to the pretensions of the subject to know itself by immediate intuition" (Ricoeur 1981: 123), we are not masters of meaning. Rather, the signs of humanity deposited in cultural works mediate our understanding of ourselves and our world. Ricoeur stresses that we ratify the positivist prejudice that reality can be empirically observed and scientifically described when we deny this capacity to cultural works. When thought is at work, works of imagination penetrate reality and break open new paths. "Imagination at work—in a work—produces itself as a world" (Ricoeur: 1991: 123). As the horizons of these worlds intersect with those of our own, cultural works both shatter and remake reality through the power of thought and imagination at work in them.

Ricoeur's and Gadamer's philosophical insights open new vistas for contemporary music criticism by inviting us to think more about music's power, its meaning, and its significance. The continuing separation of the historical or sociological question, what did the work mean, from the hermeneutical situation in which we now find ourselves only perpetuates an outworn philosophical schema that opposes reason and knowledge to myth. So long as both musical formalism and socio-historical critiques overlook the subjectivization of aesthetics, they can only continue to discredit music's exercise of thought and imagination. Music criticism need not remain in the service of either formalist dogma or the social decoding of political agendas. Through its reflections upon these works of imagination, music criticism joins the adventure of hermeneutical reason and its quest to understand justly the conditions and possibilities of thought and action.

Conclusion

The vistas this adventure opens transect boundaries dividing music theory, historical musicology, ethnomusicology, and cultural studies. For a hermeneutics of music criticism, the meaning works have is inextricable from the power they exercise. Without reducing aesthetics to ideology, this hermeneutics rejects culture's strategic utility as a weapon in the struggle for social position and power. Instead, it renews the creative mediations between works and world in the midst of social and political conflicts by rejoining philosophical hermeneutics' call for self-understanding.

This conclusion points in several directions. First, it indicates the path of an inquiry into aesthetics and ideology opened up by the hermeneutical critique of the subjectivization of aesthetics. The concept of ideology has been unnecessarily restricted to ideology's dissimulating function. Both aesthetics and ideology would benefit from an expanded concept of ideology, which acknowledges reality's fundamentally symbolic constitution to be the inescapable condition of all action and thought. Aesthetics and ideology are related through the social and cultural imagination.

Following this path of inquiry, music's ideological significance could be related dialectically to the aesthetic prefiguration of alternative possibilities.

This first path intersects a second. Every interpretation of a work is caught up in a history of effects. The experience of belonging to history precedes every attempt at ideological critique. Conversely, critiques of singular works stand in a horizon of past understandings and future possibilities. The replies that individual works provide for the questions, problems, or perplexities to which they are the answers also create a history that affects them. Criticism brings out the work's singularity when, in interpreting a work's place in history, it discerns the thought at work in the work. In this way, criticism participates in the creative renewal of cultural heritages through understanding the history singular works effect.

The third avenue of inquiry raises anew the question of the work's truth. The question of the truth of the work and of its creative rendering of reality runs ahead of existing concepts of social or historical truth. The invention of new worlds and new realities calls for judgment and imagination. By giving voice to the mood of the times, music discloses a historical disposition toward the past and the future. At its limit, music refigures the time of thought and action. Freed by the work's power to remake reality, the truth of the work is also bound to the future it opens up. In discerning this truth, criticism, judgment, and imagination converge.

NOTES

1. An earlier version of this paper was presented at the annual meeting of the American Society for Aesthetics, November 1998.

REFERENCES

Adorno Theodor W.
   1976   *Introduction to the Sociology of Music*. Translated by E. B. Ashton. New York: Continuum Publishing.
   1997   *Aesthetic Theory*. Translated by Robert Hullot-Kentor. Minneapolis: University of Minnesota Press.

Bourdieu, Pierre
   1977   *Outline of a Theory of Practice*. Translated by Richard Nice. Cambridge: Cambridge University Press.

Dahlhaus, Carl
   1989   *The Idea of Absolute Music*. Translated by Roger Lustig. Chicago: The University of Chicago Press.

Gadamer, Hans-Georg
   1991   *Truth and Method*. 2nd revised edition. Translation revised by Joel Weinsheimer and Donald G. Marshall. New York: Crossroads.

Habermas, Jürgen
   1987   *The Philosophical Discourse of Modernity*. Translated by Frederick Lawrence. Cambridge, Mass.: The MIT Press.

Hanslick, Eduard
 1986 [1891] *On the Musically Beautiful*. Translated by Geoffrey Payzant. Indianapolis: Hacket Publishing.

Kramer, Lawrence
 1992 "The Future of Music." *Repercussions* 1 (1): 5–18.

Kretzschmar, Hermann
 1990 [1902] "Suggestions for the Furtherance of Musical Hermeneutics." In E. A. Lippman, ed., *Musical Aesthetics: A Historical Reader*. Vol. 3. New York: Pendragon Press, pp. 5–30.

Kretzschmar, Hermann
 1990 [1905] "New Suggestions for the Furtherance of Musical Hermeneutics: The Aesthetics of Musical Compositions." In E. A. Lippman, ed., *Musical Aesthetics: A Historical Reader*. Vol. 3. New York: Pendragon Press, pp. 31–45.

McClary, Susan
 1991 *Feminine Endings: Music, Gender, and Sexuality*. Minnesota: University of Minnesota Press.
 1993 "Narrative Agendas in 'Absolute Music': Identity and Difference in Brahms's Third Symphony." In Ruth A Solie, ed., *Musicology and Difference: Gender and Sexuality in Musical Scholarship*. Berkeley: University of California Press, pp. 326–344.

Nietzsche, Friedrich
 1967 [1886] *The Birth of Tragedy*. Translated by Walter Kaufmann. New York: Vintage Books.

Ricoeur, Paul
 1981 *Hermeneutics and the Human Sciences*. Translated by John B. Thompson. New York: Cambridge University Press.
 1991 *A Ricoeur Reader*. Edited by Mario J. Valdés. Toronto: University of Toronto Press.

Contributors

Paul Attinello is a lecturer in the International Centre for Music Studies at the University of Newcastle upon Tyne; he has also taught at the University of Hong Kong. His 1997 dissertation from UCLA considered the aesthetic implications of European avant-garde vocal music from the 1960s. He has published in the *Journal of Musicological Research, Musik-Konzepte, Musica/Realtá, MLA Notes,* the revised *New Grove,* and several collections.

Annabel Cohen (B.A. McGill; M.A., Ph.D. Queen's University) is a professor of psychology at the University of Prince Edward Island and an adjunct professor at Dalhousie University in Halifax, Nova Scotia. Her research focuses on the effects of music in multimedia (sponsored by SSHRC) and the acquisition of musical grammar (sponsored by NSERC). She serves on the editorial boards of *Music Perception, Musicae Scientiae, Psychomusicology, Psychology of Music,* and is a Fellow of the Canadian Psychological Association.

Frank Heuser is the director of the music education program at UCLA where he teaches methods courses, supervises student teachers, and conducts an outreach program that brings violin instruction to elementary students and provides Music Department undergraduates with early field experiences. His research includes work in the motor activation patterns in the facial muscles of musicians playing brass instruments, in the relationship between inner hearing and performance skills, and in music teacher education. He serves as a guest conductor and clinician for public school ensembles and is a wind and brass instructor for the Idyllwild Arts summer music festival.

Roger A. Kendall is a professor in the systematic musicology program in the Department of Ethnomusicology at UCLA. He has published numerous scientific research articles and book chapters in music perception and cognition, psychoacoustics, and acoustics. His computer program, the Music Experiment Development System (MEDS), permits flexible and real-time design of experiments in music science and is used internationally.

Scott D. Lipscomb, Ph.D., is an associate professor in the School of Music at Northwestern University, jointly appointed to both the music education and music technology programs. In addition to his primary research interest in film music perception, he is currently collaborating on a variety of investigations related to the surround sound presentation of cinema and musical sound, the affect of music in video game contexts, tonality judgment in elementary school children, and the development of interactive instructional media to enhance the music learning experience. Dr. Lipscomb is currently serving his second term as president of the Association for Technology in Music

Instruction (ATMI), serves as a member of the executive board and chair of the research committee for TI:ME (Technology Institute for Music Educators), serves as a member of the executive Board of the Society for Music Perception & Cognition (SMPC), and served as conference organizer for the 8th International Conference of Music Perception and Cognition in 2004.

Brana Mijatovic received her Ph.D. in ethnomusicology from UCLA. In addition to her research on the music of the Balkans, and the relationship between music and politics, she is an active performer on piano, drums, and percussion in various genres of world music.

Kengo Ohgushi is emeritus professor of Kyoto City University of Arts. He organized the first International Conference of Music Perception and Cognition held in Kyoto in 1989. He served as the president of the Japanese Society for Music Perception and Cognition from 1997 to 2001.

Lillis Ó Laoire lectures in Irish Language and Literature at the University of Limerick, where he also directs an archiving and performance project in traditional song. Currently on leave, he is a visiting assistant professor at Loyola Marymount University. His book, *On a Rock in the Middle of the Ocean: Songs and Singers in Tory Island*, is due from Scarecrow Press in 2005.

Angeles Sancho-Velázquez is an assistant professor of arts and humanities in the Department of Liberal Studies at California State University, Fullerton. She did graduate work in systematic musicology at UCLA, in the area of aesthetics and philosophy of music, receiving her Ph.D. in 2001. She is currently working on a book on the disappearance of the practice of improvisation in the Western Classical tradition.

Roger W. H. Savage is associate professor of systematic musicology in the Department of Ethnomusicology at UCLA. He specializes in aesthetics, hermeneutic philosophy, music criticism, and twentieth-century music. His research focuses on intersections between music, politics, and imagination's role in the formation of personal, cultural, and social identities.

Haruka Shimosako received the B.A. degree in psychology from the University of the Sacred Heart, Japan, in 1994 and the degree of Master of Musicology from Kyoto City University of Arts, in 1996. From 1998 to 2000, she was a research fellow of the Japan Society for the Promotion of Science and studied perception and cognition of music. She currently works at the National Institute of Advanced Industrial Science and Technology, Japan.

Pantelis N. Vassilakis studied electrical engineering in his native Greece, music composition and technology at Kingston University, England (BA, 1993), and music cognition and acoustics at UCLA's Ethnomusicology Department (MA, 1997; PhD, 2001). Dr. Vassilakis has composed for the English National Ballet and the London Chinese

Orchestra and, since 1997, has been presenting regularly at U.S. national and international academic conferences, publishing numerous abstracts and articles in conference proceedings as well as one article in the December 2004 issue of *JASA*. In 2002 he received a post-doctoral fellowship at UCLA's Physiological Science Department to work on hearing, and is currently holding a digital music specialist position at DePaul University's School of Music (Chicago, IL).